AROUND THE WORLD

DAVE BIDINI

IN 57½ GIGS

McCLELLAND & STEWART

Library and Archives Canada Cataloguing in Publication

Bidini, Dave
    Around the world in fifty-seven and a half gigs / Dave Bidini.

ISBN 978-0-7710-1465-9

    1. Rock music – 2001-2010. 2. Bidini, Dave – Journeys. I. Title.
ML3534.B56 2007   782.42'1660905   C2007-901047-4

We acknowledge the financial support of the Government of Canada through the Book Publishing Industry Development Program and that of the Government of Ontario through the Ontario Media Development Corporation's Ontario Book Initiative. We further acknowledge the support of the Canada Council for the Arts and the Ontario Arts Council for our publishing program.

The lyrics on page 276 are reprinted by permission of Lansanah Mansaray (Barmmy Boy) and Lustinjay Abdulrahman Jalloh.

Typeset in Sabon by M&S, Toronto
Printed and bound in Canada

McClelland & Stewart Ltd.
75 Sherbourne Street
Toronto, Ontario
M5A 2P9
www.mcclelland.com

1 2 3 4 5   11 10 09 08 07

FOR JO

"Sing me a story I haven't heard yet"

– "My Favourite Chords," The Weakerthans

CONTENTS

ACKNOWLEDGEMENTS

The author wishes to acknowledge the help, support, kindness, and efforts of Jason Sniderman and family, War Child Canada, Mikko Keinonen, Andy and Yu Fei, Yulia Ochetova, Haddon Strong, Alun Piggins, Jay Santiago, Dawyne Gale, Steve Clarkson, Rheostatics, and Six Shooter Management, without whom this book would not have happened. Also, the Africa chapters were written for Ed Sawyer, who died shortly after this book was submitted. Thanks as well to *Reader's Digest*, the *Toronto Star*, *TORO*, *Swerve* magazine, *Post City*, and One Yellow Rabbit.

And to Janet.

EDMONTON

THE RHEOSTATICS BROKE UP QUIETLY. BASSIST TIM VESELY stared out the window of an Edmonton hotel on a cold, sunny morning, then turned and told me that it was time for a change, that twenty-five years of playing with us had been enough. My immediate reaction was to wonder why these kinds of things always seemed to happen in Edmonton. Next, I danced the dance of the spurned, asking obvious questions about what we could do to still hold it together and arriving at obvious answers. Then I stopped battling the inevitable and looked on with a certain ennui as things spiralled down from there. A few weeks later, Michael Phillip-Wojewoda, our drummer of five years, packed it in. Guitarist Martin Tielli and I and a friend – Ford Pier – scrambled to piece together a future, but none of our ideas had any glue. While the end hurt and burned a hole in my stomach, it pushed me out of my musical nest and set me on a solo walk through the greater world of rock 'n' roll.

In a way, perhaps I owe Tim for putting our band to sleep. Had we stayed together, I might well have indulged in one of those frontman laments about needing to bust out of band prison so that my self-expression could be better served (one of the reasons why our bassist felt the need to fly the coop). But my self-expression had been given more than enough attention over all of those years of Rheostaticdom, and going solo seemed to me to be the domain of those who were sick of working with others, or who weren't trying hard enough to play the hand that the rock 'n' roll gods had dealt them. Besides, since 1978 I had only ever played with my friends, and going solo would have meant breaking loyalty and tradition.

This isn't to say that I hadn't ever considered it. I think every musician in every band has moments on stage while watching their bandmate singing to the adoring throng when they consider what might happen if a two-ton lighting rack fell from the ceiling struts and obliterated him, leaving the dreamer to respond to the pleas of the hungry crowd. Moments of great self-satisfaction only feed such a fantasy, and it's not until you choke on your lyrics or butcher your drum part or bust a bass string that you feel blessed to have other players behind or beside you.

Over the years, I had from time to time tangoed with the notion of setting out on my own, if for reasons more geographic than artistic. For decades, our band had subsisted on consecutive tours along the same maple road, playing middling clubs in cities named Saskatoon and Antigonish for dudes named Rob and women named Alice (and a few dudes named Alice), whose faith in us brought the Rheos relative success in Canada but nowhere else. The Rheostatics had always been worshipped by a devoted audience and respected by more, but the mainstream ignored us, and we did little to curry favour. Still, had we been invited to the party, we probably would have loathed attending. I remember turning on the television one afternoon to find that the corner of Queen and John in Toronto – a hotbed of Canadian youth culture, and two shakes from where the Rheos had cut their teeth at the sop-carpeted, broken-staged Beverly Tavern – had been roped off so that teeming thousands could gather for the worst of American pop culture: Jessica Simpson and Johnny

Knoxville. Women from Beamsville, Mississauga, and Napanee competed in a Daisy Duke–lookalike contest ("I'm Allison, and I want to ride you like a cowboy!"), their images piped into the country's living rooms, where fourteen-year-olds from coast to coast to coast lapped it up. That I felt only cynical – not suicidal – was a wonder.

Still, I had kicked around the idea of exploring the World of Rock the way the Rheostatics first explored Canada on our inaugural tour in 1987, discovering out-of-the-way places that harboured crazy promoters and drunken drummers. In my twenties, I heard a campus radio interview with a veteran local guitar player whose brother – a singer – had died just as their band was starting to get some attention. It was a good interview, and then the host asked if he had any advice for young musicians. He paused a second, then said, "Yeah, quit. With a few exceptions, it's a miserable life." I swore that I would never be that guy. But now here I was, a forty-two-year-old Canadian guitar player, showing signs of crust and poison.

I'd known for a while that both the Rheostatics and I needed a break, so when Tim pushed, something told me not to push back, not to fight or declare emotional warfare, as I had previously with other members who'd left. Perhaps leaving my Canadian band to play for other faces and fans in different pop cultures would bring back some technicolour to those old road dreams of exploring, learning, and living, which are the only reasons anyone goes anywhere, guitar in hand or not.

Years before any of this had come to pass, I came back from yet another Canadian tour and groused to Blue, our booking agent at the time, about the need to widen our gig map. Blue had done lights for Led Zeppelin at the Masonic Temple in 1969 and had run the notorious Cheap Thrills ticket agency with Michael Cohl in the 1970s. He was old enough to remember the days when bands hit the road with neither a marketing plan nor a compass, their guitarist asking a half-soused crowd in a small, dark place miles from home, "What about this one?" before playing a new song in hopes of getting a free beer or a pickled egg or a kiss from a tall, freckled girl. Sitting in his office, surrounded by Boston Red Sox and Grateful Dead paraphernalia (Blue stood in for the late Jerry Garcia in *Half Baked*), I told him, "What I want to do is go on a world tour to all of those places I've never been before, play to people who have no idea who the frig I am."

Blue rubbed his scrubby grey-white beard. "Around the World in Eighty Gigs?"

"Ya, more or less."

"Okay," he said, resting his arms on his desk. "Let me work on the routing."

LONDON

WHEN MOST TOURING MUSICIANS STUDY THEIR GIG MAP for the first time, they almost never tremble with excitement, wave their passports, and shout, "Finland!" They are more likely to drag a forefinger down the page and, after coming to the Nordic leg of their tour, sigh heavily. But once I'd decided to head out into the world, there was no question about where my global spin would begin.

I owe my inspiration to journalist and filmmaker Mikko Keinonen, who lives in Tampere, the third-largest city in *Suomi*. Sometime in the early 2000s, Mikko wrote to me, suggesting that, should the forces align (i.e., if some government cultural agent ponied up the cash), he would be interested in mounting a Finnish stage version of the Rheos' psychedelic children's album, *The Story of Harmelodia*. I knew that were I to suggest that he set up, arrange, promote, and shepherd me around on an eight-city tour of Finland, he would not treat it as a preposterous idea, at least not as preposterous as a Finnish stage version of our album. So I told him my plan, and within weeks Mikko had a tentative gig list ready for me. Without a clue about any of the towns, except that they all had vowel-riddled names, and even less of a clue about the venues, I told him that it all looked great.

A while later, I broke the news to Mikko that I'd be bringing Al with me to Finland. Mikko wrote back, asking whether Al was the pet name I'd given my guitar, like B.B. King's Lucille or Stevie Ray Vaughan's Lenny or Willie Nelson's Trigger. I told him that Al was, in fact, Alun Piggins, my old defence partner on our hockey team, the Morningstars. Al is a wild-haired, crook-nosed, pirate fetishist who once tried to poison me between games by putting cubes of frozen aquarium water in my shandy. Off the ice, Al is a Canadian songwriter whose reputation – one of them – is for having written some of the world's finest, most beautiful songs about pornography. Once, while on tour with the Rheos in Dawson City, Al played a song in a church about getting manually pleasured in a church, making him an instant hit. On the last night of our stay, I wrestled him drunkenly down a hill and we rolled to within inches of a roaring, ash-spitting campfire. I knew that if we could survive Dawson, we'd romp through a tour of Finland.

For years, Al had studied the ins and outs of the solo racket, touring Canada by Greyhound bus and putting in innumerable hours gigging at places such as the Townehouse Tavern in Sudbury, Ontario's salty northern rock bar, where, before we were friends, Al became entangled in Rheostatics lore. When we played the Townehouse, we thought the graffiti in the basement of the band room was so bad, we couldn't bear to look at the walls. We spent what little money we had renting a hotel room for the night, so that we could avoid the sight of an enormous drawing of a vagina, signed by the artist: Hugh Dillon, Headstones. Years later, Al told me that he'd scrawled Hugh's name next to the Magic-Markered hoo-ha. We'll never know who did the actual drawing, but we at least know that Hugh Dillon didn't.

Because Al had played to almost every kind of Canadian audience, I knew that he would be excellent protection in case my solo experiment resulted in total suckdom. Even though Finland was a great place to launch the solo Bidini virus (I figured that if I messed up the lyrics to a song, the audience wouldn't notice, and if I ended up bellowing like a sea lion, they'd simply think that this was how a Canadian singer was supposed to sound), I needed Al in case Finnish audiences proved to tolerate nothing less than sonic perfection.

Before we hit the road, I leaned on Al for advice about performing solo. His pearls of wisdom included, "Playing solo is all about adapting to certain situations," and "Always start with a song you're comfortable with; it'll help you get your voice to where it has to be." It was good advice, but I wanted to know what to do if things went badly.

"I thought I sucked for two years before I had any confidence," he admitted. "I spent a lot of time on stage looking around, wondering where my band was, but pretty soon the gigs got good. And even when I had bad nights, at least I didn't think that I sucked." He paused, furrowed his brow, then added, "These days, when things go badly, the Quitters [his electric band] play our loudest song and then tell the crowd, 'Thank you, and fuck off.'"

"You've done that?"

"Oh, a couple of times," he said offhandedly, as if it had happened a lot more than a couple. "Once, we were playing the Northern Lights Festival in Sudbury, opening for Valdy. The folkie crowd wasn't into us, to say the least. They were arrogant and hostile, the worst kind of crowd, really, so we played '(Goin' Down to) Cougartown' [about having a one-night stand with an older woman], and when I yelled, 'Fuck off,' [Steve] Clarkson, our soundman, looped those last two words. The folkies just sat there as my voice kept going and going."

"This means two things," I told Al.

7

"What?"

"We've got to stay away from Finnish folkies. And we've got to learn how to swear."

Touring solo proved to be a joy, at least for the distance from my front porch to the airline terminal. For the first time in my rock 'n' roll life, there was no thumping on the guitar player's door at an ungodly hour trying to wake him, no helping the drummer haul his clunky cases into an already overcrowded van, and no awkward phone calls to the bassist, feigning a worrisome bowel disruption so that he'd take my place pounding on the guitar player's door. For the first time in my gigging life, I felt light and free, unencumbered. Al and I and our gear fit easily into one taxi, and as Toronto's greyscape disappeared in the rear-view mirror, I told Al that I simply loved touring solo.

When we arrived at the airport, and I got a good look at Al's guitar case, my enthusiasm dimmed slightly. It was patterned with band stickers and old gaffer tape and looked far more troubadourish than the shiny new case I'd bought especially for the trip. Even worse, Al sported what can only be described as a folksingers' cap – the kind Bob Dylan used to wear in the early days – and completed his folk-rock arsenal with a zippered pouch containing a dozen harmonicas. Not that our musical journey into the northern reaches of Europe was any kind of competition, but Al looked far more like a man destined to leave his musical mark on the world than yours truly in my winter coat, fedora, and showroom guitar case. I grabbed some red airline tape and dressed the edges of the case in an attempt to make it appear time-beaten, but it just looked messy. Clearly, such a fine patina couldn't be forced. The two cases trumpeted that we were master and novice, and I was happy when they disappeared at the end of the baggage ramp.

For months, Al and I had tried to book a departure show in London – we would be there for twenty-four hours before flying to Tampere – but nothing came through until the Canadian High Commission in London put me in touch with a fellow named Scott, who runs the Maple Leaf tavern in Covent Garden. It didn't matter to us where we played, as long as we played, so when Scott offered the Canadian Thanksgiving slot to us – with the warning that the Maple Leaf had never staged a live show before – we gratefully accepted.

Landing in London for the purpose of rocking (well, at least folk-rocking) was a thrilling moment. Our ride into the greater city took us into a galaxy of rock 'n' roll: Jam songs triggered by the names of streets and tube stops and curry takeouts; Kilburn High Road, which gave its name to Ian Dury's first band; countless Kinks moments, from "Waterloo Sunset" to "Johnny Thunder" to "David Watts"; Squeeze's "Up the Junction"; Gerry Rafferty's "Baker Street," and how it regrettably plugged AM radio playlists during the summer of 1975; Roxy Music's "Do the Strand"; "Savoy Truffle," and the famous hotel's glowing green marquee; the Battersea Power Station slumming over the Thames as it does on the cover of Pink Floyd's *Animals*; Pete Townshend in his Union Jack blazer standing in Trafalgar Square; the Sex Pistols signing their EMI contract on the Embankment; and, above all, the Members' white reggae/punk album, *At the Chelsea Nightclub*, which taught me as much about British life as the entire P.G. Wodehouse canon.

I'd visited London twice before, once in a musical capacity, once not. After spending most of the summer of 1985 in Dublin as a student attending Trinity College, I wasted a long, lonely week while London batted me about like a mouse in its cage. It was too big, too expensive, too crowded, too everything. I stayed at Chelsea College, then ran out on my bill in what I then thought was a fitting protest against the brashness and arrogance of the big city. The highlight of the week was seeing John Cooper Clarke and Slim Gaillard play at the Chelsea Town Hall. I was familiar with Slim – the self-proclaimed inventor of "vouty," and author of songs like "Atomic Cocktail" and "Cement Mixer, Puti Puti" – because he'd played Toronto several times. A friend of mine, a female journalist, was once invited by the old bluesman to his hotel room for an interview. She expected to hear stories about what it was like to be a musician in the 1940s and 1950s, but when she arrived, the wiry, grey-bearded Slim opened the door wearing nothing but a smile and a phallus that suggested he hadn't been sitting around writing "vouty." Watching Slim play at Chelsea, it was hard to drive that image out of my mind, but it was still a fine show. What was even finer was getting a tap on my shoulder mid-set. It was Van Morrison asking for a light.

I was next in London in the summer of 1994, just after the Rheostatics' fourth album, *Introducing Happiness*, was released. This visit couldn't have been more different from the first. We stayed at our road manager's elegant flat in Chiswick, drank at the City Barge (Nick Lowe's favourite pub), and gigged at the Borderline, the Mean Fiddler, and the Soho Cafe, where we played to Paul McCartney's son and where the club owner phoned Tim's mother in Etobicoke after our set to complain that we hadn't included "Fan Letter to Michael Jackson" in our set (which was actually my song, not Tim's, but I didn't have the heart to tell our gregarious host).

We were joined in London by our management team and Dave Bookman, the popular Toronto radio host. On his inaugural trip from Chiswick to the West End, Dave emerged from the tube anxious to do one thing before he did anything else: find a way to watch, or listen to, the Buffalo Bills' opening game of the 1994 NFL regular season. On one street corner, he saw a fellow standing next to a table loaded with radios, TVs, and other electronic knick-knacks. These were prizes for a raffle he was hawking tickets for, a short-wave radio included. Dave eyed the radio, bought a ticket, then followed the man into a big, dimly lit hall where a few people had gathered around and a mountain of prizes was stacked on stage. Someone slung a lock across the door, then the raffle began. A barker came on stage to coax people into doubling-up their bids, and within moments, Dave was handing over wads of his vacation money in an attempt to get the radio. An eternity later, he emerged from the dark into the bright sunshine carrying a suitcase wrapped in a garbage bag that contained two salt-and-pepper shakers, a lady's shaver, and a few other gewgaws, including the radio. When he tried to install batteries – all the while holding close his dream of reclining in the safety and comfort of his hotel room listening to the Bills-Dolphins football game – the back fell off the radio, revealing a hole where the wiring was supposed to be. At first Dave told us that he'd only lost a few pounds in the deal, but he later confessed to falling victim to a £200 sting in the cruel heart of the big city.

The day we arrived, Al and I rolled over Waterloo Bridge on a double-decker bus at dusk, our noses pressed against an upstairs window. At Covent Garden, we swung our guitars down the winding staircase and got off below an enormous billboard of John Lennon (yet another greatest hits album was being released in time for Christmas). We dodged the busy, end-of-the-work-day traffic and ambled up the cobblestones of Maiden Lane to the Maple Leaf. It was swarming with Canadian Thankgivingers. To our dismay, the Maple Leaf proved to be not much of a tavern after all. On Maiden Lane – the kind of street where you expected to see John Gielgud strolling around the corner, tapping his umbrella on the cobblestones – Al and I had speculated whether the Maple Leaf would be a crooked-floored, Wawa-via-Blind River, pickled-egg joint in the middle of jaunty England. It wasn't. It was bright, clean, and glossy, its floors hork- and sawdust-free. Worse, the crowd of well-cologned and nicely dressed people were smoking and sipping pints under a wall of televisions showing a week-old Leafs–Habs hockey game. Toronto Blue Jays and Winnipeg Jets uniforms and pennants were tacked around the room, and on one wall, an entire Mountie uniform was framed under glass, giving the so-called tavern the look of a museum about Canada curated by someone who'd never been there.

After depositing our guitars, pedals, and harmonicas (that is, Al's harmonicas) backstage beside an open box containing a pair of snowshoes, a sled, a Hudson's Bay blanket, some hockey sticks, and an old set of wooden skis, we were rescued by a friend, Ian Blackaby, who took us out for dinner by way of a thrilling taxi ride through the city. It was dark by then, and London suddenly brimmed with drama. I experienced that emotional rush well known to travellers that comes from being dropped into a strange town where the tempo is much quicker and the life more lively than at home. Because the theatre hour was approaching, crowds had amassed along sidewalks and under marquees. I relaxed in the backseat of the taxi and let the bright lights paint my face and the early evening's song of busy voices and thrumming engines fill my head.

We devoured fish and chips at a corner stand, then made our way back to the Maple Leaf to find it still busy. The realization that this crowd would be my audience threw my nerves and stomach into disarray. We were booked on the bill with another hoser minstrel – the long-haired, wiry Hamiltonian Mayor McCa, who'd moved to London in hopes of finding the audience that had eluded him at home. I knew there was a chance that both Al and I might look and sound bizarre by way of our songs about dead hockey players and lustful cougars, but the Mayor came across as weird before he'd strummed a chord. One of Canada's rare one-man bands, he was an oddity among musical oddities. In fact, the modern, self-contained outfit has become so unusual, the Mayor was able to count on one hand those artists whom he considered his peers: the Lonesome Organist ("a musical genius – and a great tap dancer – who plays a full drum kit as good with one hand as most other guys can with two"), Eric Royer ("a one-man bluegrass wizard with a guitar-playing machine where he presses pedals to move the pick across the strings"), and Bob Log III ("probably the superstar of all one-man bands"). I thought that being able to transport one's gear – microphones, a small keyboard, tambourine, bass pedal, guitar, guitar effects, and tap shoes – in the hull of a single bass drum was the perfect way to travel, and that the sheer courage of one-man bands elevated them above all other musicians, but the Mayor told me that it was, in fact, a pretty tough rock 'n' roll life. He said that a lot of London cabbies thought twice about picking up guys with synthesizers strapped to their backs and holding tubfuls of percussion, and that one of the prices he'd paid for testing the conventions of musical dexterity was a hernia, which he'd suffered while winding his limbs around a half-dozen instruments at once. This made me keep quiet about my own concerns: that the Maple Leaf's rented speaker towers had the sonic hoist of my kids' Close 'n Play, that the evening's turkey dinners and lagers had left the crowd heavy-lidded, and that the Maple

Leaf stage was nothing more than a patch of carpet wedged between two wooden Mounties and set against a backdrop of televisions showing Memphis versus Michigan Tech.

Al was the first to take this stage, playing a short set. He trained his songs to a handful of people sitting close to the stage, winning their hearts, as he would pretty much every night of our tour. I was on next, and decided not to wait for the pageantry of my solo debut to reveal itself but to simply plug in my two cables and tuner – which were as lacking in shopworn credibility as my guitar case – and get the frig on with it.

When I first pencilled London in on our tour map, I'd thought about it as a pre-tour, warm-up gig. Even now, given that the room was full of Canadians drinking and gabbing as if it were Wednesday night in St. Catharines, I still had reason to believe that's how it would play out. But, in the end, the crowd had little to do with it. Standing in front of an audience for the first time in my life without two musicians to my left and a drummer behind me was an exercise in cold, unwanted fear. Whether my songs were good or bad and whether this test run proved that the newborn Solo Me was built to withstand the roaring winds of time was all beside the point. I spent most of my thirty-five minute set worrying: Did my voice coming out of the pea-shooter speakers sound as dry and squawky as I feared? Was my guitar staying in tune despite what my tuner told me? Did the small woman with the ponytail at the nearest table laugh or was it a cough or was she mocking me? What were Al's impressions before he mysteriously disappeared, and had he gone to the bathroom or was he overcome with boredom, and how was he going to stomach two weeks of this sonic misery and will he ever come back, oh please, oh please, Al, please come back . . .

The set ended. There might have been some applause; I'm not sure. Al found me in the corridor saying "Fuck" over and over like an angry chicken. I grabbed him by the shirt and made him promise to tell me if I'd sucked or not. He offered some friendly positive words, but I heard none of them. I lay my guitar in its case and peeled off my hat and jacket, both covered in a terrible hot sweat.

Then, the beers came. Scott had supplied us with an iconic case of twenty-four Export, but it seemed wrong to drink what we could find at home in the boozy hub of the British Isles. After Al fetched two frothy-headed pints of Guinness, I cheered up enough to join in a salute to ourselves for having got the first gig out of the way. The beer helped me find solace in the fact that I had at least survived the show. Still, it wasn't until Mayor McCa took the stage that I understood what survival meant, and how far from rock 'n' roll death I'd actually been.

The Mayor performed while sitting on a foam wedge on top of a bass drum, which he beat using a reverse bass pedal, and simultaneously played an Echoplexed guitar, blew into a kazoo, and rattled a tambourine with his other foot. Early on in the show, he announced, "If any of the women in the crowd would like to come and touch my hernia, I'd welcome it," a line that won a laugh from a table of hockey players (the London Racers), the Mayor's brother, Troy, among them. At one point, the Mayor reached behind him and picked up a clarinet. Now, every bone in his body was either pressing, stomping, chewing, or sliding full tilt to produce his sound.

It was a musical parlour trick appreciated by everyone in the crowd except George, whose disdainful yowl cut through the cheers and whistles. I hadn't noticed George until he approached the stage from the end of the bar, his stomach protruding toadishly and plaid shirt buttoned tight to his neck, which was as puffy and red as his face. He had small black dots for eyes that stared out from under a frown, and they seemed to harden as he neared the Mayor, shouting, "You are pathetic, man! Worse than worse. You couldn't even sing a good song if you tried!"

While everyone was watching George, the London Racers were slipping off their watches and rings in anticipation of what might come to pass. The Mayor swept his hair from his face, nodded at George, and told the crowd, "Ladies and gentleman, here comes a real-life angel." This only further enraged George, who was unaware that fifteen young Canadians with the ability to pit his head like a plum had risen on their haunches, ready to knock over their table and pounce. The Mayor kept at his detractor, saying, "You've got to live your life, sir. Be happy, fall in love, and dance a little." Then he slid off his bass drum, slipped into a pair of tap shoes, and approached George, clicking and clacking and continuing to exhibit the positivism in the face of potential failure that is part of every one-man band's creed.

Flustered and turning a deeper, more violent red, George retreated, followed by the tap-dancing Mayor. "Here, sir, come on, it's fun," he said. "It's easy, and you'll look great doing it!" George stole a look behind him, where his mates were leaning against the bar and laughing, then broke into a fitful jig. He might have intended it as a parody, but it drew cries of delight from the crowd. Sensing for the moment – relishing it, even – that the whole of the Maple Leaf tavern was with him, George continued to clip and clop like a tippled mule, not once realizing that it was the Mayor's ability to diffuse a bad situation that we were cheering. By reaching for his studded shoes, he'd saved fat, loathsome George the pounding of his life.

HÄMEENLINNA

THIS BOOK ISN'T INTENDED AS A TRAVEL GUIDE, BUT HERE'S some advice anyway: if you're on a literary budget and have no choice but to fly Ryanair, don't bring anything with you heavier than a sardine tin, and do not get into the line at Gatwick Airport that leads to the jerkwad with the tapeworm moustache and lemon-sucking sneer who has as much respect for the foreign traveller as Oasis had for Blur. After trilling around the airport, crowing about our thirty Euro-to-anywhere-on-the-planet bargain fare, Al and I were tagged with a 300 Euro weight violation, shunted into a holding room without seats, and left to fight through a tangle of miserable, tired tourists onto a festival-seating aircraft helmed by scowling flight attendants and dour pilots.

Our mood was black until we arrived at Tampere (pronounced "Tampa-ray") Airport later that day, where we were met by our hosts, Inka and Risto, who drove a clunky car stuffed with junk and spoke very quietly and very rarely. After taking us to their apartment, where we slept fitfully in different three-hour stretches, we hooked up with Mikko, who turned out to be not insane even though he spoke more often, and more volubly, than the entire population of Lapland.

Mikko drove an old bronze Nevada, with a charming spilled-stuff decor and an enormous shopping bag of old cassettes peeking over the backseat. He was tall, thirtyish, had close-cropped blond hair, blue eyes, and spoke in a low, almost fearsome tone, the kind that made James Earl Jones sound like Elmer Fudd. His voice coming from the front seat sounded as if a great man in pelts wearing a Viking helmet was commanding a stag-drawn sleigh, rather than Mikko steering a small car while postulating on the effect of the European Union on Finnish cultural life or how one Russian prog rock band or another had avoided imprisonment during Soviet times or what happened when he ended up putting too much ketchup on his plate during a dinner party in St. Petersburg. Mikko was a documentary filmmaker, journalist, former manager for the Finnish industrial group Cleaning Women, and a graphic design instructor, and he knew as much about the Finnish pop scene as anyone, and lots about the Russian scene too. One of his films had been shot in Russia. It told the story of Yuri Shevchuk, "The Black Dog of St. Petersburg" – and his most recent project concerned the history of education in Finland. This meant two things: one, the easygoing nature of this project had allowed him to take time off to whisk two Canadian guitar players around his country, and two, those guitarists would learn more than any Canadian needed to know about the history of education in Finland. Still, we listened keenly, or at least pretended to, as we headed for our first show in Hämeenlinna, a town between Tampere and Helsinki, the golden birch forests and swimming pool skies drawing our gaze through windows chilled with late-October cold.

One hour after leaving Tampere, we pulled up in front of O'Maggie's bar, which occupied the ground floor of a small, stone-walled inn across from the town's main park. We were greeted by a goateed impresario with thick glasses named AP, who'd been waiting on the sidewalk in anticipation of our arrival. AP wore a Glasgow Celtic scarf and tweed cap and had an enormous cross slung over the mouth of his jacket collar. Al immediately asked him what he thought Celtic's chances were in the upcoming Scottish premiership. AP stared at him.

"What do you think about Celtic going after Roy Keane?" Al said, trying again.

"I do not know what you mean," said AP, shaking his head.

"Celtic. Your scarf. The soccer team."

"Oh, I wear this scarf because it's Irish," he replied. "My life changed when I was ten years old, which was the first time I heard the Dubliners."

Inside the dark, wooden bar – as exact a copy of an Irish pub as the Finns could possibly muster – framed Cafferys, Kilkenny, and Guinness beer mats and watercolours of the west of Ireland hung on the redwood walls. At the front of the room was a compact stage with the flag of Ireland tilted across the back wall. Some generic Irish fiddle music was playing over the stereo, and huddled in various corners of the room were pale, blond-haired Finns sipping Jameson whisky or Harp lager.

"You know, I am not a soccer fan, but, of course, I love hockey, like all Finns," said AP, barely getting the words out before collapsing in a fitful cough and telling us that he had bronchitis. Al and I reared back. "But, you know, I am as tough as a hockey player," he said, coughing some more. "You know who my favourite hockey player is?"

Al and I ventured a few obvious guesses: "Esa Tikkanen? Jari Kurri? Teemu Selanne? Teppo Numminen?"

"No," he said, shouting us down as best he could. "My favourite hockey player is Wendel Clark."

AP was a man of few words who spent a lot of time coughing into his scarf, but I took his pronouncement as an omen that Finland's musical climate would be good to me. Not in my wildest dreams had I expected that the first promoter we'd meet would profess love for the one Toronto Maple Leafs hockey player about whom I'd written a song.

I explained this to AP. I told him how Wendel had drawn me back into hockey in my twenties and how I'd written about him in song and in books that were studied as scripture in many of the great learning institutions at home, figuring that if I couldn't get away with saying this kind of stuff in Finland, I never could. Taking a second to measure the weight of my story, AP added, "I also very much like Kelly Buchberger!" before bringing us up to the stage.

We were booked to play a multi-band bill with four Finnish acts, among them Eero Raittinen, once considered the Elvis Presley of Finland. Al and I were thrilled to see "CAN" bracketed next to our names on posters and placemats spread around the bar as if we were ski jumpers touring the World Cup circuit. I noticed that my name was positioned above the others, but though I explained to AP that this was only my second solo engagement – surely the Finnish Elvis or Al or anyone else would be better suited to headline – my appeal fell on deaf ears. He told me that word of my rock 'n' roll adventure had spread around town, and that a full house was expected for the evening. My intestines pretzeled into a knot of worry. I begged AP to let me go on earlier, but he just smiled so I implored Al to weigh in on the matter. He showed me his toothy pirate grin and told AP, "Well, don't put him on last, but at least put him on after me." Then the two of them ordered pints and clinked glasses, toasting my rookie hard-folk baptism while I slid into a corner and scribbled out set list after set list, the gig a mere five hours away.

By showtime, the club was packed with Finns speaking in whispers but drinking in great volume. Every table was full, and there were lineups at the bar. The first act was a comedy duo who performed an amusing playlet using emphatically brutish voices that everyone in the club seemed to enjoy except Mikko, who stood at the back of the room and glowered at the stage through deep-set blue eyes. He told me later that the play had been, more or less, a parody of his hometown – Heinävesi, in the Savo region – and the actors had made fun of the regional dialect. I told him that it didn't seem like much of a premise for a skit, but it didn't make any difference. "There are people in other parts of Finland who speak with far more amusing accents," he said in his emphatically brutish voice. "Like people in Karelia – very fast, with lots of confusing words – or people in the southwest, around Turku. The way they speak, it sounds like they're barking."

The next band was called Antsmusic and, as one of the few Irish-Finnish groups in existence, they were born to play O'Maggie's. They sawed out a dozen or more reels and songs (including an inexplicably moving version of "The Hills of Donegal") over a wild, thirty-minute set, and the evening started to happen. The husband-and-wife duo of Ilona and Lasse, and bassist Jukka of the Finnish prog band Kingston Wall, threw themselves into their set. The crowd occasionally clapped along, only to retreat into subdued Finnishness after a bar or two. Still, the whole scene appeared to loosen.

After the show, I cornered Ilona, who told me that a few years ago she and Lasse had left their son with Lasse's mother and departed Finland for the Emerald Isle. "We sold everything we owned and bought an old post office van that we hoped wouldn't die on the road," she said. "The first place we went was the Shipper's Tavern in Donegal. It turned out that the proprietor of the club admired the fact that we were a Finnish trio playing Irish music, so they gave us one gig, then another, then another. We eventually played thirty shows, but came home because of our young son. Still, we hope to go back again very soon," she said, winking. "You know, back to the homeland."

Ilona's instrument was a 105-year-old violin given to her by AP, who'd got it from his grandfather. It originally came from Viipuri, an old town near the Finnish-Russian border that had become Russian territory after the Second World War. In Viipuri, there was a famous restaurant in a medieval tower, where a live orchestra performed on the weekends. In 1905, a fire in the restaurant damaged most of the orchestra's instruments, and the bandleader decided to sell them in an auction. That's how AP's grandfather got his violin. The old man played regularly with a town band, whose members included the local vicar, doctor, and lawyer, but after AP's grandpa died the violin was put away until 1998 when AP, himself a musician, was given it to celebrate the release of his first record. AP said, "I'd known Ilona for quite some time, but I never told her about the violin because I thought it was just rubbish. Then, during a session at my home, Ilona noticed the violin case in my study. To my astonishment, she said that the violin had an excellent and powerful voice, and she fell in love with it."

Before Ilona packed up her cherished instrument and Antsmusic left the stage, they thanked the crowd in Finnish, and then, in English, told the patrons of O'Maggie's that they were in for a rare treat, having such talented Canadian musicians in their midst. It was a nice thing to say, but it only made my guts tighten harder. Their last song was "Farewell to Nova Scotia," which I should remember as one of the most beautiful gestures of my minstrel's life but barely remember at all, as I was still balled up in a corner, trying to hammer out just what the frig to play.

It was my turn on stage, and I was greeted by a crowd that possessed both the best and worst qualities, for not only were they attentive and quiet, they were also *attentive and quiet*. Canadian audiences have a reputation for being reserved, but compared to the crowd at O'Maggie's, they are like guests at a Dennis Rodman pool party. Every beverage in the house sat on a coaster, and there were no wheezing soda fountain guns or eight balls smacked stick to pocket by bearded men wearing motorcycle T-shirts. I stared out from the stage nervously tuning and retuning my guitar, fully aware that this crowd was not only poised to hang on to every nuance of my songs but on to the mistakes too.

If it hadn't been for the audience's churchmouse focus, I wouldn't have been intimidated. It was the least self-conscious crowd I've ever seen or played to. O'Maggie's attracted people of every age and persuasion: teenagers with teased hair sitting with their grandparents, a gaggle of likeable drunks, folkies with grey ponytails rocking with their eyes closed, people in wheelchairs fisting pints, and as many women as men. To a person, they stayed silent during each song until its end, when they applauded softly, but generously, a tall wave falling and pooling gently over a beach. I played seven songs (among them "The Ballad of Wendel Clark"), told a few jokes that may or may not have been understood, made fun of the police (a universal ploy), and ended my set by walking down three steps to the side of the stage, only to be called back by a slightly taller wave falling with a degree more weight over the sand.

I was too busy trying to figure out what to do next to bask in the glory of getting an encore at my first Finnish show. I decided to call Ilona to the stage, hoping she might know what to do, but her suggestion was that I play what I liked, which made me suspect that Al had told her I needed to exhibit some sort of self-determination as an artist. Unthinkingly, I started strumming a G chord, and, as often happens whenever Canadian songwriters strum a G chord, I came up with Stompin' Tom Connors, almost immediately disappointing myself.

I'd wanted to break from regular form, and since Tom had been the Rheos' default encore music, I felt like I was doing

Ilona of Antsmusic and the Stompin' Tom of Finland
(*Terho Aalto/Hameen Sanomat*)

something I'd already done a thousand times before. But about
halfway through the song, I realized that no one in the whole of
Europe, save for a handful of misty-eyed backpackers – maybe a
homesick Swiss League hockey player or two – had ever heard
Stompin' Tom Connors. By the halfway point of "Bud the Spud,"
the audience was clapping on time, a small, steady metre that
never grew any louder than it had to be. During Ilona's solo, I
walked to the lip of the stage, threw my guitar against my hip,
and made a series of twisted, Connoresque faces as my accom-
panist gamely soloed in a song she'd never heard before. The
person sitting nearest to the stage quickly scraped her chair back
as I leaned forward into the crowd, the neck of my guitar stabbing the air. My act was something performed by a hundred different singers at a hundred different clubs across North America
on a hundred different nights, but I felt like Screamin' Jay
Hawkins in front of the timid Finns. Which isn't to say that they

didn't like it: the folkies rocked with a little more velocity and the drunks (with whom, I noticed, Al had blended in nicely) were considerably drunker. I was tearing the room apart.

Eero Raittinen was the last performer to take the stage. With his big silver hair swooped back above the Lisa Loeb–glasses that the Finnish seemed to favour, he looked exactly the way I pictured a Finnish rock god. The typical Norseman's image had recently been betrayed by a modest wave of young star performers, among them the Rasmus, HIM, and Nightwish, who could have been Greek or Croatian for the darkness of their features. I wondered whether their appeal was similar to what I'd discovered in Transylvania in 2000, where in the lobby of the Hotel Harghita a group of young Magyar kids sat, enraptured by Britney Spears videos.

But Eero's Norse roots burned deeply, and because he'd been responsible for the very first wave of Finnish rock 'n' roll, it was his job to hold up the side. When AP told us who was going to be on the bill, he singled out Eero, saying, "People cry when he sings" and nearly crying himself. People in the club approached Eero as if he were guarded by a velvet rope, the carefulness of their movement and the quiver in their voices signalling that this was an encounter they would remember for a long time.

"I did very badly in high school," Eero told me over dinner before the show. "I was a failure, really. People said I was the stupid kid, and so I did bad socially because nobody wanted to be around me. Then I discovered rock 'n' roll: people like the Sound '63 and the Jerry Kings. The first record I bought was *Golden Records, Volume 1* by Elvis Presley. Suddenly, I found a way to say all of the things I'd been thinking. At the time, there was mostly Finnish pop music around – there was no rock 'n' roll, with maybe a few exceptions – so when we did 'Be-Bop-A-LuLa,' pretty much every teenager in the country responded. It was a glorious time. It was the birth of Finnish rock 'n' roll.

"But it wasn't just Finland. We went to East Germany in 1964. We played 'Twist and Shout' in a theatre and the kids starting rioting. Like in Russia, they'd never heard anything like it before. It was almost frightening, the impact of the music. But it's what rock 'n' roll should be about. It's the reason anyone ever plays: to have the feeling that you're changing the way someone thinks by the way you're playing."

Eero and his brother, Jussi, signed their first record deal, at sixteen and seventeen respectively, with Fazer Records in 1960. Afterwards, they started a new band, the Esquires, with Eero behind the kit and Jussi singing, performing traditional Finnish songs or tangos in the guitar-twanging style of Hank Marvin and the Shadows. This gave way to the Raittinens' most acclaimed outfit – Eero, Jussi, and the Boys – who recorded Finnish translations of Beatles songs. Around the same time, Eero established a solo career, scoring with one of Finland's biggest records of all-time, "Old Arch-Church," a Swedish song. His interest in the blues deepened and soon playing with Jussi and the Boys became a sideline. AP expanded on this, telling me, "Once the Boys started inching toward widespread commercial acceptance, Eero quit to maintain the music's essence. He spent a lot of time without making big money because of his decision. His brother became much more successful than Eero, but Eero was more respected. He chose to play music that wouldn't get played on the radio. He chose to go his own way, the only way."

Eero's set featured a young slide guitarist who played sitting on a stool during their forty-five-minute set of blues standards, sung howlingly by the Finnish Elvis. There were two stools on stage, but Eero spent most of his time standing in front of the stage, feeling the heat of his followers as he growled and barked

The author with Eero, the Finnish Elvis (*Mikko Keinonen*)

songs like "Back Door Man" in phonetic English, the Deep South becoming the Deep North while maintaining the essential solitude and courage of the blues. I'm not much of a blues guy – a condition I blame on having spent most of my formative years listening to bands for whom the blues was finding the bong empty at the beginning of the weekend – but there was something wonderful about seeing this sixty-year-old Finnish legend throw himself into the music. I've seen my share of legends perform before: Peggy Lee entering and exiting the stage by wheelchair, looking like a great silver Cleopatra at the New York Hilton on 50th Avenue; eighty-year-old Bill Monroe walking into the Apocalypse Club to a standing ovation while wearing a stars-and-stripes blazer and carrying a stars-and-stripes guitar case containing a stars-and-stripes guitar; Sly Stone showing up two hours late to the Colonial Tavern, then slamming down six unforgettable songs before wandering off into the wings, never to return; and Johnny Cash playing with June Carter at Roy

Thompson Hall in Toronto, Bible videos playing behind him as he caught his breath in a captain's chair mid-set while his son performed. In each case, the shows were glazed with melancholy, but Eero's performance eschewed all of that. He ripped through his repertoire, came back for an encore, then drank with his fans. It was how most young musicians like to envision themselves in the twilight of their art, yet very few actually realize.

Before leaving O'Maggie's, I thanked AP, who by now had fought through his chest-rattling cough and was drinking with gusto. He told me, "Some people said that my dream to present Irish music in Hämeenlinna was impossible. But I did it, and look: those same people are here listening tonight. This is the best club in Finland, Dave, the best," he slurred. Then he spotted Al and threw him into a headlock of love.

As I neared the doorway, one of the O'Maggie's drunks broke from his group and grabbed my arm. He was missing a few teeth and had a tight face weathered by the cold, but his eyes glinted with mischief. He brought me close and, in hackneyed English, said, "Your music, yes, very good. I liked your voice very much." I thanked him profusely, then admitted that it wasn't too often that my voice got singled out for praise.

"No, good, good," he said. "You pronounce English very well."

TAMPERE

WHENEVER I TALKED ABOUT FINNISH ROCK 'N' ROLL WITH anyone who either played or lived it, the conversation always veered to one performer: Matti Nykänen, the Olympic ski jumper and pop star. Matti's story was on everyone's minds, as he had recently been sprung from jail after doing time for stabbing his friend while playing *sormikoukku*, a parlour game in which one person tries to hook the other with a finger. Matti apparently couldn't stand losing, and after falling behind and being taunted by his friend, he shivved him. This was typical of the Flying Finn's post-Olympic life, and as Risto and Inka drove us back north to Tampere for the second date of our tour, the news came over the radio that he'd suffered another dust-up with his wife and was looking at four months of jail time if found guilty of assault.

Matti's pop infamy embarrassed the Finnish musical community. As an outsider, I was intrigued with his rise and fall without having to suffer through its daily permutations, which many Finns found tiresome. After Matti's run as a golden-haired alpine star throughout the 1980s, he'd turned to music as a vehicle for sustaining his stardom. It worked for a while until his several mistresses were found out, some of whom ended up launching recording careers themselves. Matti's star dimmed, but the Finnish public was still drawn to him in the same way that motorists are drawn to a flaming Toyota stuffed fender-first in a ditch. Matti continued to gig, and Finns continued to fill arenas, then concert halls, then small theatres to hear him. At one point on the downward slope, his manager suggested that he incorporate striptease into his act. Matti, ever the body-proud ex-athlete, agreed. The shows still got smaller, eventually settling into clubs, taverns, and finally restaurants, but his act remained the same: disrobing to his briefs in an attempt to give his performances the kind of show-stopping element that his voice or songs could not. Then a few minutes of video shot in a restaurant showed him stripping with tears pouring down his face. The tape made the national news. Matti was disgraced but continued to hang on. Now, he'd decked his wife, and everyone was talking about it.

Darkness and melancholy pervaded a lot of Finnish musical culture, which might explain, in part, why the darkest of genres – death metal, speed metal, metal, thrash, shred and hard rock – still held huge appeal for the sombre Finns. Even when these musical siblings lagged in popularity in North America, they held on to their fans in Scandinavia and Finland. Death metal rose in popularity in the 1990s and bands like Dio still toured Norway, Sweden, and Finland, and sold a mountain of tickets. In 2005, Deathchain, Amorphis, Apocalyptica, Sentenced, Malicious Death, and Pain Confessor were serious forces, while the Children of Bodom – whose fans are known as the Hate Crew – scored consistent number-one singles on the national charts. In 2006, the rockapocalypse band Lordi, led by the former president of the Finnish Kiss Army, captured the Eurovision song contest using pyro and costumes to steal the title. Swathed in gruesome latex, Lordi are like Gwar lite, with each member of the band representing a monster from a different universe.

Al and I spent our first day in Tampere strolling around town. It is a pleasant, mid-sized city built around two canals and a river where old brown-brick factories have been reborn as art galleries and performance spaces. We kept coming across packs of middle-aged Tamperites wearing black Motörhead T-shirts, which stood out, naturally, against their blond hair and snowy complexion. Assuming that the local headbangers' chapter was holding its semi-annual gathering, we thought nothing of it. Then a day later, we discovered that Motörhead had performed at the Ice Hall the night before, supplanting the city's two hockey teams – the Ilves (lynx) and Tappara (battleaxes) – for two hours of classic British riffology.

I was disappointed that I'd missed a chance to document Finnish hard rock culture full bore, but nowhere as disappointed as Al. Many years back, Al's old band, the Morganfields, were performing at the Backstage Club in Montreal (opening for the Headstones) when the club's soundman told Al that because Motörhead were in Montreal for a concert the next night, there was a good chance they'd stop by the club and take in the gig. "The soundman seemed a little too excited that the club was going to be graced by a real-live rock star," Al said, so he had been nonchalant regarding the potential drop-in.

In the middle of the Morganfields' set, the soundman announced over the club's monitors, "Lemmy [Motörhead's lead singer and bassist] wants the stage now! Lemmy wants the stage now!" Al's nonchalance instantly turned to cynicism, then rage. During the band's final few songs, he juiced his fuzz tone and screamed his lyrics to protest the fact that his set was about to be sabotaged by a rock star. The soundman turned off the PA in an attempt to get the Morganfields to stop playing, all the while parroting his command through the monitors. At the end of his set

Al, true to his word, shouted, "Thank you and fuck off!" to the crowd. Lemmy was standing in the wings, looking, in Al's words, "like a big fucking rock star waiting his turn." Al threw all of his stuff off the stage and loaded out. "I walked right past Lemmy, saying nothing," said Al. "A little while later, Motörhead's road manager found us and asked just what the fuck my problem was. I was so pissed off I didn't say anything. Then he told us, 'You know, Lemmy really dug you guys. He was actually dying to sit in with the band.' The soundman, it turned out, was French Canadian and had misinterpreted Lemmy's request, thinking he wanted the stage all to himself."

Finland's other great musical love is tango. Introduced in 1913 at the Börs Hotel in Helsinki by a Dutch couple during a demonstration dance, the tango's deep melancholy and heavy rhythmic tread captured the Finns' imagination. Local musicians eventually slowed the beat and pushed the sound into a minor key until it resembled a woozy waltz, unlike its sexually energetic South American cousin. Because the rise of tango coincided with Finland's independence from Russia in 1917, it came to represent a kind of liberation music and became the music of choice for the pre–Second World War generation. During the war, Arvo Koskimaa's "Syyspihlajan alla" was played continually over Finnish radio as a way of mocking the Russians' attempt to intercept broadcast frequencies. Postwar, pretty much every village in Finland had a tango club around which social life revolved. One Finnish musician told me that in the late 1950s there was such deep allegiance to the tango that rock 'n' roll bands were ordered to play it – once at gunpoint. In 1974, Frank Zappa and the Mothers of Invention won the Finns' eternal hearts by playing a Finnish tango at the Helsinki Concert Hall. While Finnish musical tastes had broadened immensely since then, there was still a degree of mania about the tango. Currently, festivals like Tangomarkkinat, in the country town of Seinäjoki, attract about 100,000 people annually.

Tango historian and broadcaster Maarit Niiniluoto once told David Atkinson of the *Financial Times* that because "Finns are not very verbal, nor prone to easy communication, tango expresses the distance that Finnish people feel in their lives. The sadder the tango, the more Finnish people love it." Some fans hold that the tango brings colour and life to the country's long, dark winters, while others think its deeply blue mood mirrors Finland's suicide rate (the second highest in the world). The unbending bond between tango and the soul of Finland was best articulated by singer Laura Hihnala, who told Atkinson, "When I sing, I feel the pain of tango. Finns reach out through this music – it's like musical therapy." Sounding like the lead singer of Deathchain, she added, "I want to take Finnish tango to the rest of the world, to share our pain."

It's not surprising that the Finns had looked beyond their borders for musical influences – particularly in modern music – because for decades the indigenous scene had been dominated by copycat bands and celebrity *schlagers*. Until the late 1990s, and with the exception of Eero Raittinen and a few of his peers, they'd made very little popular rock 'n' roll of substance – a cultural conundrum shared recently by countries such as Canada and Australia. Johanna Vehkoo, a journalist for Tampere's local paper, said, "As late as 1999, a lot of Finnish bands were disco-dance bands who tried to copy Ace of Base and Roxette: successful Swedish bands. For a while, Finland became notorious for sending performers to Eurovision [Europe's annual song contest] who traditionally scored the lowest. Only Norway had more songs that scored zero points."

Then, Vehkoo explained, "Slowly – very slowly – all of this started to change. In older times, you'd notice the Spice Girls and Britney Spears on pencil cases that kids brought to school. Now it's Finnish pop stars like Hanna Pakarinen, the girl who won Finnish Idol. She's pretty mild, but she wears black, has chains on her belt, and sings in English, a big improvement on the national charts, where traditionally albums recorded by celebrities have been very big. Not so long ago, the Cuban wife of a former member of parliament released a best-selling record, and then, of course, there's Matti Nykänen." It was inevitable his name would come up. When I asked Vehkoo what she thought of the fallen Olympian, she said, "He was once a huge star, but now people pay to go and laugh at him. I feel very sad for him. He and his wife are always either fighting violently or making up. But every now and then he'll release another song about ski jumping to glory and people eat it up."

This weird cocktail of Irish-Finnish groups, British metal bands, tango heroes, and pop idols gave me the impression that Finnish soundtrack was wildly extroverted music played by painfully introverted people. After hanging out for a few days at Telakka – Tampere's most well-regarded venue and the site of our next gig – this dichotomy became easier to understand.

A converted, century-old shipyard, Telakka had a live room, a theatre, an art gallery, and a movie house (and sauna, of course). Because of its old, dusty floors, candlelit tables, and the great wooden beams supporting its low ceilings, it felt like a place that had shouldered countless hard winters and cold, wet autumns, a fortress resistant to the wild Nordic elements. When we arrived at the club after walking through the city's labyrinth of central railyards, it seemed that everyone inside was wearing a turtleneck, smoking, drinking Koff beer, and murmuring to one another. The tables were matched with old schoolhouse chairs, a push-button cigarette machine sat in the corner, and the room's low light and porthole windows made it feel as if the hour were forever at dusk.

We were treated to a meal of salted herring with mashed potatoes, which I ate while studying posters in the club's vestibule announcing upcoming gigs – I WAS A TEENAGE SATAN WORSHIPPER, BONGO RHINO, MENTAL ALASKA and a myriad of other artists. I'd never heard of any of them. New bands in new towns always beguile me, at least until they turn out to be Toto cover groups. Tampere had those too, including a few who were performing at "Toto Night" at another club on the same evening as our gig.

Below the jigsaw of gig posters was a CD jukebox stocked by Tomi Salmela, the Finnish actor and star of Jim Jarmusch's movie *Night on Earth*. It boasted records by Miles Davis, Tabu Ley, Lee Dorsey, the Dixie Chicks, Townes Van Zandt, Randy Newman, Joni Mitchell, Jackie Mittoo, and countless Finnish bands. Since there was nothing perfunctory about its programming, I spent much of the afternoon at Telakka feeding Euros into the machine, my ear bent toward the doorway to the vestibule. When I ran out of money, Al and I asked where we could crash for a few hours before the gig. The women who ran the lunch counter and poured Koff and Karhu beer at the small stand-up bar suggested we try the band room upstairs, where two cedar benches and three chairs sat outside a sauna.

I grabbed a bunch of sauna towels from hooks with the names Jussi, Tuukka, Jere, and Peltsi plated below them and covered one of the benches with them. Al, flaunting his troubadourness, chose the tile floor. As I lay on the bench, trying to sleep, I noticed that the sound coming from Telakka's jukebox had given way to a classic rock radio station. The keening sound of the Finnish disc jockey's voice – to say nothing of the exoticism of the station's commercials and stings – ensured that even though I desperately needed to sleep, it was impossible for my brain to shut down. Had I been listening to classic rock radio in North America instead of northeastern Europe, I might have been numbed into submission by so many "Radar Loves" and "Rocky Mountain Ways." Instead, I listened to the announcer's looping ramble, and to my great delight and satisfaction I recognized a few words – "Stevie Wonder" and "Motown." The station was playing eight of his songs in a row, occasionally interrupted by the announcer, presumably telling the story of Stevie's life.

It was a rare connection with classic rock – or oldies – radio for me. My affection for the format ended the moment I realized that all such stations repeated songs over the course of their programming day, as if to suggest that there haven't been enough good records released over the past four decades to keep a playlist fresh. After suffering through a barrage of "Venuses" by Shocking Blue and "Horse with No Names" by America, I concluded that these playlists are filled with songs that you or I never have to hear again; songs that should be forever banned from the radio; songs that, when you hear them, make you want to get out of the supermarket as quickly as possible. My personal list of banned songs begins with "Time of the Season" by the Zombies. Not only does this mothball include the most unfortunate of all middle-eight alternatives – the 1960s organ solo – but its lyrics are pedophialiac. Classic rock or oldies radio steals precious airtime from vital new bands, and touts songs that not even your aunt's dentist could love. In the right hands, retro radio could probably be a great thing: music junkies dipping into the fourth track on side two of that Great Album by that Great Neighbourhood Band that no one outside of Your Town has ever heard of. Instead, it's become just another way that big business is attempting to squish the world into one compliant white mass jiggling to a nostalgic soundtrack tied to product placement and the lie that one generation's music is superior to another's because its songs, like millions of pop cockroaches, cannot be killed.

I wouldn't have guessed it, but lying on a slab of wood covered in sauna towels on the top floor of a club in western Finland was the perfect place to hear "You Haven't Done Nuthin'" from *Fulfillingness' First Finale*, Stevie Wonder's sixth album. The song's woozy groove, its pecking clavinet, striding horns, and the Jackson Five's choral singalong – "Doodawop! Whombappa!" – comforted my sleepy head and bones. As the radio ran through "Superstition" and "Don't You Worry 'Bout a Thing" to "Sir Duke" and "Master Blaster," my ears feasted while my body slumbered. Then we were called, too soon, down to the club.

Back downstairs, Al and I sound-checked on a three-foot high, narrow wooden stage, then sat down to meet the headline band, Laurila, a young power pop band originally from the north of Finland. The group's singer was Janne Laurila, a young, quick-smiling, dark-haired fellow who continued what must be the Finnish tradition of asking visiting Canadians to guess the name of their favourite hockey player.

"I'll give you a hint," said Janne after I'd missed on several attempts. "It is a player named Jokinen."

"Olli Jokinen?" I guessed.

"No!" shouted Janne, shooting out a finger. "It is Jussi Jokinen! He comes from my hometown, Oulu."

After we'd established Janne's connection to the Jokinen of the north, I sat down with his band and talked rock. When I mentioned something about the audience in Hämeenlinna being the quietest crowd ever, Laurila's drummer, Antti Hietala, was quick to warn me not to mistake Finnish reserve for a lack of interest or dearth of spirit. "A lot of people who come here get the wrong impression," he said. "Some people think that because we're quiet, we're being devious or deceitful, but it's not true. Because someone isn't speaking, it doesn't necessarily mean they're withholding wild and wonderful things. It's just that the Finns aren't very good at small talk. But who needs small talk? Small talk is very overrated. It's for Americans and western Europeans who are uncomfortable whenever there's any kind of silence. Finns, on the other hand, allow themselves to be quiet. To us, filling the air by saying things like 'have a nice day' is more suspicious."

The conversation turned back to music, and to Laurila. Antti and Janne stressed that they played positive and energetic power pop for a new generation of listeners tired of melancholy Finnish music. "When I was growing up, there was one very popular singer, Topi Sorsakoski, who did a sort of rock 'n' roll/tango thing," Antti said. "He was the prototype of the sad, alcoholic Finnish man singing about being a sad, alcoholic Finnish man. He always looked and sounded like he had a terrible hangover, but fans loved him because they saw themselves in his music. But our band – and other bands like ourselves – are trying to destroy the stereotype. We're singing about how life can be great, and we're singing in English. Believe it or not, this is still a revolutionary thing in Finnish music."

It was exciting to hear talk of revolution in rock 'n' roll, coming, as Al and I did, from a continent where the notion of a revolution in music had long ago been wrenched from the culture. I got the sense that in Finland because the culture was opening up, you could still talk about revolution without choking on your granola. But Antti's optimism was nonetheless guarded. "I've been hearing for the last ten years that Finnish rock 'n' roll is going to be the next big thing," he said. "I'm still waiting."

I told him what was happening in Canada, how bands such as Arcade Fire and Broken Social Scene were making a serious imprint on the American alternative music scene, drawing attention to the greater national sound as a whole, but Antti was wary about how a Finnish star system would affect his country. "Finland has become more celebrity obsessed than ever before," he said. "Newspapers and TV are becoming more American-style, and a lot of successful record companies who promised they'd sign young Finnish bands after the successes of HIM and the Rasmus are only signing groups with the potential to grab headlines. In a way, it's great that we have our own pop stars, but there should be room for everyone. Unless you look and sound like you're capable of appealing to lots of people, the press and the industry don't really want to know about you."

After a while, Laurila excused themselves and took to the stage to sound-check a couple of big-beat songs that reminded me of the music of Fastball or the Lemonheads. By gig time, Telakka was filled with murmuring turtlenecks, their faces drawn in the flickering candlelit. The stage had one feature that struck me as terribly Finnish: a single wooden post standing dead centre, blocking the singer's view. When I got up to play, partly to appease my solo butterflies and partly in an act of extroverted North Americanness, I moved the centre microphone two feet to the right, revealing the entire room save for an empty table near the front.

While tuning up, I noticed a figure in blue and white sitting at the back of the club. I peered closely and saw that it was a person wearing not an unusually colourful turtleneck but a Toronto Maple Leafs sweater. I was so astonished, I unplugged my guitar and walked over to where a man named Timo was sitting with three Rheostatics CDs and a copy of my first book, *On a Cold Road*.

There are a handful of phrases common to people the world over, and "What the fuck?" has to be one of them. Timo, who had rock 'n' roll hair and a goatee, got the gist of my outburst and laughed. "I know about you from Rush," he said, explaining that he'd discovered the Rheos after reading on the Internet that drummer Neil Peart had played on one of our albums. I asked Timo if he knew a lot about Canadian music. He told me that while he loved Max Webster and was probably the only person east of the Maritimes who owned every Goddo record, it all came back to the Guess Who.

"I first heard 'Dancing Fool' in 1974," he said. "Well, it wasn't their version – it was a Finnish band who covered it – but I loved the song and decided to find out more about the band who'd written it. Then, last year, I made the pilgrimage: I went to Kitchener, Ontario, to see them perform. It was the greatest concert of my life."

I told Timo that I considered meeting him a great stroke of luck and climbed back on stage feeling secure that even if the evening betrayed me, at least one person in the crowd would think of the show as adding a footnote to the annals of Canadian rock 'n' roll. But while Timo was a great talisman, it turned out that I didn't need him after all, for the audience in Tampere was as lively as the Hämeenlinnians had been shy. Whenever I asked the crowd a question between songs, they shouted back. Early in the set, I introduced the song "My First Rock Concert" – a litany of formative rock 'n' roll experiences sung over G-C-D – and polled the crowd to name the first band they'd ever seen perform live. For a moment, there was only silence until a single deep voice boomed from the darkness of the room, "Remu and the Hurricanes!"

I wouldn't have known Remu or any of his Hurricanes had I found them sitting in my kitchen on Christmas morning, but it didn't matter, because the mere mention of the band triggered wild laughter, which sounded particularly lively coming from an audience of hushed Finlanders.

Then came another voice: "BTO!"

"BTO?" I asked incredulously. "Tell me, sir, are you a 'Taking Care of Business' or 'You Ain't Seen Nuthin' Yet' kind of person?"

"BTO!"

From that point forward, every song I did was preceded by a short discussion. Either that, or I made fun of Matti Nykänen, which would prove throughout the tour to be an engaging device. Later on in the set, one fan who'd been working on his English over the course of four or five songs answered my first question, announcing from a table near the stage, "My first rock 'n' roll show was watching the group Queen." I told him that I was impressed, and a little jealous, having never seen the great cabaret metal band perform live.

"Yes, Queen," he repeated. "A hundred thousand people in St. Petersburg!" at which parts of the crowd *ahhhhed*. I felt suitably far from home, knowing that if I'd asked that question of a hundred different Canadian audiences, few if any of them would have said that Freddie Mercury strutting across the stage of a St. Petersburg soccer stadium was their formative rock experience. From this point on, the evening got better and better. During Al's set, the same Remu-loving fan approached the stage. Al stepped to the floor and hugged him, proclaiming, "I love Finland!" before sinking the fifth of Scotch that he drank every show. Later, during Laurila's set, a tall, older gentleman and a dark-haired woman in a pinstriped suit walked out of an unlit corner of the room and slow-danced in front of the stage for two verses and a chorus before withdrawing to the darkness.

Near the end of his set, Al invited me and Risto – who, despite being a drummer, was among the quietest persons I'd ever met – to join him for a version of "Freight Train" by Fred Eaglesmith. Risto tiptoed behind Laurila's kit, settled nervously on the drum stool, tentatively picked up a pair of drumsticks, and, after a four count, proceeded to smash the skins into sub-mission. He was a blur of arms and legs and hair, the drums rattling and shaking from the force of his playing. I'd never seen someone so wispy and featherlike become so frenetic in such a short time. After he finished, Risto gazed through his long, matted hair into the crowd, then fired his sticks off the front of the stage. Minutes later, he was back at his table with Inka, smoking and staring off into the dark in utter silence. I decided that Finland needed rock 'n' roll like the rest of us needed food, beer, and air.

HELSINKI

AFTER TAMPERE, AL, MIKKO, AND I HIT THE ROAD FOR
Helsinki, a two-hour journey accompanied by the sound of tapes
rattling across the Nevada's dashboard. Finland's capital was
beautiful. Enormous wedges of Precambrian rock jutted out of
the street like great stone foreheads with grassy sideburns,
making it seem as if buildings like the Nokia block or the Kiasma
Museum or the Temppeliaukio Church – a modern, domed
building hewn from solid rock – were merely guests of the land.
The city gave way to a lovely, leaf-strewn neighbourhood called
Kapyla that was impossibly well forested, given that it was
located minutes from downtown. This is not to suggest that the
tempo of the big city made it unlikely for so much mellow to
exist so close by, because while Helsinki's core purred with
people, it never roared. There was a calm about it that reminded
me of Toronto in the 1970s.

Later that day, we wandered around the city with Mikko's
brother-in-law, Paul. Before Paul set me loose in the city to
explore its book and record stores, he took me to Kaivopuisto
Park. There, we climbed a hill and looked into the Finnish Gulf,
where ships made daily crossings to Tallin, Estonia, just eighty
kilometres to the south. Helsinki is the only city other than
Buenos Aires where disembarkment leaves the seafarer in the

43

centre of town, and I could see the modest onion domes in the
heart of the city behind me, as if both welcoming visitors and
pushing the Finns to look beyond.

We were booked to play at the local art college, opening for
Cleaning Women, Mikko's old friends with whom he'd travelled to Russia. Mikko's excitement was palpable. He had made
the drive to Helsinki a constant storytelling session in which he
related Cleaning Women's experiences in China (one of the
members had mistakenly called the crowd in Shanghai a "cow's
vagina") and Moscow (where the singer told the Russian
crowd, excitedly, "This is our worst concert in Russia," trading
an "fi" for a "wo"). We discussed the possibility of Cleaning
Women one day travelling to Canada to open a national tour for
the Rheostatics.

I'd first heard Cleaning Women at Risto and Inka's and had
liked them. We'd screened an animated short to which they'd
contributed a skronkish instrumental soundtrack, and I'd liked
that too. They were promising on record, and the chances that
Al and I would meet our kindred spirits at our third show in
Finland seemed pretty good.

The club at the art college – Kipsari – was a smallish room
with lots of ceiling pipes, exposed steel, black lights, and couches
and tables strewn around. The polar opposite of Telakka's
brown boat barn, it was the kind of bar I would have immediately walked out of were I pushed into it by club-crawling
friends. Once inside, Al and I immediately noticed that Cleaning
Women's equipment contained as much bare metal as the bar
itself. I would have been more impressed by their industrial
Jungle Gym, however, had the entire breadth of the stage not
been taken up by a row of laundry racks, except for a three-foot
gap where Al and I were supposed to stand and play. Dominating the back of the stage was a cumbersome drum kit built out

of old tire rims, stove doors, colanders, roasting pans, bits of iron detritus, and metal cylinders that looked as if they would be fun to hit. The stage was like a robot's graveyard, where the skeletons of old machines had been assembled and reborn into a dazzling musical arsenal. But the sight of it was dimmed for me by the fact that I had no room to stand without one of the drummer's crooked stove pipes poking me in the caboose.

The first thing I did was ask Mikko whether CW could take down parts of their construct to give us a bit more room to perform. Al warned me against doing this, saying, "Dude, we're playing with an industrial band!" sounding as if he was relishing the situation just a little too much. But I thought I'd give it a try because good gigs generally happen whenever the headlining band and opening act share a certain regard for what it takes to make each other's show hum. Without mutual respect or admiration, the atmosphere can be poison. Once, the Ben Folds Five were opening for 1990s grunge popsters Everclear – an awkward pairing, to say the least. Near the end of the tour, the guys in Everclear asked BFF if they'd videotape their concert for them. They said they'd be glad to but instead filmed themselves swishing their penises around in Everclear's rider: the gua-camole, salsa, etc. They shot some of the show, then filmed post-gig as Everclear and their entourage tucked into the fouled chips and dip.

When the Rheos were a young band, we opened for a group called the Kinetic Ideals. We were booked to play a show in Waterloo, but when we got there we discovered that one of us had left our guitar strap and cables at home. We asked the head-lining group, with whom we'd played many shows, if we could borrow these items. They held a meeting behind closed doors and decided that we could not. Their decision was so absurd that we thought it was a joke until we realized they'd consulted their manager and that he'd advised them not to, for whatever reason. Tim and I ended up sharing straps, and the gig was fine, but during the Kinetic Ideals' set, we took a measure of revenge. We drank their beer and savaged their deli tray, singing Kinetic Ideals parody songs while our friend Gordie strummed their warm-up acoustic guitar so hard that he broke three strings and spidered its body in threads of blood.

I ignored Al and suggested to Mikko that it would be a lot easier for Al and I to do our thing if we didn't have to worry about falling into one of Timo the drummer's bedpans. He looked grave and told us, regretfully, that it would be impossible because Cleaning Women's show required precision electronics and hours of set-up. It seemed like a reasonable argument in principle, but that the news was delivered to us by Mikko, not the band, made me suspicious of their sense of diplomacy. Then, the promoter, who wore a Gunter-esque black turtleneck and shark's tooth necklace, broke the news that because of the planned length of the CW's set, Al and I had less than an hour to share between our two sets.

As it turned out, Cleaning Women were nowhere to be found (making it very hard to find their warm-up acoustic guitar). By gig time, a modest crowd had gathered under the black lights, attempting to outdour one another in their ironic T-shirts, laced leather boots, and sci-fi hair. Once Al took to the stage, I was chilled by how purposefully they ignored the crazy-haired, crook-nosed Welsh-Canadian singing about freezing to death in the woods. They were as loud as they were bored, particularly three lesbians on a couch set near the front of the stage who ran their hands up one another's shirts when they weren't throwing eye-rolling glances of disgust at the stage.

To his credit, Al played as if to the lemur cage. One thing I'd noticed about his set was that he didn't let crowd indifference get the best of him, another pro move, I figured. He asked the crowd in Helsinki the same question he would have asked had he been gigging in Sudbury, Pender Island, or Chattanooga: "Anybody here from Guelph?" Before performing "Janefield," one of his most moving songs, he introduced it as being about a high-school friend who owned the world's largest collection of pornography ("way before Dave started his," he sniggered). It was a litmus test for Al, because he knew that audiences who laughed or giggled uncomfortably at this were his for the taking, while those who didn't would have to be worked a little harder. But in Helsinki, the crowd responded to the word *pornography* as if he'd said *pot pourri*: yawning, draining glasses of cheap beer, and smoking.

Every musician in every genre has a way of dealing with hostile or unattentive crowds, but there's a certain "fuck you" in a solo act that is different than with a band. Sure, basses and doubleneck guitars are convenient when it comes to taking out that jackass spewing venom from the front row, but a single performer dealing with a heckler can be far more confrontational. As I made my way to the stage before throwing myself to Helsinki's chronically hip, I remembered a story that Al had told me about Stan Rogers, the late Canadian folk singer. Stan was built like an ox, had a surly temperament to match, and he didn't easily suffer fools. One night in the early part of his career, he was playing in a folk club where someone in the audience kept requesting Morris Albert's "Feelings," another one of those songs that we should never have to hear again. Stan was polite at first, reminding the fellow ad nauseam that he didn't play cover songs. But the guy wouldn't let up. "You probably won't play 'Feelings' because you can't play 'Feelings,'" he sneered. Stan got up from his chair, put down his guitar, walked up to the fellow, grabbed him by the ears, and punted him out the door into the street. Then he returned to the stage and asked, "Now, does anybody else want to hear 'Feelings'?"

With no choice but to position myself in the middle of the stage with Cleaning Women's mechano-works surrounding me like bayonets, I began my set. Then I stopped. The person working the monitors had forgot to wire my voice to the stage. I managed to work it out with the soundman, but no matter how well I described the way I wanted my voice to sound in the monitor, it came back at me like a hen squawking into a paper bag. My guitar sounded dead and dry too, clearly the victim of a rock rig that responded best to dudes screaming over twenty-five jackhammers. This isn't to suggest that I don't enjoy a little jack-hammer every now and then. It's just that I felt terribly under-equipped, knowing that not even David Lee Roth hollering in his red rhinestone jumpsuit could have got a rise from that crowd.

One of the discoveries I'd made about playing solo was that I fidgeted with the microphone stand whenever I talked, some-thing I'd never done before on stage. I would run my hands over its metal as if searching for fingers to clasp for comfort. Even worse, on the cool stage of Kipsari I called attention to this tick by rambling on about it to the crowd until one of the stand's rods gave way with an ugly thud.

I felt humiliated and walked off stage. I'd fully intended to head to the back of the club and throw my gear into the white-walled closet that passed for a band room, but I stopped at the lesbian couch, demanding as best I could, that they look away. "Here's another in a long line of Canadian songs about pornog-raphy," I groused, pulling the plug and singing, as Tony Bennett might say, "in the air."

"It's also about George W. Bush," I added as the girls' buried their faces in one another's armpits. I strummed a D chord and kicked my foot against the black tile floor and was about to start

"Pornography" when Marco, a pale, chrome-domed Buddha sitting across from the girls, threw his arms wide into the air and sang, "Oh, George Bush, I fucking hate you."

I shuffled over to Marco and played for him. I was so close that I could have leaned over and licked his head. After every chorus, I asked Marco what he thought of George Bush, and he provided the appropriate vocal. By the last verse, he was clapping his hands trying to get others to join him in his opera buffo. One by one, a set of bored Finnish faces came alight like a string of patio lanterns. Pushing my luck, I swanned back to the lesbian couch and slid across an arm of the chesterfield while playing, but they were in no mood to be serenaded. So, of course, I stayed, shouting to Marco, "Who do you hate?"

"Oh, George Bush, I fucking hate you."

I invited Al into the crowd to help me sing the next song – "Bridge Came Tumblin' Down" – and it went down as well as the previous one, so we dared returning to the stage, playing "Freight Train" and ending with "Horses." For "Horses" – a song that sounds best when accompanied by a propulsive rhythmic whomp – we called for Timo, Cleaning Women's drummer, who had wandered into the club during my set, along with the rest of his bandmates. Before laying into the song, we shouted, "Timo! Timo! Come and help us invent Canadian-Finnish folk-disco!" We hoped he'd bolt to the stage, as Risto had in Tampere, but Timo never appeared. We finished the song anyway, congratulating ourselves for turning a nothing gig into something.

I headed backstage to stash our gear and threw the door open to find Cleaning Women sitting around on a bunch of stools, smoking. Timo was crouched in front of a wall mirror, staring deeply at himself and putting on eyeliner.

"Timo. What happened, man? Me and Al, we were calling for ya out there," I said by way of introduction.

Timo looked at us the way a dog looks at a monkey.

"It would have been great to have you," said Al.

"Ya, really great," I told him. "What happened, man?"

Tero, another of the Cleaning Women, answered for his drummer.

"Timo could not play. As you can see, he is busy putting on his makeup."

Cleaning Women's conceit was that they were from outer space, from the Planet Clinus (rhymes with penis). While gigging with them the following night in Lahti – a hole of a town where the local speciality was *kippkoff*, or "meat mug," as Mikko called it – we were amazed to watch them backstage, pulling on nylons and skirts and applying makeup in an attempt to look both womanly and alien (another detail: they all wore black bikini underwear). To make absolutely sure that audiences understood their concept, Terro started each show by announcing, "We are Cleaning Women. We come from Planet Clinus in outer space!" Mikko and his friends thought this was a brilliant concept, and while I was reluctant to call into question Mikko's taste – after all, he liked Al and me well enough to bring us to Finland – it was unfortunate that he'd tried to convince us that Cleaning Women was Finland's best band. Because, alas, I didn't like them.

Musically, it was all concept, no song. And even the concept of a futuristic electronic band seemed trite. I'm sure we could all name a handful of artists, some good, some not, who claim to be from a place other than Earth: David Bowie/Ziggy Stardust, Gwar, Man or Astroman?, Kraftwerk, Gary Numan, BB Boris, Parliament-Funkadelic, Spaceman 3. Nor was the shtick of men dressed up like women original: entertainers have been doing that since before Milton Berle. Maybe it's the BTO in me talking,

Pre-gig ritual in Helsinki (*Mikko Keinonen*)

but I probably would have been more absorbed by their set if they had not been dressed like female extras from Fritz Lang's *Metropolis*.

Had the Cleaning Women seriously rocked, none of this would have mattered. There were a couple of moments backstage when I was drawn in by the sound because I couldn't see them, and they were occasionally heavy sounding despite their skirts and hairbands. Risto, the bassist, played a long-necked instrument with a body made from the very tin tub in which he'd bathed as a child. Despite his JC Penney outfit, he had a severe look – a sharp-browed, gaunt Rutger Hauer – and at times he made his souped-up bath sound like a roaring jet engine. Beside him, Terro played a laundry rack with such speed and precision that he sounded like a Nordic Adrian Belew, expertly working his delay pedal while melodically bending the laundry struts. Timo, the drummer, was the band's weak link because, like the group, he believed that being surrounded by found objects was enough to win hearts and power a brand-new sound. But if it ain't got that swing, whacking a hunk of metal only sounds like a hunk of metal being whacked. Unfortunately for Timo, there were more interesting rhythms being made in the quarries of Finland than in the clubs where the Cleaning Women played.

Mikko seemed disappointed that we hadn't connected with his favourite band and we drove home from the gig in silence. In the dressing room in Lahti – which was no bigger than a tissue box – the Cleaning Women had purposefully set up their wardrobe racks and warm-up area away from where Al and I were eating fries, drinking pop, and already longing for the charms of Tampere and Hämeenlinna. The club in Lahti also revealed that grimy, low-ceilinged, graffitied rock clubs crowded with fickle kids swilling cheap beer are rock 'n' roll constants the world over. I could have been in Bristol, Toledo, Waga Waga, or north Hamilton, and Cleaning Women were just another band I was destined to leave behind.

Mikko and I were still getting to know each other, and our relationship had come to the point where we had to push through each other's quirks of personality in order to keep our rock 'n' roll train on track. One of the wonderful things – yet also one of the perils – about going around the world playing music is being more or less at the mercy of one's host. It's a mild occupational hazard for anyone who relies on the kindness of strangers to get from place to place. In this case, Mikko went beyond all expectations to make things right for Al and I. He drove us everywhere, booked the gigs, arranged accommodation, introduced us to musicians, and made sure we knew absolutely everything there was to know about Finnish and Russian rock 'n' roll. But therein lay the problem. Our first few days were filled with Mikko's colourful illuminations of Scandinavian culture, and I listened carefully. Then I realized that this torrent of end-lessly valuable information and storytelling would not cease. This was a good problem to have, and I learned loads from Mikko I probably would never have known otherwise. But part of touring and travelling is about making one's own path: deking down this street, over that bridge, behind this wall. There's a delicious freedom that comes with being tuned into your own instincts, riding on an endless reel of interior musings.

The following afternoon, we left Lahti and our Cleaning Women shows behind and headed farther north to Jyväskylä. Ferreting through Mikko's shopping bag full of cassettes, I found a tape by countryfolk singer Townes Van Zandt and popped it into the stereo. I'd met Townes once before, at the Horseshoe Tavern in Toronto. Dave Bookman's band, the Midi Ogres, opened for him

(I played drums). Townes was in rough shape that day. He came
on stage, played three songs, then disappeared into the band
room where he drained the backwash out of every empty beer
bottle in the room. My friend Gord Cumming, along with songwriter Butch Hancock, coaxed him back on stage, and he eventually got it right and finished a marvellous set. The highlight for
me was jamming with the great songwriter in the dressing room
before the show, playing drumsticks on a heating pipe to a duet
sung by Townes and Butch. But Gord came away with the best
memory of the night. After thanking him for his help with the
show, Townes asked Gord to hold out his hand, then reached
into his pocket. He took out a pair of invisible dice, and pressed
them into Gord's hand, telling him to keep them safe. Maybe
Townes knew he wouldn't be needing them any longer: he suc-
cumbed to a heart attack a short time after the gig on New
Year's Day 1997.

Despite their East Texan roots, Townes's songs were the
perfect autumnal Finnish travelling music set to thick forests and
blue lakes of water pure enough to drink. As the day gave way
to night and the temperature dipped to the lowest it had been
since we'd arrived, his sombre, soulful tenor and songs of
heartache matched the beauty of the journey and the disappointment of the last few shows. I finally felt like we were wandering
a little off the prescribed path, and in this regard Townes music
sounded right too.

Before we arrived at Jyväskylä, a town of 80,000 in eastern
Finland, Mikko warned us, "You aren't really playing a club. It's
more like a restaurant, or a place where you would get a coffee
or a beer. You are playing with Sirkus Kosmonautti, and my
hopes, well, they aren't terribly high." The club – Vakiopaine –
was a small café with a large storefront window lit by cande-
labra. Inside, there were four or five tables, a laptop computer,

and seven or eight people sitting around drinking and doing what appeared to be their homework. They looked surprised that we'd shown up. There was no stage, just a carpet at one end of the room where a tiny man, with a freshly shaved head and wraparound Bono sunglasses, wearing an aquamarine jumpsuit with orange piping and white spats, was fiddling with a beat box and sampler wired behind a portable lectern. This was Sirkus Kosmonautti.

Our fingers crossed that our encounter with another musical spaceman would go better than the last, Al and I introduced ourselves to Mr. Kosmonautti, a one-man band who proved to be far more amiable than the women of Planet Clinus. Mr. K had taken his name, he told us, because he'd recently studied the circus arts, fuelling our hope that he might incorporate high-wire or acrobatic bedazzlement into his act.

It turned out that Kosmo's only nod to the big top was his trapezist's jumpsuit, but his performance was amazing in other ways. He started his set just after 10:00 p.m. when there were only a dozen patrons in the club, among them a greasy hoodish type with a drooping moustache, a few peach-faced students reading rock magazines, and an amusing Harry Dean Stanton-esque drunk and his cross-eyed girlfriend, whose table was obscured by giant glasses of beers. As soon as the cross-eyed woman discovered where Al and I were from, she parroted the two English words she knew: "Right! Wrong! Right! Wrong!" They were exactly the words that were running through my head as our tour meandered from weird to weirder.

Once Kosmo began playing – standing behind his lectern and fiddling with his beat boxes and synth loops – the hood refused to look at him. He stared off into a cloud of bitterness, as if trying to muster the anger and energy required to take out, if not Kosmo, than the entire room with the hunting rifle that I feared he had stuffed down his trouser leg. But he left after two songs, which the elfin singer played on a green, homemade tenor guitar using three-finger chords set to "Pop Goes the World" keyboard parts and programmed Casio jams. Harry Dean Stanton and his sweetheart were quite taken with Kosmo's wobbly pop. After each song, Harry shouted, "Play more! Play more!" while his cross-eyed girlfriend mooned over him as if he were the most charming creature to ever drink a giant beer.

At the conclusion of each song, Kosmo came out from behind his lectern and bowed, telling the half-empty room, "Muchas gracias!" then laughing to himself. Almost all of his songs sounded like the first one I ever wrote: "Radio 80 Fantasy," a keyboard-blipping anthem about the future based around a two-note guitar solo. One of the numbers, which he said was about Africa, started with a keyboard that went *byoab, byoab, byoab* before giving way to a "doot-doot-doot!" vocal, which he repeated as if it were R2-D2's mantra. It doesn't sound like much, but after the manufactured gravity of Cleaning Women, Kosmo's performance sounded pure and real and inno-cent. Nothing was contrived: in fact, his dipping-bird bows and corny Spanish patter made it seem like to him the whole notion of being a pop performer was fresh and new. This became obvious at the end of his set, when Harry Dean once again shouted, "Play more! Play more!" Kosmo took it as a call for an encore and played five more songs, including a strange hyper-speed cover of Steppenwolf's "Born to be Wild," before giving the stage to Al and me. On a cold Sunday night in a nearly empty club in a nowhere town in northern Europe, we played unplugged and had the time of our lives.

At the end of the night, we sat with the remaining audience members, mostly students from the local university. Kosmo told us that he'd played "Born to be Wild" as a musical tribute to our homeland. The Steppenwolf nugget deserves to be pushed into that category of songs that we should never have to hear again, but if it's going to be played at all, it might as well be performed as a salute by a musical spaceman in a café in small-town Finland. Kosmo also admitted that he'd never been called for an encore before, that it was his only fifth gig ever, and that most of the others had been for small children. With this, we ordered giant beers in his honour and listened to the students complain about modern Finnish bands and how too many of their songs were about the sorrow of life. Kosmo looked pleased throughout the conversation. Not even a storm of rocks and garbage could have dented his excitement.

At one point during Kosmo's set, I'd looked at Mikko to see his reaction. He was rubbing his face in embarrassment, so I'd assured him that the music was totally cool – in a totally uncool way – and that Al and I were digging the show. At the end of the evening, he was anxious for us to get on the road. But we were reluctant to abandon a club we would not see again and kept telling Mikko, "One more beer!"

Then a rough and bewildered just-been-booted-out-of-a-bar fellow stumbled into the club. The students weren't bothered by him, so I wasn't either. He introduced himself as Philip.

"Why does Finnish music have to be so depressing?" lamented one of the students, echoing the words of Janne Laurila. "I am happy, you are happy," he said, poking Philip, who had certainly drunk enough to be happy. "Why can't Finnish rock 'n' roll be happy? Why does it always have to be so stupid and sad?"

Phillip slid his elbow across the table and looked each of us in the eye.

"You know what the best kind of sad music is?" he asked.

We looked at him, wondering what the drunken interloper had in mind.

Philip drew a deep breath, pointed a finger at the ceiling, and announced, "Townes Van Zandt."

I was astonished.

"Townes Van Zandt," he repeated. "That is good, sad music. Perfect for Finland."

JOENSUU

IF YOU WANT TO SEE MY PENIS, YOU'LL HAVE TO MARRY ME. Some men, after finding themselves in a group with other men, are not shy about waving their business around like a sock puppet. But I'm more of a sit-and-hide-it kind of guy, so I wasn't thrilled when Mikko and Al decided we needed to have a sauna (or "sow-nah," as the Finns say). I relented, however, once we arrived at the most perfect one imaginable.

After our show in Jyväskylä, we drove for an hour, then turned onto a dark wooded road before settling at the top of a hill in front of an old converted schoolhouse, the weekend retreat of Mikko's sister-in-law's friend, Merja. It was an opulent place with high ceilings, bear-skin rugs, a baby grand piano, miles of oak bookshelves and glass cabinets, and walls adorned with antique axes, hammers and scythes. In the candlelit sitting room, where warm Karelian pies, cheese-and-nettle pastries, and freshly baked spanikopita were waiting for us, there was an old orange-and-white jukebox from the 1960s stocked with records by Finnish artists, as well as the obligatory Toto platter ("Don't Chain My Heart"). The song that was playing as we walked in sounded exactly like "All the Young Dudes" by Mott the Hoople, only with a Finnish singer and Finnish words. Merja told me that the singer's name was Hector, and that he was very famous in Finland. When I asked her what the song was about, she said that it was the singer's plea to his troubled friend not to take his own life. "In the end, he does," she said, which didn't surprise me. "I don't know if you know, but there are many songs like this in Finland."

After gorging ourselves, Merja showed us to our quarters: a warm, wood-panelled room with huge beds and thick blankets. We slept a sleep as good as death. After twelve hours we awoke to breakfast served in the piano room. We sat at a long table set with fine china and crystal glasses and feasted on porridge, grain bread, eggs, salami, five different local cheeses, marinated white-fish, and more Karelian pies. And then we went to the sauna.

Saunas are everywhere in Finland. Mikko had one, Paul had one, Telakka had one. In the hotel in Hämeenlinna I'd watched a film on television showing fifteen naked preteens cavorting in the woods. For a moment I thought I'd happened upon child pornography, but swiftly realized that it was a Finnish film. The kids were headed to a sauna, where they read books and had a great old time.

For Finns aged eight to eighty, the sauna is a way of life. The 2002 census showed that there were 2 million saunas in a country of just more than 5 million people. At one time, pretty much the entire world used the sauna as a means of getting clean: the Russians had the *banya*, the Turks the *hamam*, the Japanese the *onsen*. Today, thanks to forces such as the Refor-mation, which obliterated the sauna in greater Europe, and the genocide of aboriginal peoples in North America, which margin-alized the use of sweatlodges, the sauna survives in only a few enclaves. In Finland, the sauna was once the only place, espe-cially in the brutal winter months, that was warm, germ-free, and social. It was where women gave birth and doctors tended to patients – many corpses were prepared for burial there – and while the bathhouses of the world fell prey to the inevitable sins of the flesh, the Finns adhered to the dictum, *"Jokaisen on kayttaydyttava saunaa samalla tavalla kuin kirkossa"* (*"In the sauna, one must conduct himself as he would in a church"*). Leave it to the Finns to take the grindy-grindy out of what happens when a bunch of nude people get together.

Al, Mikko, and I walked down a set of stairs behind the schoolhouse to the sauna, a wooden shack nestled in a bramble patch overlooking the Kymi River. There was a late-autumn bite to the air as we got out of our clothes in the unheated outer room, then climbed starkers into the sauna proper. The heat slapped us as we walked in, then Mikko ladled water over a pile of hot rocks that gave off a steamy sigh before blasting us with a great gathering heat. As I sat there still as a potted plant on the cedar bench, the steam pushed its way into my lungs and pores in a slow process of wonderful suffocation. I approached that feeling of heady release promised by saunians the world over, sweating to the nth degree. This felt fine until I realized that I was nearly drowning in my own secretions. I looked over at Al, who had fallen silent, apparently robbed of his personality by the heat. Mikko, too, was quiet, for once unable to conjure long, colourful stories out of the smallest detail of our surroundings. He sat with his legs to his chest, staring at his toes. Because the others had become so withdrawn, I gave up the idea of starting a conversation and dwelled on the fact that I was sweatier than Iggy Pop and how really wet and uncomfortable I felt. But I couldn't stay mum forever, and I asked Mikko if anyone had thought to put a television in here. A DVD player? A radio? Maybe some old *Hockey Digests?* Mikko chuckled and told me that the whole idea was to relax and let the world peel away while you stewed in your own fluids. I remembered something Paul had said during our afternoon drive around Helsinki: "A typical Finn would like nothing more than to go into the forest in the winter, take a sauna, and sit by himself for hours." This sentiment was echoed by a woman I'd met in Kuopio, who said that her dream vacation was "to go up to Lapland with my father and say no more than six words to each other."

When the temperature inside the sauna reached nearly 60°C, Al, desperate for a breath, climbed off the bench, ensuring that, for me, the single enduring image of this culturally significant moment would be his sweaty ass. It was at this point that it occurred to me that there was another very Finnish quality to the sauna: it's a way to get terribly sweaty without doing anything exciting to get terribly sweaty. Mikko and I poured buckets of warm water over our heads, wrapped ourselves in towels, and walked outside to join Al. Leaves and branches crunching under our bare feet, we made our way down to the river where I stood like Matti Nykänen in my bath towel and let the wind tickle my berries. The feeling of standing half-nude in the Finnish wilderness was a great antidote to the smoky clubs Al and I had played the previous three nights. It was all I could do to stop myself from shouting, "Cow's vagina!" I was engulfed by a feeling of total submission and relaxation, but instead of embracing true Finnishness and wandering off into the brambles to die, I made my way back to Merja's cottage. There, I poured several consecutive cups of coffee and let this looseness of body and mind give way to a torrent of writing, which I did while sitting in a plush, big-armed chair with a hundred-year-old birchbark canoe hanging over my head.

It seemed like a good time to ponder the differences and similarities between Finns and Canadians. On first blush, studying Finland was a lot like staring into a mirror, but after a handful of days in the world's second-most literate nation, a few distortions started to appear. The characteristics that my country and

Mikko's shared, I thought, were largely cosmetic: the endless wonder and beauty of the land, the poise of the cities and propriety of its citizens, the slow, careful emergence of an indigenous culture, and the ubiquitous moose antlers (there was a pair above the entranceway to Merja's dining room). Other than that, I wasn't sure that Canadians were much like Finns at all. Finnish people were how Canadians saw themselves, but weren't: quiet, clean, friendly, timid, unflinching. Canadians often characterize themselves as skittish mice compared to the oafish Americans, but next to the Finns, we were loud and loutish, reckless and rude. Among Mikko and his friends, I felt far more brash and extroverted than I ever had at home. This, I realized, was the Americanness of my personality. Living close to such a bombastic country had coaxed some vigour and personality in me. Previously, I'd seen the quiet reserve of Canadians as virtuous, but watching it dominate the Finns' personality, I worried whether too much northern introspection was unhealthy, given the Finns' suicide songs, their search for solitude in a place that was empty to begin with, and their cultural isolationism in the face of Russian and Swedish influences. And considering that while the Finns were the most coffee-obsessed people on Earth – drinking nine cups a day on average – they were also the least verbal, *Suomi* struck me as an emotionally unhealthy place. We left Merja's the next day, and our tiny rock 'n' roll caravan drove east to the small city of Joensuu, which for the sake of Finland's literary portrait arrived not a moment too soon.

The first person I noticed at the Hotel Jokela – the site of our last Finnish gig – was an African woman staring out of the window of the bar. She was sitting with friends in one of the tavern's old red-leather booths, their table busy with glasses even though it was only late afternoon. The entire tavern was filled with people, and for the first time all trip I was in a place high and lively with voices. Instead of quietly deliberating their own mortality, the men and women of the Hotel Jokela seemed to be arguing and telling jokes. The bar had dark, creaking floorboards, fat clouds of cigarette smoke, a cranky jukebox, and a television that looked like it had to be hit with a stick to work. Like most honest taverns, the walls of the Jokela were hung with photos of people drinking there seventy years ago; even better, a few of these patrons were still around. They'd tipped ales in this room from the day the Jokela first opened in 1927 to the moment Al and I showed up to present our pesky hard-folk repertoire. Since the hotel staged shows only once a month – and because we were the first North American performers ever to play there – I felt privileged and made a mental note to myself not to suck.

On the other side of the hotel entrance from the main bar was a lounge with a smaller bar, where a tinfoil basket filled with delicious looking fried whitefish and a pitcher of iced orange juice had been set out for us. Beyond the lounge was the hotel's live room – the *Sointu* – where more red-leather booths and tables with white tablecloths faced an open area with a juke joint piano and two modest speaker towers, almost like a little jazz lounge. A small, dark man with brown teeth and wearing a beautiful suit was sitting at the piano. He was Kemal Achourbekov, the hotel's Azerbaijani pianist. After quick introductions, we gathered in the lounge, where we destroyed the basket of whitefish – it was immediately replaced by another – and listened to the story of the building told by those who lived and worked there.

Heidi and Hannu, who for some reason insisted that we call him Charlie, were the middle-aged proprietors of the Jokela. Bespectacled and neatly groomed, Charlie had a dry wit and gravitas that held the business together. Heidi was the radiant matron from whom the bar staff, including her daughter, Anita, sought guidance. In 1928, they told us, Charlie's grandparents were married in the bar, so his family had a deep connection to the place. During the Second World War, the Hotel Jokela was the only building in the region with a telephone. Because the Finns had allied with Germany against their greater enemy, the Russians, the hotel often harboured German soldiers. Once, when a drunken German officer tried to strong-arm a local woman into his bed, one of the young men of Joensuu took exception. A terrible knife fight ensued, and the German soldier ended up lying in a pool of blood on the tavern floor. Many years later, another visitor to the Jokela was equally smitten by a local maiden, in this case actor Omar Sharif, who was filming *Doctor Zhivago* a few kilometres outside town. He was supposed to stay with the rest of the cast at a larger hotel, but Sharif spent most of his time at the tavern with Lisse, one of the Jokela's beautiful young waitresses. Sharif and Lisse carried out their romantic tryst in room number four, which Charlie occasionally showed to visitors.

Kemal Achourbekov was the latest global wanderer to have found a home under the Jokela's old tin roof. With dark, riveting eyes and a bulldog's jawline, Kemal had a life story that could have been lifted from a novel by Turgenev or Dostoevsky. As a musical prodigy growing up in Azerbaijan in the 1970s, Kemal had had a reasonably happy young life until, like a lot of gifted children, his love of performing was nearly quashed by an abusive music teacher. Taking extreme measures, he fled to Moscow as a teenager, where without any further study he took the Moscow Academy of Music entrance exam and passed. After he graduated, his stellar reputation as a pianist led to work playing at social events, including palace concerts for Brezhnev's daughter. "She was always very drunk, very loud," Kemal said.

"I could have played any music in the world, but she wanted to hear mostly crazy gypsy songs and drinking music."

After a time, Kemal was required to put in his military service, at which point his life took a wild spin. "My troop commander was a very vain and jealous man," he told us, sipping a glass of wine. "After he discovered that he had a famous musician in his ranks, he decided to organize a concert in Chernobyl, in the Ukraine, in an attempt to impress his fellow officers. He pulled me out of the barracks and put me on a train to Chernobyl, where I played on the very evening the nuclear power plant erupted. At the time, nobody told us anything. They kept it a secret, so it was hard to know what had really happened. There was a young ballet company who also performed that night, and the flowers they were given after their show glowed in the dark from the radiation. Even though the plant was outside of town, the whole city was overcome with the poison of radiation."

Mikko mentioned that his friend Jari, who would later accompany us to St. Petersburg, had a similar experience while attending university in Kiev. When I met Jari in Russia, he told me the story first hand.

"Three days after the disaster," he said, "all of the Finns were evacuated from Kiev, as well as other nationalities (except, of course, those from the Third World). Two weeks later, I was called to Moscow to take the entrance test for the Russian Film Academy. During the test, I was accused of betraying the Soviet Union because I hadn't stayed in Kiev after the Chernobyl accident, which happened eighty kilometres from the city. They decided to take me in as a student, but only after I asked why my interviewers hadn't travelled to Chernobyl or Kiev after the accident themselves.

"When I arrived in Kiev to do my final exams in May, the town looked the same, but there was something strange going on. After a while I realized that there were no children in the streets [they had all been evacuated] and that everyone was drunk. When I went to my dorm, my Ukrainian roommate, Jura, opened the door and started yelling at me, 'You fucking idiot! Why did you come back? It's not safe here.' Before he'd let me in, I had to take my clothes off and shower to wash away whatever radiation I might have picked up. After the shower, I was forced to drink *samogon* [Russian moonshine], which people in Kiev were convinced would protect them from radiation. Jura told me that his friend of his – a fireman – was among the first rescuers who went to Chernobyl, and that four out of five crew members got drunk before the operation. The one who stayed sober had died. This quickly became a legend, and everybody started drinking. Mothers all around the Soviet Union were making *samagon* and giving it to their sons and daughters. Jura had already received twenty bottles from his mother, and in this sense Kiev turned into a kind of drunken Russian paradise."

When I asked Kemal if he'd been directly affected by the radiation, he touched his fingers together and said, "No, not personally. But some of the people I was with that night lost all of their hair and teeth. Others became impotent, or had some other ailment. The day after the explosion, we were scheduled to perform at the power plant but no one expected that we would go. Still, because information about what had happened was so hard to get, they put us on a bus and we drove to the plant, where we sat for twenty minutes baking in the radiation before turning back."

After Kemal's release from the army, he met a Finnish woman who brought him to the Jokela, and that's how he ended up eating fried whitefish and telling his story to two hosers. We were so giddy from talking with a Russian-Finnish-Azerbaijani musician in the lounge of one of the world's greatest taverns that we were spurred on to our most spirited performance of the tour.

The gig was successful in part because I finally managed to get my voice around another of Finland's scrappy, low-wattage sound systems and nerves no longer balled my strumming hand into a claw at the start of the set. But the real reason for the success of my performance was not owing to my skronk and yowl, but to Wendy from Zambia – the African woman I'd seen staring out the window when we arrived.

Wendy was as tall and thin as a dandelion, with firefly eyes. When I took to the stage, which, like at the storefront gig in Jyväskylä, wasn't a stage so much as a clear space at one end of the room, I was greeted by Wendy and a tableful of chatty Finns sitting near the front. Were this any country other than Finland, I would have viewed them as the solo artist's bane – the kind of people for whom the quiet parts of dramatic songs are the ideal times to ask friends about long-lost relatives or discuss global economics – but this was the first crowd we'd played to that had life and energy.

At the start of my set, the chattering stopped, and at the end of my first song, Wendy and her friends began peppering me with questions about my guitar, Canada, my journey around Finland, and my hat. I welcomed their curiosity. One of the struggles of playing solo and acoustic is the constant need to retune one's guitar: without a veil of electric fuzz to disguise them, its wonky harmonics are often laid bare. This is a routine that sometimes results, at least for me, in long dead spots, which in front of crowds as quiet and observant as those in Finland felt as interminable as side three of *Tusk*. In other places, I'd tried to fill the tuning gap with witty patter – provided I hadn't already made fun of Matti Nykänen – but in Joensuu, I was kept busy verbally Ping-Ponging with Wendy and her friends. One of her tablemates, who'd been described to me as a famous Finnish writer, asked if I knew how to play any Van Morrison songs. I told him, while keeping an eye on my tuner's light, "Sorry, I don't do fat Irish leprechauns." He laughed outrageously; so did Wendy. Things rolled on from there.

Before playing "My First Rock Concert," I asked Wendy to name hers. Instead of answering straight away, she stood up at the table, rotated to look at the crowd behind her, turned back to the stage, flung her arms into the air, and shouted, "Miriam Makeba!" She then proceeded to sing some Miriam Makeba, but I managed to stop her before she sang the entire song. Still, she stayed on her feet during "My First Rock Concert," providing operatic harmonies and waving her arms as if being attacked by bats. She kept up her impromptu vocal arrangements for pretty much the entire set, and when I finished, she got to me before I'd unplugged my guitar and commanded, "Hug now, please!" Later on at the bar, she asked if she could draw something in my book, and when she handed it back to me, I saw that it was a sketch of a nude woman with enormous breasts with the words, "Loving you always" scribbled below. Even later still, she demanded another hug but this one came with some pelvic grinding, so I peeled myself away and thanked her for all of her support.

There would be no legend of room number two.

Kemal joined Al and me at the end of Al's set. He looked even smaller seated at the black piano, but his arms spanned the whole of the instrument, his fingers dancing across the keyboard like fish splashing in a stream. It was obvious from the first note that he was a virtuoso. When the time came for him to take a solo in the last song of the evening, "Horses," the piano exploded in a storm of notes. Hunched over, his shoulders pinching the air, he landed heavy, then light, then heavy again across the battered keys. After his first twelve-bar solo, we cheered him on to another, then another, then another, until a smile stayed creased across his face. The crowd barked and rallied behind him, their voices growing louder and more excited with each solo. Wendy shot out of her seat but resisted trying to sing above the frenzy. The whole scene was one of the beautiful moments that only music can produce: the former Azerbaijani child prodigy, a man who'd been shepherded to near-death during one of the world's worst nuclear accidents, playing a Canadian protest song about worker's rights and the demise of prairie justice for a raucous Finnish rock 'n' roll crowd led by a tall, drunken Zambian flower. For the first time in my life, the Rheostatics seemed like an afterthought.

At song's end, Kemal, Al, and I crashed into the final chord, grinning as it faded away. Then we hit the bar, played a few more songs, and drank until we were sore. Just before we left to collapse face-first into our pillows, Heidi poured us each a shot of a strange pink liqueur that tasted like liquid bacon. She insisted upon pouring us another, but I demurred. Al whirled around and shouted, "How often do we get to come to wherever the fuck we are?"

I admitted that he had a point.

And then we went to Russia.

VYBOURG

I FIRST WENT TO RUSSIA IN THE FALL OF 2004. GROWING up at a time when Russia was demonized in the West as a cold, alien planet lurking at the end of the universe, I had never dreamed of going there. And now here I was again: on a train racing from Joensuu to St. Petersburg for my third visit to Russia in twenty months. When we switched from a Finnish to a Russian train somewhere in the Karelian interior, Al confessed, "I feel like Frodo going into Mordor." Al had gone from behaving like little Charlie Bucket in Finland – savouring even the dullest Nordic detail as if it were a wonderful new candy – to a cowering mass of denim, hair, and worry. I was reminded of my initial emotions on being in the former Soviet Union, how fear of the unknown had made everything I'd seen and done seem profound.

Before travelling to Russia (where I was making a film about hockey) in 2004, I was warned by people who didn't know their Yakushevs from their Khrushchevs: "Just try to not get murdered while you're over there." At the time I'd chalked this up to typical North American xenophobia, so I was surprised to hear the Finns, who share a border with the former Big Red Machine, say much the same thing. "Be careful," had been the Finns' refrain (Mikko's mother had actually crossed herself when she'd said it). I knew enough from previous visits to take this advice with a grain of salt, but it still sobered me, coming as it did from people who had had first-hand encounters with the dangers of modern Russia. Paul told me, "Russia is a place divided between those who pour all of their heart into whatever they're doing, and the worst kinds of criminals imaginable." Jari, the filmmaker who'd survived Chernobyl, told me about attending the St. Petersburg film festival, leaving the theatre for a pee, and being forced at gunpoint by four dirty cops to trade his money for his life. The Russian mafia or mob was and is largely misunderstood by almost everyone outside of the Federation. It's not made up of sunglassed, shaved-head behemoths named Yuri waving Uzis; it's a term that covers corrupt governmental officials and white-collar criminals, and it is pretty much a given that a lot of Russian soldiers and cops are crooked, mean, and underpaid. Because it is hard to tell the difference between these two pillars of Russian law enforcement – they all wear the same greatcoats and official khaki issue – they seem to be in abundance, which on my first visit only fed my suspicion that I was *this* close to taking a plug in exchange for my passport, ID card, and money stash.

During my second trip to Moscow, Michael Mainville of the *Toronto Star*, a journalist working in Russia, asked me if I'd ever seen a dead Russian. I told him that I had, in the winter of 2005. The film crew and I had just descended by escalator for what felt like a vertical half-mile into the Kievskaya Metro (built in Stalinist times to effectively double as a bomb shelter). I was swept away by the cathedralesque grandeur and baroque flair of the subway, which was decorated, as many of the Russian metros are, by ornate lamps and glass chandeliers, turning a simple station into a proletariat palace.

While taking in the opulence and the golden light, I looked across the platform at a group of five policemen who were standing around smoking and laughing. Being in a blissful state of mind, I wondered for a moment whether all of the bad press about dirty cops and soldiers was just that. Then, I spotted the reason for their laughter: a man in a trenchcoat lying stiff at their feet, a blanket obscuring everything but his face. Ashes from the policemen's cigarettes fell on the body as if knocked there on purpose, and their laughter was so relaxed it sounded cruel. I quickened my pace and reached my train, my heart and mind set spinning by this remarkable contradiction. This, for better or worse, was Russia in the twenty-first century.

The Russian train that delivered us from Finland into old Leningrad was darker and rode the tracks more ruggedly than the sleek Finnish dart we'd boarded in Helsinki. In the dim light of our compartment with constructivist scribble–patterned seats, Al was struck with the true gravity of our journey. While my mind busied itself with thoughts of green sorel borscht, the Museum of Contemporary Art, the Maly theatre, *kvass*, hockey in the Red Army practice rink, and Uzbeki food on the Arbat – all Moscow pleasures; I'd never visited St. Pete's before – Al glumly considered the stories that Mikko and I had told him during the low hours of driving around Finland. We'd meant to get him excited, but what we'd really done was scare the shit out of him.

I can imagine what he was thinking then, when about sixty kilometres east of St. Petersburg in Vybourg, the former capital of Karelia, Finnish territory before the Second World War, I was escorted off the train. It was only a matter of getting my entry visa stamped, but the late hour and the lightless train platform made it look as if we had arrived in a John le Carré novel.

One of the things that Mikko had stressed was that in order to gain access to Russia by train, it was important to have all of your papers signed, but I hadn't realized until we left Helsinki that my customs declaration form hadn't been stamped. So, I stepped into the corridor and waved the tiny paper square as if drying a Polaroid, hoping to catch the attention of someone important. The train's conductor found me quickly. He was a small man dressed in royal blue and he wore a broad, sweeping moustache, a kind of great facial swoosh. When the train stopped in Vybourg for a respite before heading full steam to St. Pete's, he gestured for me to follow him, and so I did, staying closely behind him for the full length of the iron rooster, past a panoply of faces illuminated by the sallow light of the train.

After the fourth or fifth car, the inevitable questions started to pop into my head about where we were headed, what the fellow was planning to do with me once we got to wherever we were going, and whether I'd been pinched as an easy mark for my all-too-obvious exhibition of Western impatience outside of our compartment. The sound of the cold steel doors sucking shut behind us as we stepped between cars only added to the intrigue. Russia's dark palette had replaced Finland's clear northern light, and those old impressions of demonic Russia crawled forward in my mind. Was this the wrong turn I shouldn't have taken, with the kind of person I never should have followed? At the same time, all that was happening around me was so interesting that I wanted to take in all of the impassive deep-eyed faces staring at us as we shuffled through the train.

We passed through eight, nine cars – I counted each numbered plate that rattled as the conductor pushed open the doors – before we reached the brightly lit dining car, where I stepped out of the spy novel back into my world. Sitting around a couple of tables strewn with dinner plates was, clearly, a rock 'n' roll band. I knew they were musicians partly because it takes one to know one, but mainly because they sported the right symbols: tattoos, piercings, T-shirts with cut-off sleeves. They also had the long, bored faces that come only from touring life, to say nothing of Russian touring life, to say nothing of Russian touring life by train. I made a mental note to stop and get the goods on them if and when I returned as the conductor helped me off the train, gesturing with a tug of his neck for me to follow him along the concrete platform.

Suddenly, the train made a sound as if clearing its throat. I thought for sure that it was about to leave without me. I shouted at the conductor like an excited preschooler, "Train! Train! Train!" He gave me a goofy look, then grunted at me to pick up the pace. I did, and moments later we turned into a room in the station house.

It wasn't so much a room as a large, unlit hall with a single desk, some filing cabinets, and two uniformed Russian women, their blonde hair backcombed high above their heads. I hate to generalize about sex or religion or race – especially about the Russians, whose citizenry spans the greatest slab of land on Earth – but I find Russian women very intimidating. Which I kind of like. A travel weakness of mine has always been that I think that the most beautiful women in the world live in whatever country I happen to be visiting. It's partly because they're forbidden, partly because they're unfamiliar, and partly because I'm usually travelling in a group of men who reek of beer and smokes. Still, after years of falling for women the world over, I'd decided that surly Russian blondes spin my wheels the fastest.

It's not so much the look – the long Slavic nose, deep starry eyes, skateboard-ramp cheekbones, and full lips (though it's not *not* about the look) – as the attitude, which requires Russian women to look at every man with disdain, even contempt. My relationship with Russian women was consistent: I'd offer them my good-guy-in-a-hat-hey-how-ya-doin? grin and receive in return a pooling stare that would tighten into a deep killing gaze that dissolved into an indignant huff before they paraded away, as they inevitably did, leaving me convulsing on my knees in the middle of Dzhambula Street. Worse were those times when that killing stare melted into a slow, smoky smile, making their game crueller than you can possibly imagine.

So, as the two uniformed women to whom I'd been presented fixed me with a stare in the cold hull of an empty room while the train snorted as if it were about to pull away – with Al no doubt pressing his forehead against the window of our berth, sobbing with anxiety – I was tortured two ways. I was both entranced by them and fearful – yet hopeful – that I might have to spend the rest of my life in some kind of Russian love-slave camp.

The conductor, God bless him, grunted at the sexy administrators and indicated that I should hand over my unsigned form. I did, and – glory of all glories – they grunted in return, produced a stamp and a stamp pad, and got the deed done. The conductor hurried me back through the train (sadly, the band had disappeared, making me question whether they'd been there in the first place) to where Al was waiting dry-eyed in the compartment. Within an hour, we were driving with a handful of Mikko's friends, who'd also made the trip from Finland, from the St. Petersburg train station into the nighttime city.

Frodo had made it into Mordor.

ST.PETERSBURG

THE SEX PISTOLS, THE CLASH, THE DAMNED, ET AL. MIGHT claim to be the first punks, but having researched the history of musical rebellion for the purpose of placing the Russian rock scene between the 1950s and the 1980s in context, I know this to be untrue. This is not to disparage these mighty One Hundred Clubbers and all they begat, it's just that strutting around in garbage-bag blouses and zippered pants seems slightly less punkish when you consider that the only rules they flouted were those of taste and style. In Russia and other European countries, punks faced oppression and murderous political regimes, risking a talking-to far worse than one delivered by David Frost or the Queen Mum.

In 1939, the *Swingjugend* (Swing Kids) of Hamburg were a loosely formed group of young people who mobilized as a reaction to the institutionalized *Hitlerjugend* (Hitler Youth). The boys grew their hair long in defiance of Hitler's edict that all young men wear military-length hair, and they dressed in foppish scarves and English sport jackets, sometimes even carrying an umbrella in an impression of the British foreign secretary of the time. Female Swing Kids wantonly painted themselves with makeup and listened to Afro-American jazz, dancing in what writer Peter Shapiro described as "an outrageous fashion; linking arms, jumping up and down, jitterbugging to the point of physical exhaustion, (sometimes) with two (partners) at the same time." The Swing Kids were considered such a threat to the mindset of German youth that covert musical ensembles such as the Reichs Music Chamber were recruited by the Gestapo to report any signs of Swing Kids gatherings. As a result, the movement was forced underground, at least until a 9 p.m. curfew was imposed upon all young people and their activities. This led to the mass arrests of 1943, which saw hundreds of Swing Kids (and their wartime French counterparts, the *Zazous*) purged and sent to work camps.

A decade later in the 1950s Soviet empire, Russian kids known as *stilyagi* (in Poland, they were *bikiniarze*; in Hungary, *jampec*) prowled dance floors in wild dress in an attempt to shake loose the conventions of Communist times. The *stilyagi* took American names such as Bob and Peter and introduced the art of "hanging out" to Soviet youth. Alexei S. Kozlov, a former *stilyagi*, told broadcaster Artemy Troitsky for Kozlov's seminal book *Back in the USSR*: "We had three dance styles – the atomic, the Canadian and triple Hamburg – that were similar to boogie woogie." The *stilyagi* reacted exuberantly whenever orchestras dared play something other than the state's recommended dances, sneaking in a foxtrot in place of a waltz or a polka. Since there were more male *stilyagi* than female *chivikha*, men often spun each other around the dance floor, creating a physical maelstrom. The *stilyagi* wore dark, tight-fitting zoot suits and skinny ties, and their hairstyle was known around Russia as the Tarzan: long hair combed straight back and smeared with grease. "The back was turned up with a curling iron," said Kozlov, "and I remember I constantly had burns on my neck."

In Moscow, the *stilyagi* patronized the Dynamo skating rink in the wintertime, a daring social gesture given that Dynamo was the social arm of the KGB. Kozlov and his friends went there because it was one of the few places where you could dance – or at least skate – to jazz. Wearing long checkered jackets with white shirts and ties, they would "skate out in full regalia, just as we did for the dances," said Kozlov. "We wore high-topped skates (in imitation of their trademark tall-heeled shoes) and moved together against the flow, slipping in and out among the couples in their heavy outfits and hats." Troitsky wrote that the *stilyagi* were also magpies for Western art, reading copied Hemingway and Dos Passos texts, and collecting reproductions of impressionist art. Kozlov remembered, "Even though we spent a lot of time in cafés and at all kinds of parties, we drank very little. We talked all the time; we found it more interesting to exchange new ideas than to get drunk."

But, as with the Swing Kids in Germany, the *stilyagi* also had their adversaries: the "Golden Youth" of the Stalin era. Made up of the children of government officials, they drank to excess and partied violently. After a young girl jumped out of an apartment window during a Golden Youth party, the government spun the incident in the press into anti-*stilyagi* propaganda. Posters appeared on city streets – one of them read "We Will Clean Our Streets of This!" while showing a group of grey-clothed proles recoiling in horror at the sight of a *chivikha*. Before long, the group's hangouts were subjected to so-called "cleansing raids." The raids, however, weren't quite as fearsome as one might imagine, certainly not anything like what the KGB had inflicted on its political opponents. Troitsky says that enforcers would push the *stilyagi* against the walls of the club while drawing a pair of scissors, which they'd use to clip a lock of their hair or slice a jagged opening up their trouser legs.

By the 1960s, the *stilyagi* gave way to Russian *beatnicki*, a movement largely born at the 1957 epochal Seventh International

Festival of Youth and Students, which is widely recognized as the event that pushed Moscow from being a provincial arts town into an Eastern European cultural mecca. Remarkably, thousands of young men and women from around the world were allowed and encouraged to attend the event: poets, painters, and musicians among them. One of those young artists was Gabriel García Márquez, who remarked to Troitsky upon his return to Moscow in 1979 how much more lively and sophisticated the city was compared to the late 1950s. After the festival, the first signs of rock 'n' roll started to show up on Russian radio: "Rock Around the Clock" and "See You Later, Alligator" by Bill Haley and His Comets, as well as "Love Me Tender" by Elvis, and hits by Pat Boone and Paul Anka. None were as well loved, however, as songs by the Italian boy crooner Robertino Loretti. Alas, his ascent into maturity robbed his voice of its boyish innocence and caused a season of mourning among Soviet pop fans.

With their passions for rock teased, fans of the music tried desperately to get their hands on recorded material. Because there were few pressing plants, and because state music releases were tightly controlled, an industrious few converted their record player into a record-cutter and etched songs into circles cut from old hospital X-rays (the emulsion on the X-ray surface was perfect for sound reproduction). For decades, much of the Soviet populace first heard Western rock bands on these "ribs" – seven-inch flexi-discs (*Roentgenizdat*) played at 78 RPM and purchased for kopecks (pennies). Soon, a national underground was born in which the sounds of the Ventures floated up from fractured spinal cords and the Animals played on shattered femurs. Few listeners could identify which band was which as most of the flexis came without credits or liner notes. The quality of the recordings was poor, but because they were relatively inexpensive, patrons listened past the fizzes, crackles, and muted tones. But their affordability didn't lessen the disappointment of the occasional rib buyer who, after putting the needle to a new flexi, was treated to a few seconds of music followed by a voice mocking them for buying a defective record, followed by five minutes of silence.

Through ribs and rib-swapping, the rock 'n' roll revolution in Russia took hold. Troitsky points to the Revengers in Riga, Latvia as the first Soviet rock 'n' roll band. Czech-made electric guitars appeared in music stores in the early 1960s, but other instruments remained scarce. The Revengers built their own basses, stringing them with piano wire. This obliged the bass player to wrap his fingers in duct tape to play them. The Revengers' repertoire, like most early Soviet bands', was primarily gleaned from whatever they heard on ribs. Pete Anderson, who translated songs for the Revengers, would travel three hundred kilometres every weekend to Tallin, Estonia, where he kept abreast of the new sounds by watching a pop-music program beamed in from Finland. Kolya Vasin, who's known today as the patriarch of Leningrad rock fans, was equally desperate for new music. He told Troitsky, "I had a Jubilee record player upholstered in blue velvet and a friend who used to bring me records on ribs in a shoebox. They cost fifty kopecks each and I couldn't afford to buy them, but I listened to them like a drunk on a binge." Perhaps even more extreme were the experiences of a bassist identified only as Viktor, who told Thomas Cushman for his book *Notes from Underground* that he sold his motorcycle to buy a T. Rex album on the black market for forty rubles.

When Russia first heard the Beatles in the mid-1960s, everything changed. After hearing the Beatles, Kolya Vasin wrote, "All the depression and fear ingrained over the years disappeared. I understood that everything other than the Beatles had been oppression." Veteran Moscow musician Alex Gradsky was of like mind: "Everything except the Beatles became pointless." Soviet Beatlemania was such that the *Beatlovka* look became hugely popular, and trading Beatles memorabilia (press clippings, and so on) was a favourite pastime. In some instances, photographs were rented so that fans could enjoy them without having to pay the exorbitant black-market charge to own them outright. There was even a term invented for the Beatles' fanatic – *Bitloman* – and Soviet Beatles' bands ruled the pop scene: the Guys, the Little Red Devils, the Scythians, the Melomanes, and the Winds of Change.

Troitsky theorized that "Elvis and rock 'n' roll were nice, but too exotic for our public. The rough black rhythm, the fast tempo, the shouted vocals or hypersexual intonations were all magnificent and ideal for new dances, but how could we identify with them? They were as remote as America. The Beatles were closer, not just geographically, but also spiritually. The Beatles had melodies, and for the Russian ear this was mandatory. Good rhythm and a strong, full sound are always welcome, but without beautiful, melodic lines the chances of success here are minimal. That's why the Rolling Stones were never rivals to the Beatles here."

To get a sense of what the Beatles meant to Russia, you have to remember how you felt on hearing them for the first time. Then you have to magnify that sensation twentyfold. Even then, you'd fall short of comprehending their music's impact on the East. Under Communism's grey umbrella, discovering the Beatles was like opening a jack-in-the-box of sound and colour. The impact of the music was intensified by the fact that it was clandestine, making it ever sweeter and more powerful when absorbed. The Beatles were an entirely new artistic experience for a citizenry raised on literary tragedy, classical ballet, and the state-approved Melodyia recordings of DUMA party speeches and Ukrainian folk songs that filled record shops (Paul McCartney and Wings' 1973 album, *Band on the Run*, was Melodyia's first Western release, which saw the light of the Russian day in 1977).

I lost interest in the Beatles as a teenager after embracing the One Hundred Clubbers and their rough, angry world. Punks and mods (who were effectively portrayed as Nazis by Russian news agencies in the 1970s and 1980s) always had more affinity with bands like the Who and the Stones than the Fab Four, whose posthumous commercialism overshadowed the inherent wildness of their art. There were a few punk/new wave bands – Siouxie and the Banshees, Psychedelic Furs, the Feelies – still devoted to the Beatles, but as a rule it was uncool to dig them, especially after rumours of a Beatles reunion surfaced. My friends and I groused about the pointlessness of such a nostalgic exercise, and the Beatles themselves obviously agreed.

My opinion changed, however, one winter's night in Winnipeg in 1988. It was the second time, I think, that I'd ever heard music on CD. The first time, a record executive had played "Manifesto" by Roxy Music for me in his office, but this instance was more revealing. The red Afghani hash probably helped, but it was "Across the Universe" on a gleaming digital platter that sucked me in like a penny through a vacuum hose. I don't think the Beatles had ever struck me as weird, or even mildly psychedelic before, possibly because I'd been exposed to songs like "Lucy in the Sky with Diamonds" and "I Am the Walrus" through Saturday-morning cartoon shows, revivalist tribute acts, and those blue-and-red "Greatest Hits" packages that stripped away the band's knotty shell and left only the gooey centre. Psychedelia and experimentalism were deep forces throughout many of their musical concepts, but they were made innocuous by the banal gossip surrounding LSD references and the "Paul is dead" gobbledygook. The only time I'd ever thought the Beatles were even mildly heavy was when I saw my older cousin well up with tears on the day their breakup was announced. I may have paused a moment to consider how a rock band could have such a serious affect on human emotion, but mostly I thought that being deeply wounded by the demise of something that existed in cartoon form was absurd.

But after getting swept away by "Across the Universe," I understood that the Beatles were one of the few musical entities with the power to influence a person twice in their lifetime, each time on a completely different, yet profound, artistic level. My appreciation of the band as a preteen amounted to glorious miles of vertical flight springing up and down on a mattress to "Yellow Submarine" or zooming down the street on my CCM bike with "Hello, Goodbye" playing on the handlebar radio, and my second Beatles' epiphany was no less ecstatic, if played out in a stoned fog in my friend's cold apartment. As an adult, I'd redis-covered Led Zeppelin, T. Rex, and Mott the Hoople too, but those moments only confirmed my appreciation of them. There was no second curtain pulled back to reveal a whole other essence of sound, as there was this time.

Afterward, the Beatles kept coming. I remember being emotionally restored by the radiant conclusion of "Abbey Road" while idling in a van with the Rheos outside a hotel in Burlington, Vermont, after humping boxes of unsold T-shirts through the night in the cold shadow of an opening set played to uninterested Tragically Hip fans. Another time, I was rescued by the wonky tri-tone guitar lick – "Rain Dogs" thirty years early – in the bridge of "Here, There, Everywhere" as it played on a ceiling speaker above the pay phone at the Essex County Husky Truck Stop (the one where BTO got their name) while explaining to my parents that our car had overheated and left us stranded south of Windsor. Also, sitting alone as a twentyish kid in an empty movie theatre listening to a prefilm mixed tape with John Lennon butterflying the ceiling paint on "Money," his fierce, shivering lead vocal rendering the cinematic experience moot; or hearing my wife whispersinging "I Will" to our newborn daughter while cradling her down the hallway, then, years later, listening to the little girl sing "Got to Get You Into My Life" while falling asleep, and even later still, my son demanding to hear "Ob-La-Di, Ob-La-Da" as he bounced up and down.

My Russian Beatles moment came in old Leningrad during our second day there. I was wandering through the streets just before nightfall looking for Pushkinskya Prospekt, which I hoped would lead me to a club called Fish Factory, where Al, Mikko, a collection of Mikko's friends, and I were meeting before going to Cynic, the site of our prospective first Russian performance. (We'd shown up at Cynic the night before to discover that the promoter, a kid named Sergei, who also worked the bar, was unaware that any show had been scheduled. Cynic was a low-ceilinged hovel with a concrete floor and a few scattered tables – the perfect hard-folk setting – so we were crestfallen when Sergei balked. We stayed for food and drinks, and he finally relented, telling us to come back the following evening to play.)

St. Petersburg is a classical, yet unprecious, city. If Moscow is the brick and limestone capital that leads with its fists, St. Pete's draws you to its bosom through a tangle of canals and what feels like one long, endless neighbourhood, peppered with the occasional cop wanting to relieve you of your money. The city's famous palette of rich yellows and blues, mint greens, and caramel-coloured buildings helps brighten long streets that seem tired, even ruined, by war and a difficult post-glasnost era. She is an aging doyenne who, in her soul, refuses to be ground down.

My quest to find Fish Factory was a happy exploration of the city one wrong turn after another. I'd left Al and Mikko back at the hostel in an attempt to clear my head after days of travelling together in our host's compact car. At the corner of Nevsky Prospekt and Kazanskaya Ploshchad, I sat on a bench in the cold drizzle of the afternoon and admired St. Petersburg's warm, sunken beauty. Looking north down the Kanal Griboyedova, my eyes followed a line of tour boats like bobbins on the water until they fell upon St. Basil's bejewelled facade, bright and glorious despite the weather. An office building painted eggshell blue stood to my right and across the street towered a shopping arcade that housed one of St. Petersburg's biggest bookstores. The centre of the building was capped by a huge glass globe held aloft in the charcoal sky by green copper vines. (When I later effused about the building to Mikko, he told me that originally there had been two washrooms inside the globe and the women's had stared directly over the street, providing St. Pete's with one of its most astonishing views.) Slouched at my back was the Kazanski Church, a great stone colossus with enormous pillars and blackened walls that dared you to enter. By contrast, the Hermitage Museum, or Winter Palace, waited coquettishly around the corner and gave way to the golden spires of the Naval Academy, which gave way to a web of busy roundabouts that, in turn, gave way to the great, hiccupping sea.

While I wandered the streets, it dawned on me that my crooked path mirrored the experiences of early Soviet rock fans for whom finding a venue was a matter of great mystery and intrigue. The first official rock venue didn't open until the late 1980s. Before then, concerts were held without any advance notice because of government suspicion. Shows were staged in factories from midnight to 2:00 or 3:00 a.m., after the last shift had ended, all signs of the performance disappearing before the plant reopened in the morning. Yuri Shevchuk, the "Black Dog of St. Petersburg," told Thomas Cushman, "I remember going to Siberia alone, with the guitar, or to Kazan. A man who was meeting me would be standing at the corner. Wanting to avoid the cops, he'd say, 'Turn around that corner, and other people will lead you farther.' I'd do that, and then I'd enter a basement without electricity, but with hundreds of people . . . no microphones . . . and candles everywhere."

During my walk, I looked for traces of the Leningrad Rock Club, the famous, defunct Nevsky Prospekt venue operated in the 1980s under the auspices of the Intercouncil House of Artistic Activity (a Communist organization). Formed by local musicians, the club was an example of the modern Soviet Union's policy of "repressive tolerance." It was the first decent, aboveground venue to showcase rock 'n' roll, and gave the state firsthand surveillance of the scene, its bands, and leaders. Its board was made up of local musicians, but those who refused the invitation to join were harassed. Musicians were required to submit lyrics for approval before performing, and some had their tapes seized by Rock Club officials. When Black Dog was asked by officials to provide the state with a sample of his recordings, he handed over a homemade reel weary with distortion on which he'd sliced awkward bits of scratchy Indian classical music into his own tunes. It was a cross-cultural train wreck. The authorities thought the music was so bad – and unlikely to corrupt – that they left him alone.

I found no remnants of the Club. I almost didn't find Fish Factory either. It wasn't until I passed through a black iron gate off the main street and walked along a grotty passageway, down a set of stone steps to a long, dirty laneway postered with show announcements that reflected Russia's modest rock boom – the

Tony Montanas, Hostile Breed, the King Kongs, and a classic rock tribute band with the name: Let's Eppilin – that I came to a small, open-air courtyard. There, four Sergeant Pepper–era busts of John, Paul, George, and Ringo were crudely rendered. It was the John Lennon and Beatles Museum of World Peace, and Fish Factory was a few feet to my right. Before joining my friends, however, I lingered for a few minutes in the light rain under the gaze of my heroes, feeling as if I'd travelled a great distance over the planet, yet not very far at all.

After a meal of dumpling soup and fried garlic bread at Fish Factory set to a CD of Jimi Hendrix's *Greatest Hits, Volume II*, we taxied to our performance at Cynic. The unmarked club lay on the other side of a heavy wooden door, the polar opposite of the House of Blues–style neon facades favoured by North American pop venues. When we pulled the door shut behind us, we were surprised, and thrilled, to find the room squirming with life. When we had first visited the club a day earlier, there had been only a handful of us – including Sergei – drinking and hanging out. The social climate may have changed radically in the former USSR, but Cynic still possessed a hint of rock 'n' roll cloak and dagger and for that, I was thankful. Buried in an old, crumbling building, it preserved the mood of what it was like to experience rock 'n' roll in secret. As Al and I searched for Sergei to ask him where to set up and plug in, I looked forward to pretending to play music in a time of illegal hammer-ons and lawless whammy squeals.

Sergei was nowhere to be found. Mikko was at his wits' end trying to find out where he'd gone and what he'd promised us, for there was no PA or monitors or direct boxes anywhere in the club. In Sergei's absence, responsibility for running the club had fallen to a fiftyish woman in a green dress whose hair was assembled in a lumpy cone above her head. She had florid makeup and lipstick trowelled across her bemused half-smile, and she stood impassively behind the bar answering Mikko's Russo-Anglo-Finnish questions by shrugging. Mikko got nowhere with her and gave up. After he peeled away through the crowd (comprised mostly of young people drinking and smoking in unreasonably heavy proportions) I approached her with my guitar, pointed at it, and told her, "Guitars! We play!" With the kind of slow, dramatic action perfected by Russian women, she shook a cigarette from its pack, drew it between long red fingernails, laid it on her protruding lower lip, lit it with a match, looked away at a distant speck of nothing, and said in a Slavic drawl, "So, play."

Realizing that no sound system was going to materialize any time soon, Al and I took our guitars from their cases, found a room in which to tune – we had to crawl through a tiny door in the wall to get there – and went back into the club to roam the room and play as if we were accordionists in an Italian restaurant. Lucky for us, the first table we approached was buzzing with people celebrating Alexei's thirtieth birthday. You could tell who Alexei was because, in a group of eight or ten, only he was wearing an orange baseball cap with a pair of clapping hands clipped to the bill. When we asked if we could play him a birthday song, he pulled a string and the hands applauded, signalling us to start. His friends splashed vodka into a row of shot glasses, grabbed our hands, formed them in a grip around the glasses, and raised them to our mouths. One of Alexei's friends also passed me a couple of little green pills shaped like arrowheads, which I politely dropped between the bench slats. Al managed to toast the birthday boy, but begged off for the balance of the drinking session, still feeling the effects, he said, of the liquid bacon we'd ingested in Joensuu. The responsibility for appeasing our hosts, thus, fell to me, and I cast myself like a dory into a sea of booze. I'd like to report that my two previous visits to Russia had made me less of a novice when it came to drinking vodka, but it's not true.

The vodka propelled me into a car crash of a set featuring songs by Gordon Lightfoot, Talking Heads, Camper Van Beethoven, and the Ramones along with a few original compositions that could pass as party songs. We rotated around a few tables and concluded the show by playing to a group of American and French girls studying in St. Petersburg. The Americans asked what state we were from, and when we told them that we weren't American, they looked confused. They also looked beautiful, fresh-faced, and sparkling with the adventure of living in a great, strange land, so we made them guess our country of origin. Staring at us long and hard – and making me suddenly conscious of the fact that I'd spent just a little too long away from home – one of the girls guessed, "You guys are from Italy, right?"

With that, we considered the evening a success.

Our show at Cynic was our only public performance, but we spent most late-evenings jamming and hanging out in our hostel, singing to Mikko, Jari, and dozens of their friends who had materialized over the course of our stay. When I tried to calculate the number of performances for this book, I struggled with what constituted a legitimate show before deciding that consecutive evenings spent howling Canadian folk rock in a narrow Russian kitchen for a horde of strange Finns – and, it turned out, one wayward French student who'd also been booked there – was substantial enough to include. It certainly felt like a real show. Everybody got sloshed, and while I'm sure we butchered our repertoire, Mikko seemed pretty happy. By playing what amounted to a private show, we wanted to give something back to the person who'd helped get us to Finland and across the border into Russia. At the end of two weeks, we'd come to know each other pretty well; at least, as well as any North American will ever know a Finn. At one point, Mikko had taken us to his parents' country home, where we met his dad, who'd fought against the Russians in the Second World War. The old man's smile was bright despite a body creaking with age, and he seemed pleased that we'd crossed the pond to share our Canadian folk rock with the Nordic world. Mikko's mom made us coffee and served cakes, and when it came time to play, I started with something soft and winsome – "The Sky Dreamed," I think – after which Al played "Janefield." They demanded more, so we played "Freight Train," even though the setting was still and quiet, the house surrounded by the calm beauty of the woods. When Mikko's mother told us that she'd enjoyed "Freight Train" the most, Al admitted that he'd been reluctant to play such a raucous song. She responded, "You might not think so, but old Finnish people like loud songs too."

Just before 11:00 p.m., Mikko took us to the train station and put us on the overnight dart to Moscow. Al and I were excited, feeling that we were being loosed into Russia as we hauled our guitars and luggage across the busy train platform. Once we'd finally got everything into our berth, we hugged Mikko and thanked him for everything. True to form, he buried the moment in the discussion of a subsequent trip: "Well, when you come back, we will do many more things."

"Okay, Mikko, okay, great," we said, then drifted on.

MOSCOW

To say the name properly, and to give it just the right ono-
matopoeic push, you've got to scrunch your eyebrows, tense
your cheeks, harden your lips, tighten your larynx, close your
fists, and growl as if passing on troubling news:

Moss-ko.

In a club in Moscow, a beautiful young woman with aquamarine eyeliner named Maria flicked out a hand at me and
drawled in a sour whisper, "St. Petersburg? She just stands there
and looks pretty." Moscow is a lot of things – its streets, for
instance, are gloriously clean and well kept, and its architecture
possesses an operatic thunder – but pretty it is not. There are no
fluttering harps in the soundtrack to Russia's seat of power.
Instead, imagine a great anthem – the beating of snares and the
wailing of voices – that evokes New York City boiled in borscht,
Paris with a knife in its sock, Prague striding with laced boots
and a broken guitar.

Moscow has a lot to recommend itself, but more than
anything, it has Muscovites. In the eyes of many Westerners,
Muscovites in repose appear as if a great weight is pressing hard
upon their souls, their hooded eyes and hunched shoulders har-
bouring the last shred of sensitivity that hasn't been stamped flat

by the social and political tumult of the last hundred years. But, once you get to know them, Muscovites exude great warmth and character. They're as voluble as Romans, as funny as the Irish.

When Al and I arrived in the Russian capital early Sunday morning for our performance that night, we were met by orange-haired Yulia Ochetova, who had been the fixer and translator on the hockey film crew a few years earlier. We easily made our way by taxi into the city, a pleasant surprise because, on most weekdays, Moscow is a rat's nest of vehicles, its roads choked. More often than not, the source of trouble is an old rust-bitten truck – a relic from collectivist times – that's exploded in flames across three lanes, its engine parts strewn across the pavement. This time, we drove quickly to the apartment belonging to the *Globe and Mail*'s Moscow correspondent, Graeme Smith, a friend of a friend. Graeme had just come back from reporting on the earthquake in Pakistan, where he'd written his column from a mountain enclave while subsisting on walnuts and apples and bathing in hand sanitizer.

Graeme's apartment felt about as Russian as the Scarborough Town Centre. Nestled in a diplomatic corridor that housed ambassadors and embassy personnel of all stripes – Graeme's flat had previously been the home of the Iraqi foreign minister – the only distinguishing feature of the residential block was the old Soviet bus idling outside. It was full of whisky-soaked soldiers ostensibly there to protect visiting dignitaries. When Graeme's girlfriend at the time, Alison, sat us down in the kitchen in front of a Bodum of coffee and a plate of sandwiches – right after she showed us how to tap into the couple's Internet and work the cable television – I suffered a sort of culture shock in reverse. There was no sign of a samovar, no pungent scent of cabbage soup. Later, when we ate at the nearby American Diner – located strategically to exploit homesick North Americans –

the only feature that distinguished Moscow from Moncton was an old, moustachioed security guard in a corporal's uniform, who sat smoking and reading newspapers in the corner. The poor man, Graeme told us, was required to dress as a clown on weekly family days.

Back at the apartment, Graeme showed Al and I to our rooms, where we crashed after promising to rise early that afternoon to take in the big city before our gig at Jao Da, a.k.a. the Chinese Pilot. I had a deep, satisfying slumber, despite a chest cavity that had tightened because of allergies, forcing me to pinch tiny breaths. The source of my discomfort, it turned out, was a wee black cat named Pablo – an agreeable beast to many, but poison to me. I'd developed terrible allergies to animals over the years, and because they almost always put me down for three or four days, I was careful not to spend much time around pets. But while planning our journey, I'd neglected to ensure, from any of our hosts, that their environs would be pet-free, and so, on the afternoon of our Moscow rock 'n' roll debut, I spent the better part of a half-hour stewing in the steam and moisture of Graeme's shower, trying to regain the use of my lungs and sticking my head through the curtain to puff on my inhaler.

I broke the news to Al that, rather than spend our first afternoon attacking the Kremlin City with a vengeance, I'd have to take the day easy and cram our sightseeing into the following afternoon. A consummate travelling companion, Al told me that it would be fine as we left the apartment for a short stroll toward Red Square and beyond.

More than anything, I wanted to revisit the Maly Theatre while I was in Moscow. The Maly is directly across the street from the Bolshoi, about a block from Red Square. The two theatres are connected by tunnel through which, during the golden age of Russian theatre, performers dashed from one show to the

next. (Locals often refer to the Maly as "the little Bolshoi.") In
Joensuu, I'd asked Kemal if he'd ever performed at the Maly, and
his eyes grew damp at the memory of the theatre's red-velvet
seats, gold-trimmed balconies, and the velvet-curtained boxes
where both Tsar Nicholas III and Stalin used to watch performances from on high. I'd first visited the Maly in 2004 to interview Tatiana Yakushev, the wife of the great Russian hockey star
Alexander Yakushev. Tatiana – who was as flamboyant as a
Gabor sister when telling stories – had lost her only child, a
daughter, to violence in the early 1990s. Because she'd danced as
a young woman at the Maly, we had arranged to interview her
on stage.

When we arrived to set up our lights and camera, we were
guided around the great hall by the theatre's tiny, white-haired
manager. We were particularly intrigued by a bronze hammer
and sickle that hung above the old wooden stage – most
Communist-era symbols had been removed – and when I asked
why this icon had been preserved, he joked, "We thought we'd
keep it up, just in case we ever go back."

The convivial nature of the Maly's employees surprised me.
The theatre manager hadn't thought twice about letting
someone they'd met only ten minutes earlier wander the wings
of the theatre. It demolished my preconception of Russians as
suspicious and hard-faced. I almost forgot that we were within
shouting distance of both the Kremlin Bell Tower – where Ivan
Barma, St. Basil's architect, was allegedly blinded by Ivan the
Terrible after completing his masterpiece, so that he would never
reproduce it – and the notorious KGB tombs, which lurk behind
a building that houses Moscow's biggest toy store.

As I paced side-stage, readying my heart and mind to talk to
Tatiana, I came upon a mirror, gloriously tall and wide, with a
deep, ornate oak frame. I passed it, stepped back, stopped, and

looked in. The mirror held me to my spot on the worn and polished floorboards like arms to a small child.

Since landing in Moscow, I'd been searching for a portal into a country that had been veiled to me my entire life. The Maly stage mirror was this portal. Through it, I felt the sensation of standing in a place where for hundreds of years men and women had also stood before striding out on stage to lose themselves in Pushkin, Gogol, or Chekhov. While some occasionally performed for history's monsters, mostly they performed for full houses of ordinary Muscovites, whose lives had borne witness to some of the most remarkable events of our time. I lost myself in the mirror's eye.

Moss-ko.

Al and I never made it to the Maly. The route from Graeme's apartment to Red Square – about a twenty-minute walk – proved to be a trip through bronchial hell. I found that I had more of a physical kinship with the aging party geezers who lingered outside the Kremlin playing old Communist anthems on tape decks than with the hordes of kids hanging around Sbarro or any one of the fast-food franchises that ring the square. My guitar felt heavier than a Scottish caber, and I had to stop every few steps to catch my breath. My only propulsion was the force of Al's enthusiasm at visiting such a famous place, and his relief when he realized that, by day, Moscow was simply too fabulously busy and alive to give itself over to thieves and scoundrels. Too bad for them, I thought, for if ever a Westerner was easy prey for a band of miscreants, it was me, navigating the famous cobblestones step by halting step.

To get to the club, we threaded our way through the commercial heart of the city, which, post-glasnost, had been remade in the image of New York, Rome, or Paris, with designer fashion boutiques, expensive shoe shops, and tony restaurants dominating streets that thirty years earlier had seen only bread and sugar lines, not window shoppers. At night, idling SUVs and Hummers – the playthings of the new oligarchy – grumbled outside the glittering bars and discos, each with two people inside: the owner's driver and his bodyguard. Beyond Red Square at night were necking teenagers in ironic red CCCP T-shirts, and heavy-metal guitarists playing Joe Satriani around fountains and beer gardens. The kids' demeanour said as much about the New Russia as the cops and soldiers who patrolled the subways, and while their hip clothes and evident lust for anything new and Western made me feel cynical about Russia's orgy of new capitalism, there was a refreshing ebullience to them. In 2004, I'd followed a group of kids to a park in Central Moscow where the Scissor Sisters were expected to perform. It had rained constantly throughout the show, but not a single person left during the band's forty-minute set. Lead singer Ana Matronic told the crowd that she'd been named after a Russian saint and that her parents were Russophiles. As a result, it was a kick-ass show, and the crowd went wild, jumping and dancing in the mud that had collected at our feet. The symbolism was delicious: a gay New York pop band playing where a statue of Stalin had once loomed.

Eventually, we made our way to the Chinese Pilot. Like Cynic and Fish Factory, the Pilot was hidden from the street. If we hadn't been looking for it, we wouldn't have noticed the small square painting of a Second World War pilot in the cockpit of a fighterplane. It hung from a long metal awning over a passage that led off the sidewalk. The awning reminded me of those makeshift tents erected in sporting arenas to protect visiting teams from being pelted with garbage by hostile fans. The passageway led to a small set of steps that ended at a fortressed wooden door. We pushed it open and walked into a club that, at first glance, looked like a Sovietski Village Vanguard – low-lit, cool, and humming with possibility.

The Chinese Pilot consisted of three rooms. The back room was a candlelit grotto where I could almost hear voices being whispered through the walls. Groups of young, chain-smoking Muscovites who looked like they listened to Tortoise sat around tables covered by checkered tablecloths drinking coffee, reading books, and talking about whatever young, chain-smoking Muscovites who look like they listen to Tortoise talk about. As it turned out, they were waiting for the screening of an Antonioni film, which, a small mimeographed poster told me, was part of the Pilot's monthly film series, programmed by an instructor from Moscow University. When I left the club hours later, the kids were still there, gently arguing with their professor and smoking.

The middle room had a tavernesque bar and kitchen serving drafts and twenty different kinds of bliny (Russian crêpes, or pancakes). Beyond a wall that was supposed to act as a noise-break was the live room, which had a tiny dance floor and a small stage that looked like it was built from the ribs of a firkin. The tables were old public school desks and the seats were stools, while the walls had been stripped, then repainted in spots to display curious boxed paintings that ostensibly told the story of the Jao Da, the Chinese Pilot. From above the stage, red fairy lights painted the scene.

Tanya and Irina were the proprietors of the Pilot, which opened in 1999 and stayed open twenty-four hours, seven days a week. Because Tanya and Irina bore the classic features of Russian women, I found it very difficult to talk to them, let alone do business. My weakness as a road manager was exposed. Before the show, Tanya, who had a blunt blonde haircut, wore high black boots and a red sweater, asked if she might see me in her office, "in private," she said. I followed her to a dark back corner of the club where she faced me, put one hand on my shoulder, pulled me into her blue-eyed canyons, and told me, in a voice as soft as a snowflake, that, after paying the headlining band (Marimba Plus, a jazz octet), she would have no money for me and Al.

"Would taxi fare be okay?" she asked.

I was about to tell her that it was simply forbidden for me to get into a cab with her when she said,

"A hundred and fifty rubles, okay?"

I answered in English, but it probably sounded like Macedonian. I returned to the stage and told Al that while we weren't going to get paid, Tanya wanted to take me home in a cab.

Then I spotted three scruffy cats prowling the floor and occasionally rolling on their backs. I hoped I could get them banished, but it turned out that the cats lived, slept, and were fed at the club. Had I been the kind of cricket-bat wielding road manager for whom beautiful and slyly aggressive Russian women were natural adversaries (as opposed to potential tickle-mistresses), I would have demanded that Tanya hoof open the doors and make the right hissing sounds to send the felines running for their lives. But I couldn't bring myself to do it. Besides, the beatniks who filled the back room were creating enough smoke to match a KISS/Crüe double bill, ensuring that I would get little reprieve no matter how often I sucked on my inhaler. After sound-checking on the small stage, I clutched my chest like Fred Sanford and suggested to Al that we find a nice table below the ventilator that didn't exist, all the while cursing whatever vengeful rock 'n' roll god had decided to torture me with asthma on my debut show in the city I loved best.

After dinner, we strolled the neighbourhood around the Pilot. The sky had dimmed to reveal the glowing spire of one of the Seven Sister's – a set of classical towers built by Stalin the Punisher with slave labour – poking the horizon like a great electric finger. We walked to a nearby park where a tall bronze sculpture of some big gesticulating dude towered over the grass. We stood there talking and shooting the shit as night fell over Moscow. Al's Russian adventure was in full swing, and he no longer felt as Frodo had, even though a few feet across from us a duct-tapped Lada that had been chased down by police was being searched fender to fender. Still, this was the first time that either of us felt like we were just hanging out, just being, in Moscow, which is always the first step in getting to know a city. With his hands pushed into his pockets like *The Freewheelin' Bob Dylan*, Al confessed, "Man, I've just got to come back to this city," which unless you've been robbed or rousted or had your car searched by the fuzz, is pretty much the sentiment that every visitor feels when they leave *Moss-ko*.

I wanted our show at the Chinese Pilot to be the best, to end our Eastern European swing in a hail of popping corks and confetti. I wanted to prove how much I'd learned as a soloist, and to give back to Moscow all that it had given me; to match it in soul, conviction, anger, bombast, and humour. But because I couldn't breathe, I could barely sing. To make matters worse, my guitar came back at me through the club's monitors sounding flat and hard, in both tone and pitch. From the beginning of my set, I clipped long notes, strummed my guitar defeatedly, and stood rooted to a single grooveless spot on stage, as if wearing clay trousers, but aware the whole time that I was performing in one of the great clubs of Russia in one of the world's mind-blowing cities.

After the show, Al said sagely, "It's the shitty gigs, the ones that you have to fight through, that count the most." I hadn't felt that until near the end of my set, after I'd dragged my wheezing corpse through thirty minutes of disappointment. Then, for the last two songs of the tour, Al and I invited the members of Marimba Plus on stage to play "Freight Train" and "Horses" with us. We guessed that they would be up for this because during Al's set, Sacha, the drummer, and Andrei, the saxophonist, had started clapping unprompted to Al's "Drunk in America," making it sound greater and more joyful than ever. For the end of our set, Sacha and Andrei were joined on stage by Anton on bass, Sergei on clarinet, and Ilya on the flute. I was relieved that the burden of performance no longer fell entirely on me, and started to have fun.

It took several bars for our insta-band to find the groove. It's not as if any group can be thrown together and immediately gel, let alone a set of Russian jazzists and two road-ragged hosers from Lightfootland. But slowly, it happened. The Plus played softly and respectfully at first, but as they opened up, the groove widened and the attack grew teeth until we were finally in the full swing of the song. Al sang like a hound with his paw stuck in a sewer grate and I laid hard into my strumming. Pretty soon, we were seven players creating a fierce and joyful noise.

And then the PA exploded. It crackled loudly for a moment before giving way to a great and ugly *gwoooooooaam*. The soundman, whose name was Staz, flew across the room, searching for burnt wires. Al and I looked at each other with grave uncertainty – Had we destroyed the system? Was this the end of Jao Da? – then Sacha, the Marimba Plus's fine drummer, flashed his sticks, tapped out four beats, and played on. Al and I laughed a high laugh, then kerranged through the song's final chorus. The crowd saluted us with an outrageous cheer.

It was time to go home.

NEW YORK

ALMOST EVERY MUSICIAN IN NORTH AMERICA – AND probably lots outside it too – sees New York City as the place where careers are established or validated. This was true during the 1980s and 1990s when Toronto musicians dreamed of conquering the Big Apple – as well as London and, to a lesser extent, Los Angeles. The highway heading to the border was jammed with broken heroes and all that, and for a while bands couldn't leave quickly enough for the glittering stages of Manhattan.

Because I was a kid with a strong sense of nationalism and an anti-American punk ethos, this seemed like so much misguided energy and enthusiasm. The goal of "making it" in New York had the veneer of an older generation's dream, a deluded idea of fame that seemed beside the point when Canadian music was finding its identity. To me, it stood to reason that a band should try selling a few tickets in Sault St. Marie before they set off to make it in cut-throat New York where, for a time, bands were required to pay club owners for the privilege of a gig. I reckoned that if you could make it in the broken-bottle hot boxes of the Soo, you could make it anywhere.

But since Manhattan is so tantalizingly close to Toronto – eleven hours by car, fewer from Montreal – musicians have been forever drawn to its heat and the sense of artistic romance that's long radiated north. Over the years, I've experienced both sides of this romance, having played there a handful of times with the Rheos, so when I was invited to join my friend Chris Brown and his Citizens' Band for a Big Apple gig after returning from Russia, I jumped at the chance. It would give me the opportunity to revisit memories of past shows while pushing my concert count closer to eighty or seventy or fifty-seven, or whatever it would be.

Chris had gone to NYC (with singer Kate Fenner) in 1996 after years playing piano and organ in several Toronto bands, including Bourbon Tabernacle Choir and Barenaked Ladies. His home, in Brooklyn's Park Slope, was a waypoint cherished by travelling Canadian players. His couches and floors were forever busy with wandering minstrels, and his back garden – which he'd dubbed New Manitoba – provided a welcome refuge from the grit and smoke of the city.

Like a lot of transplanted musicians, Chris did what he had to do to keep busy and stay alive, gigging with Anna Egge, playing on Rick Moranis's solo album, recording bands at his home studio, dropping in on sessions here and there, performing regularly at the New York Children's Museum, and touring with his other group, Chris and Kate. For the Citizens' Band, he'd put together a heavy ensemble featuring Tony Scherr on bass, Teddy Kumpel on guitar, and Anton Fier on drums. I'd met Tony a few times; Teddy, never; and Anton, once, during his days at the helm of the alt-rock collective the Golden Palominos. I'd interviewed him on CBC Radio in 1989 when I was guest-hosting a late-night music program called *Brave New Waves*, and the experience had been less than pleasant. After he mentioned that he'd recorded nothing but great albums – a suggestion that I found both preposterous and pretentious – I said, "It sounds like you're batting a thousand." Then he scolded me, "Life's not a fucking baseball game!" I told this story to anyone who asked what was my worst interview, and now, for my first New York appearance in more than a decade, Anton would be sitting on his leather drum stool, laying down the backbeat to one of my songs.

When I told Chris I was reluctant to play with Anton, he assured me that he'd probably forgotten about our interview, and that Anton was a changed man. If it was good enough for my friend, then it was good enough for me, so as I settled in to watch the show – the venue was the Living Room, one of the Citizens' Band's regular haunts, and where Chris kept his Hammond organ – I felt good about what was to come.

Watching Chris play reminded me of the Rheos' fourth or fifth "showcase" gig in 1991, when Chris had joined us for a few songs at a small shoebox bar with three lights called Little Tramps. That night, we were given thirty minutes to play for a bunch of record company executives who'd expressed interest in signing us. The show happened during the CMJ (*College Music Journal*) conference, a week-long derby of independent bands trying to pole-vault over one another for whatever contract lay at the edge of the mat. Also playing that night were a Manhattan band called El Nino and a group from Queens called the Raw Poets, who had a six-foot-tall lead singer and two tiny brothers on bass and guitar and who sang hilarious songs about high school.

Because we'd already done our share of "showcase" gigs – and because I thought of bands who treated the pursuit of fame and status as so many morons sprinting after a flaming bus – I approached our show with eyebrows raised and a strong sense of caution. But, as fate would have it, our gig at Little Tramps romanced me harder than any other. Our set was proceeding normally until about halfway through the performance, when I found myself standing on top of the bar, playing my guitar and lording over the crowd. I don't know how I got there or what I'd been thinking. I just knew that I was very excited to be playing "Legal Age Life at Variety Store" in a packed club on a Saturday night in New York City and had rushed at the bar like Nathan Lane charging into the footlights. Then I realized that none of my bandmates had followed my paroxysmal dash, a rare occurrence considering how eagerly we supported one another's lead, and how we tried not to let the lead singer get too far out of sight. I wasn't sure whether they'd remained on stage because, in light of the song's brevity, it would have taken them too long to hoist themselves atop the bar; whether they'd concluded that my sudden showbiz zeal could be best enjoyed at a distance; or whether they'd decided that, since I'd worked my way into a perfect, joyful place – and since they were good bandmates, after all – they would stand back and let me channel my inner Springsteen. Whatever the case, I held form above the crowd, singing, stomping my Converse, and howling at the ceiling lamps that swayed along my eyeline. And then I climbed down.

We finished our set and headed back to the bar, where everybody wanted to know my name. Our manager told me that the record company folks had liked the band, but that they thought that the guy in the hat was the group's "true star." It was funny, ridiculous, absurd, and embarrassing having to hear this. I easily brushed the praise away, then found my bandmates, who'd allowed me my New York rock 'n' roll moment because they knew I'd react the way I did after being told I was the Next Big Thing.

Still, as I reminisced while watching Chris, I felt just a little regretful, the way one remembers ignoring the overtures of a beautiful woman, or behaving like an ass in the presence of someone wise and important. Not to belittle my gig with the Citizens' Band, but I wondered whether the circumstances of playing in New York for the first time in ten years would have been different had I followed the trail of musical romance offered to me that night, or had the Rheos, as a band, not been so proud or idealistic or stubborn or allergic to the notion of "making it" in the big city. I wondered whether we'd been too principled – or precious – for our own good, especially during those showcase days, when the evenings were separated by long afternoons at ridiculously fabulous restaurants being fêted by record executives and A&R scouts. We once dined with the staff of Arista Records at a restaurant where the lead singer from Fine Young Cannibals was having a heated discussion with two silver-haired pythons wearing expensive watches and gold cuff-links: his lawyers. Sometime during lunch, the company's A&R rep asked what bands I liked, and I told him, "XTC."

"Oh, I loved their *Lemons & Oranges* record," he effused, trying to make a connection.

After that lunch we headed out: four youngish Toronto kids with money in their pockets hitting the record and comic-books stores around St. Mark's Square (including Dr. Psycho's 3-D House of Wax, a great, chimeric store that I visited only once, for it was gone when I returned the next time). The main thrust of our conversation wasn't about the incalculable riches or honey-haired vixens or brightly lit TV studios that would follow our union with Arista, but, rather, how the A&R rep had got the name of XTC's record wrong. It was *Oranges & Lemons*, not *Lemons & Oranges*. Because of this, the label lost all credibility for us, even though they offered us a contract later that afternoon.

Ironically, we ended up spending a few minutes as part of Artista's roster when the American label we did sign with, Sire, was merged with the bigger subsidiary in the mid-1990s. We did another showcase for their staff at the Mercury Lounge, located next to Ben Franks deli on the Lower East Side. When we arrived, we discovered that we were opening for Sophie B. Hawkins, a New York pop singer, and that Don Kerr, our drummer, was required to play Sophie's drummer's kit, which had seventy-four pieces and the kind of dead-sounding skins needed to play the singer's subdued folk-pop hybrid. We fought our way through a decent set, and did okay, but the thing I remember most was the scene around Ms. Hawkins, who'd just come out as a lesbian and had been featured that day on the cover of *OUT* magazine. When her show ended, a legion of record company personnel, magazine writers, and beautiful New York pop people rushed to greet her, as they'd greeted me at Little Tramps, fawning over her talent and beauty.

Later on, as we packed up for a long drive by van to Harrisburg, Pennsylvania, I went backstage to get my notebook and found the hallway still crowded with people trying to get to Sophie. I managed to elbow my way to our room, where, outside, Ms. Hawkins and her group were arrayed against a wall, their arms wound around one another, as photographers kneeled in front of them, their flashbulbs flooding the dim backstage. Sophie appeared to be swimming in gold light, her eyes starry, her hair perfectly set. The evening was supposed to serve the same purpose for both of us: to impress upon our record company that our music was worth championing inside the label and to the public. But in rock 'n' roll, while one band poses for the camera, another climbs into the van. For some reason, we were mostly in the van.

Remembering this only added to my rock 'n' roll regrets, which were also partly a condition of age. Recently, I'd worried whether I could still move around like I used to, and whether my scissor kicks had become a parody of their former selves. The Rheos' demise had induced a crack-mirrored reflection of my artistic life, refracting missed chances and wasted opportunities. That our friends and peers had enjoyed the fruits of rock 'n' roll romance only darkened my view: the Barenaked Ladies had played a sold-out Roseland Ballroom on the day that they became the first Canadian band since the Guess Who to reach number one in the United States and the Tragically Hip performed for millions around North America on *Saturday Night Live* at the invitation of fellow Kingstonian Dan Aykroyd. The clouds had started to gather and grow thick above me, and as I waggled my guitar cable across the Living Room's stage, I concluded that not only had the Rheos failed to match these other band's achievements, but we'd lost our band trying to find fulfillment, success, and romance in other ways. And now, the famous New York drummer at the back of the stage hated me. Really, the last place I wanted to be was up there.

Bilious with disappointment, I started playing. I decided on a self-deprecating, easy-to-learn number, "This Song Ain't Any Good," which is as novel and unprobing as "A Day in the Life" is heavy and hard. I chose it because it wouldn't exacerbate my mood; I could simply play the damned song smoothly and well and get off stage without Anton Fier firing hot cymbal shards into my back.

But I'd forgotten for a moment that the musician rarely has control over a performance, despite being the author and messenger of the music; something essential rests in the hands of an outside force. Because bands exist so that a group of people can work toward shaping a single musical moment, it's hard to know when one, or all, of these people will raise the song like a cat by its scruff. Just as the members of Marimba Plus had done in Moscow, the Citizens' Band ignored my distress and fell hard into the song, filling the velvet-curtained room with its thirty or so tables pushed toward the stage as if a great sonic bird had seized my woebegone folk singer's words. My mood improved almost immediately once I realized that Anton Fier didn't hate me at all. If he did, his spider-armed, sliptime groove belied his feelings. His toms were being struck with joy, I thought, not revenge. To my left, bassist Tony Scherr, who'd just spent a year touring with Willie Nelson and Bill Frissel, crept beside me to harmonize on the song's chorus, and sensing him there – his sly, lopsided grin, smiling eyes, and right hand teasing the fat strings of his bass like an old person tickling the belly of a Schnauzer – made me more concerned that my microphone was reading his growl-throated tenor than whether the Rheos' muddled career path or self-righteous doctrine of rock had been the cause of our breakup. When I noticed that during the song's last few kicking verses, my friend Chris was rocking over his old keyboard, I gave up wondering why "One Week" had become a monster radio hit while few DJs had played "King of the Past" or "PIN," or how my vitriol regarding the music industry's policy for choosing sellable pop shit over brave and new Canadian sounds had ensured that we'd never be invited to perform at the Juno Awards or be given a bronze plaque in the nation's rock 'n' roll hall of fame. The band's low-fat groove and joyous, ebullient playing told me that if I wanted those things in my life, all I had to do was keep gigging, and gigging some more, because while the Rheos had broken up, I hadn't, and even though I'd missed seizing fortune on countless occasions, at least I wasn't running screaming from the disappointment of what I didn't have.

PUDONG

IN THE INTERIM BETWEEN RUSSIA AND CHINA, I RECEIVED word through our management that both Tim and Michael, my ex-bandmates, would come to China if needed. This only muddled an already confusing situation. Though the Rheostatics had broken up, nothing had been made official. With Tim and Michael gone, Martin and I had to figure out whether we were genuinely, 100 per cent, forever broken up or a band reduced to two prolific songwriters, whatever that band was.

Things became even more complicated when I discovered that my tour of China would be billed under the name Rheostatics. I had planned on playing solo, but the Rheos management received word from the Chinese promoters of the Maple Rhythm Festival – Andy and Yu Fei – that gigs had been scheduled in amusement and industrial parks for the May Day holiday week. They suggested that playing with a full band would be best since crowds of 15,000 were expected at many of the events. I kicked around the idea of getting the Rheos together for one last Asian fling, but soon realized that bringing a breaking-up band to China would be an exercise in melancholy, if not futility. I asked Andy, via e-mail, if a slightly wonky version of the Rheostatics would work, and he wrote back, saying, "Of course. Members change: no problem." So the idea of forming a

Rheos' facsimile cemented. This way we'd avoid the heavy personal drama of touring with original members, who would only be there because no one else wanted to be.

Assembling a band proved to be easy: I called Al. We'd already navigated two foreign countries, so I knew that Al and I could travel together without wanting to murder each other. He had only one caveat: he wanted to bring along his friend and drummer, Jay Santiago of the Quitters. Building a touring band around a chemistry that already existed seemed like the right thing to do. We added my future brother-in-law and the Rheos' guitar technician, Dwayne Gale, on guitar and bass, and booked a ticket for the Rheos' soundperson, Steve Clarkson. We had a group: the Rheos-Not-Rheos. The plan was to learn a half-dozen of my songs and a handful of Al's and pray that it would somehow work.

Before going to China, I met Andy in the Library Bar at the Royal York Hotel in Toronto. He proved to be an affable and curious young man from Shijiazhuang, the biggest city north of Beijing. He'd been to Canada three times over two years, attending music festivals and conferences, and meeting as many bands as possible. After dreaming up the Maple Rhythm Festival, Andy secured financing through his promotional company, Life Fashion, and the Canadian Embassy, then set out to assemble a lineup. On first blush, it seemed as if he'd invited the first five bands he encountered, since the only thing we had in common were our passports. There were two East Coast bands (the Sons of Maxwell and the aboriginal band Forever), one prairie blues guitar prodigy (Jordan Cook), a Mississauga grunge band (Stradio), the jazz expressionists the Shuffle Demons, and the Rheos-Not-Rheos. Since the CanRock scene is small – at least in comparison to New York or London's artistic labyrinth – it seemed odd that the only band I knew was the Shuffle Demons. Now I not only had to acquaint myself with a whole other culture of sound, but also with a handful of musicians with whom I shared citizenship.

The Maple Rhythm Festival would be the first-ever Western rock 'n' roll caravan to tour China, but it wasn't the first time Andy and Yu Fei had brought Canadian bands to China. Wide Mouth Mason, the rambunctious prairie blues-rock group, had toured there in 2002, and Toronto's By Divine Right followed soon after. When I asked Jose Contreras, By Divine Right's singer, about his experiences there, he painted a picture of crowds throwing flowers when he sang, gigs that were cancelled moments after they'd been booked, and a procession of lavish banquets silly with rice wine. By Divine Right played four shows, even though they were promised a dozen performances, and already our itinerary was nearing this fate. Originally, Andy sent a list of eight cities, but by the time we left Canada, it had been whittled down to four, then three. I was disappointed that we wouldn't be cutting as wide a swath across China as expected, but because we were forming our group on the fly, I figured it was probably just as well, particularly in a country where the rock 'n' roll touring route was still being dug.

Unlike their Communist cousins in the old Soviet Union, the Chinese had barely encountered rock 'n' roll. Forty years after their Western heyday, only a handful of Beatles and Rolling Stones songs had been sanctioned by the state for radio airplay. Andy told me during his visit that the Chinese people were familiar only with three Beatles songs: "Let It Be," "Yesterday," and "Hey Jude." Then he asked, "When you come to China, do you think you could play 'Hey, Jude'?" He said that when Elton John debuted in Shanghai in 2004, the audience sat through the show in silence until the last song of his set, the state-approved "Can You Feel the Love Tonight?" at which point the crowd went wild. Weeks before our trip, the Rolling Stones had also played Shanghai, drawing 8,000 fans, 90 per cent of them expat Westerners with the means to afford the exorbitant ticket prices. Costs ranged from 300 yuan to 3,000 yuan per seat, more than triple the average Chinese salary, which, according to writer James Nyce, had only just reached the standards of 1850 industrial America, despite China's noted economic boom. The concert turned out to be an ambiguous moment in the Stones' careers. Five of the band's songs were banned by Beijing's Ministry of Culture because of their suggestive lyrics. When he learned this, Mick Jagger wryly told a U.K. reporter: "It's a good thing the Chinese government is protecting all of those Western investment bankers from being corrupted by our songs." Still, the Stones were privileged to have warranted so much attention from the higher-ups. Bjork had played Shanghai the year before, and no more than a hundred people came out to hear her.

When we touched down in Shanghai after twelve hours in the sky, Andy was waiting for us behind the exit gate waving a camera and a cellphone and dressed in a smart blue blazer and jeans. This was a considerable upgrade from the jeans-in-pockets, Prince Billy–bearded folks driving cardboard-grilled vans who usually met us at airports back home. Andy's businesslike comportment was the first sign that in many ways China, because of its rock 'n' roll infancy, still treated musicians as if they were touring textile magnates. This was confirmed after we laid eyes on our hotel: the Oriental Riverside, a four-star high-rise in the financial district. It had an espresso bar, no less, and, even better, it sat kitty-corner to a row of fabulous restaurants and massage depots and was just a few minutes from a busy enclave where merchants prepared delicious potato and egg crêpes in open-air kitchens and sold buckets of frogs, snakes, and eels.

Once we'd checked in and humped our guitars and trap cases into our rooms, we were asked by Andy to attend a press conference on the third floor of the hotel, where our coronation continued. A canvas poster had been strung up behind a dais where six microphones stood in front of six chairs. The poster showed all of the Maple Rhythm bands, including the Rheostatics in a publicity photo taken in the summer of 2002. My temporary bandmates laughed into their hands. Jay commented that Tim's head reminded him of an Easter Island totem, and that he could probably pull off the look from behind his drum kit, because all audiences ever see is the drummer's head. Dwayne, for his part, squinched his eyes at the photo of Michael Phillip-Wojewoda, then decided it would be impossible to grow a goatee in such a short period.

Andy made a few comments in Chinese to the handful of local print and TV reporters attending the event, then he intro-duced a grinning member of the Canadian Consulate, who joined him on the dais, along with manager Norm Sharpe, whose two bands, Jordan Cook (the Jimi Hendrix of the Prairies) and Stradio, had been brokered as a package for the Maple Rhythm caravan. Norm had a hands-in-pockets way of talking and a modest prairieness that was refreshing considering that he made his living in a field busy with power vultures. Norm's comments were typically managerial, touching on rock 'n' roll diplomacy, Canada versus America, and opportunities for a free-market exchange among bands in both nations. The Rheos-Not-Rheos snickered at this, having heard these kinds of plati-tudes from industry types over the better part of twenty years.

Shanghai press conference announcing the Maple Rhythm bands
(*Dwayne Gale*)

Stradio and Jordan Cook represented Norm's hidden agenda –
to open an untapped market for these young bands. The rest of
us were just happy to have weathered the flight.

After Norm spoke, Andy asked if the reporters had any
questions. I wouldn't have been surprised if they'd lobbed a few
softies about countries coming together in song, but instead,
they grilled the panel about the purpose of the event, asking, "If
there is only one show in Shanghai, why is it called Canadian
Pop Music Week?" and "Why do Canadian musicians go to the
United States to earn a living?" and "Why are all of the musicians here men. Why are there no women on the bill?" This came
in part at the expense of Norm, which gave the Rheos-Not-
Rheos a small measure of joy.

Before coming to China, I'd imagined we'd find audiences grateful that we'd taken time out from our heightened rock 'n' roll lives to expose them to our elevated art, but the more I learned about pop music culture in China, the more I realized this wouldn't be the case. At a banquet following the press conference, I asked Andy why he hadn't chosen more modest – and reasonable – venues, such as large clubs, for the tour. After breaking the news to me that there was no such thing as a large rock 'n' roll club in China (this proved to be only partly true), he said that the only way for Western bands to gain an audience in China was to present them in the grandest theatres, the biggest amusement parks. Local bands who played in clubs, he said, were not respected by the public. Later in the tour, a Hunanese promoter we met elaborated that sub-superstar bands, no matter where they came from, were considered on the level of drug dealers and prostitutes in the same way early jazz bands or baseball players had been viewed by the American ruling class. One of the reasons for this, Andy explained, was because indie bands weren't allowed to sell CDs. "They can press them and use them for promos," he said, "but they get in trouble if they try to make a profit from them. Only state-approved bands who sign with big record companies can make a living playing music."

Chinese audiences were largely weaned on (and devoted to) Cantonese pop stars, and they weren't clamouring for something new, or Western. A lot of Chinese listeners doubted the quality and value of Western music, an attitude about foreign products in the largest consumer market in the world that had left a lot of hopeful Western businessmen gasping for air. When I brought this point up with Andy, he said that Canadian rock 'n' roll would be better accepted because he and his partners at Life Fashion had a plan: to present it as an equal to opera and theatre, in venues better suited to those classical forms.

Striking it big in China was the farthest thing from our minds – getting to the barbecued pork and shrimp spears that spun on our table's lazy susan at the post-press conference banquet was a more pressing concern – but it was important to Norm and his bands. Perhaps they'd drawn inspiration from unlikely bands finding success outside of their homeland while dreaming of pan-Sino fame. While the music of the Beatles, the Rolling Stones, U2, Tina Turner, Coldplay, Pink Floyd, and Bryan Adams makes up much of the world's pop soundtrack, there's still no accounting for what will or won't take hold in any country. One example of this is the British pub-glam band Smokie, who probably couldn't put twenty-seven people in a club in New York City but whose songs are wildly popular across Russia. Whenever I heard any kind of contemporary music played in the former Soviet Union, Smokie's hits were part of the local repertoire, on club sound systems or performed by cover bands. The Russians love Smokie so much that, in 1996, they were one of only a handful of musicians to play the Kremlin Palace in Moscow, which they did with their fourth lead singer in twenty years, another feature that distinguishes Smokie from most bands.

Boney M is also revered in Russia and beyond. When Mongolia first gained independence in 1992 after years as a Soviet satellite state, it held its first non-state-sanctioned concert. Despite being able to hire whatever Western band they wanted for the first time in their history, officials caved to the demand for Boney M. The longstanding Dutch disco band made its Ulaanbaatar debut to 3,000 Mongols packed inside a wrestling stadium, but the real story happened outside, where 12,000 more fans gathered around loudspeakers broadcasting the event.

British new wave guitarist Jack Green's debut album went gold on the Canadian Prairies, but it died everywhere else in the world, and the English prog-pop band the Strawbs continued to sell records in Newfoundland long after their career had faded. Friends in St. John's told me that because Strawbs were the only British band of their generation to play the Rock, Newfoundlanders maintained an undying allegiance to them, buying whatever music they put out, whether or not any of the original members remained.

Even though Jordan Cook and Stradio were both unknown bands who'd yet to release an album, it wasn't out of the realm of possibility that they'd find their biggest listenership in China. Part of the Maple Rhythm's intrigue would be finding out which groups would survive on China's uncharted rock 'n' roll roads, and whether any among us were the Strawbs.

The next day, our thirty-person hoser caravan was bused forty minutes from Shanghai's city centre to the city's Special Economic Zone, Pudong, an oasis of concrete constructed in a spot where ten years ago there were rice paddies and small Chinese villages. Walking around Pudong was like strolling through a perfect architectural model, so fine were its streetcorners, so vivid its lawns and trees. Swarms of workers paid a pauper's wage tended to every aspect of the civic omniverse – tilling gardens, freshening plants, righting rocks tilted in scuppered ponds, and unspecking whatever bits of trash pocked the sidewalks and boulevards. We would be playing in the Oriental Art Center and Music Hall, which, viewed from a distance, looked like five enormous tea cups knocked together. Across the street stood a monstrous concrete raptor touching down: the Museum of Science and Technology. It made me think of the Hall of the People in Bucharest, Ceauşescu's useless monolith, whose only function, it seemed, was to remind other Romanians of their insignificance. In Pudong, there was one of these every few blocks. It didn't matter that 16 million people lived within a half-hour's drive of the district. You could fill the borough with bodies, and its boulevards, patterned with hundreds of red-and-yellow star flags, would still seem empty.

Beside the museum a pathway that stretched out of sight beckoned, and Dwayne and I decided to follow it to the end. This proved impossible, however, for a security gate about two kilometres from where we started was controlled by an officious ticket taker who demanded money to stroll an empty riverfront. Walking back to the Music Hall, we heard an unusual sound coming from a stone bench along the boulevard: a young Chinese student was singing "Take Me Home, Country Roads" by John Denver into a yellow megaphone. ("Maybe it's a lament for what used to be here," opined Dwayne.) We stopped and quizzed the student and his two friends on the unusual song selection. "It's a song that an American friend of ours used to sing," he told us. When I asked him if this was really just a ploy to meet girls – pointing out that, were you to use the song to do so in Canada, you'd grow hoarse before you got any action – he insisted that it was merely for fun, and that he and his friends were only hanging out, killing time. I asked him what he thought about what had become of Pudong, but he didn't know how he felt one way or another. The conversation turned to the Rolling Stones, whose music he found "tacky," and the freedom of information, or lack thereof, in China. We were surprised when they told us that gathering information wasn't a problem. They said that they knew about the woman from Falun Gong who'd disrupted President Hu Jintao's visit with George Bush, and that they regularly read the BBC, CNN, and other Western websites to find out what was going on in the world. We'd assumed that China's access to Internet sources was quite limited. "People have the wrong impression of China when it comes to what we

can and can't see on the Internet," said the fellow with the megaphone. "In most cases, we know what we need to know. Either
that or we know how to get it," he said, before getting back to
his song.

Back at the Hall – whose long, sinuous tiers of upholstered
wooden seats were so new they smelled of lemon wax – we
walked into the sound check, which was going slowly, and
rather badly. Jordan Cook's soundperson, Ron, had caused a stir
after airing his frustrations to the Hall's local technicians, for
whom the basics of producing rock 'n' roll were as foreign as
Estonian poetry. Ron proved himself to be a bit of a pip on
landing in Shanghai, walking up to airport hostesses and trying
to pass himself off as a distinguished guest. At the Hall, he
berated the house tech (whom he called John Wayne instead of
learning his Chinese name) for not knowing the English for
simple technical terms, and had taken exception to another tour
soundperson's kibitzing with one of his artists. We talked about
this with some of the other bands while awaiting our turn to
sound-check. Steve Clarkson, our soundperson, reported that
while Andy had tried to translate between the local and international parties, there were certain terms – coaxial cable, XLR
cable, DI box, to name a few – that were comprehensible only
after much frenetic miming and gesturing. We agreed that Ron
might well go insane trying to square things into his notion of
how rock 'n' roll in a foreign land was supposed to go down.

Andy had shepherded us to the Hall at an ungodly hour
(8:00 a.m.) so that every band would be on hand (and held
captive) at the start of the long day. The idea had merit – contain
thirty wide-eyed rock 'n' roll tourists so that they'd be available
to sound-check at any time – but because the set-up was taking
so long, handfuls of hours passed while we sat and did nothing.
I walked as far as I could around Pudong – there was nothing

resembling a café or tea shop in the area, and musing by the riverbank wasn't an option – before eventually settling under a palm tree on the Hall's common, where I scraped out a few chords in a jet-lagged attempt to get some songwriting done. This got me nowhere, so I returned to the dressing room where because we'd spent so much time waiting around – a promoter's rookie mistake, Andy admitted – bands had started to gossip. The scuttlebutt focused, mostly, on Ron, Norm, and Jordan Cook, and how the Colin James of the Prairies' entourage wasn't doing the young finger-tapper any favours.

Through Norm's managerial influence, Jordan Cook sound-checked first because he was scheduled to headline the show. It didn't matter one way or another to me who played when, but it sent the message that someone had established a pecking order, and that someone wasn't them. When Norm had openly discussed at the banquet the possibility of getting a Chinese endorsement deal for Jordan, Jay had leaned over to me and said, "I'm Jordan Cook for Rat-on-a-Stick!" Jordan seemed like a decent enough kid, but because he had brown-and-blond Green Day hair, had played with musicians from Soundgarden and Kanye West, was signed to Epic, and airbrushed publicity shots of him preening into the camera flashed on the giant screen above the stage during sound check, a target had started to form on his back. At one point, Norm was heard talking to a representative from the Canadian Embassy, boasting that Jordan was "as clean and as good a kid as you'll ever meet. He doesn't drink, doesn't smoke, and is a strict vegetarian." After hearing this, Al turned to me and said, incredulously, "What kind of twenty-two-year-old kid doesn't drink?"

Jordan reminded me of another young Canadian blues guitar prodigy whom the Rheostatics met on our first tour in Winnipeg in 1987, Tim Butler. Everywhere we went in town, it

was "Tim Butler this, Tim Butler that." He was – as Jordan
Cook was, as countless prodigious T. Bones around the world
are – the second coming of Robert Johnson. Martin Tielli, the
Rheos' gifted picker, had a crisis of confidence knowing that a
young legend born to the great stages of the world was in our
midst. He suffered through a few uncertain performances because
of this, and only after we left town did our guitarist rediscover
the magic that made him so great in the first place. We saw Tim
Butler play on our last night in Winnipeg. He tore apart the
Royal Albert with his Stevie Ray Vaughan-esque *shtiklakh*
playing his guitar behind his back and winning roars of approval
from the crowd. Because I've never been a blues guy, the music
meant very little to me, but you didn't have to be Greil Marcus
to see that his show was pure retro-revue. We didn't hear of Tim
Butler again until many years later in Vancouver, when we
showed up to play at the Town Pump in Gastown. On the sidewalk outside the club, we found Tim Butler – thin, ragged-eyed,
and sunken-cheeked – playing his licks, a guitar case open at his
feet. Perhaps Jordan Cook, in his wise-beyond-his-years-
bluesman-wisdom, had decided to stay clean and sober because
he'd also seen his share of Tim Butlers. Or maybe he thought
that being a straight-edged vegetarian was just cool.

By gig time, there were about six hundred people scattered inside
the hall, under its state-of-the-art lighting racks and in its finely
cushioned seats. (Whenever anyone had plunked themselves
down in one during sound check, they'd been told to move to a
fold-up chair.) The venue sparkled like a sleek car drying in the
sunshine, but I thought that it could have used someone to kick
over an ashtray, maybe pee in a potted plant or two. After taking
a head count, Andy came out from behind a backstage curtain,

where he programmed videos for the screen with his computer, clasped his hands together, and proclaimed the event a success before a single note had been struck. In a country where, Andy told us, crowds for pop music events numbered either fifty or five thousand, it was rare to find so many fans gathered in one place, let alone at an event featuring Canadian bands. His face was flush with pride as the first band, Stradio, prepared to hit the stage.

I got ready for our show – restringing my Gibson, tuning it up, bashing the new strings like a cat savaging a tennis racket, then tuning it up again – then I climbed into the upper reaches of the Hall to take in this considerable moment in Can-Sino rock history. At the press conference, Norm had hinted that his two groups – Stradio and Jordan Cook – might play a few songs familiar to Chinese fans. This hastened Andy to ask us if we'd planned a similar program (we hadn't). So I wasn't surprised when Stradio ended their set with a medley of "Twist and Shout" and "La Bamba" which, just as Andy had predicted, got the crowd standing and cheering.

There was something very sweet about seeing the Chinese react to Stradio as if they were the Beatles, but something sad too, because, well, Stradio weren't the Fab Four, even if the sixty-watt amps provided by organizers made those songs sound much as they must have sounded in 1964. That a twenty-first-century group would cover forty-year-old songs to curry favour with the crowd made me see Stradio for what they were. Even though I'd cringed when their lead singer, a fellow named Martine, told a reporter from *Shanghai Life* that crowds could "expect good music and good looks," they seemed like decent enough guys whose idea of rock 'n' roll was just different from mine. But I believe that playing versions of your grandfather's happy pop when the world's climate is roasting and übergovernments are tearing down old villages and filling in rice paddies to build glass monstrosities where touring pop bands can break into new markets by pretending that everything is *Awwwright!* is artistically irresponsible. They'd fudged an opportunity to tell a nation who they were, what they stood for, and what Canada was like, while a lot of great bands who could have done this sat at home.

After the last grandstanding cymbal crash of "La Bamba," Stradio left the stage. Next up was the Shuffle Demons, who hucked their gear in from the wings. There are some bands that occupy a musical category all their own: the friend's band. Friend's bands could be the world's most abhorrent musical creation, but critiquing them publicly would rip up a pact. It's something that friends shouldn't do. If I wrote positively about the Shuffle Demons, it could be considered an inside job, as I've known the band for a handful of years. On the other hand, panning them would mean having to walk on the other side of the street to avoid them at home. I was damned if I did, damned if I didn't. With the friend's bands, it's best to keep quiet.

After the Demons' set, Forever, the Mi'kmaq rock band, played next. When I first saw them at Pearson International Airport, I thought they looked more like a crew bound for the oil fields of northern Alberta than the stages of central China. They were big men with Stock Ale paunches who'd travelled farther than any band to get to here. Forever's perpetually sunglassed drummer, Keith, had a laugh like a hyena on Prozac, and I'm pretty sure that Pete, the one-eyed bass player, was drunk for all three flights and two days of travel. Two of the guys had mullets, and one of them, Bernie, had a mullet top but no tail, the result, I suspected, of cleaning up before meeting the authorities who'd handed over the little girl he and his wife had adopted in China just a few months earlier. Forever was rounded out by Ken, who played keyboards, and Dennis, the group's singer, whose day job was managing the local hockey arena in the band's reserve of Eskasoni, Nova Scotia. Dennis was excited to be in China because he'd heard that the Mi'kmaqs had originally come from parts of Eastern China. Standing on the land of his ancestors was already a thrill, let alone playing his songs to fans to whom he might be remotely related.

Dennis had won the job with Forever after beating out another contender, known to everyone around Cape Breton as Screamin' Bob. Bernie told me that Bob showed up loaded at the audition wearing a police hat and a white leather jacket. He dropped to one knee and sang "Sweet Child of Mine" through three harmonizers. After the song, Keith told him, flat-out: "Bob, you're terrible. You can't fuckin' sing. The harmonizers make you sound three times as bad." Derek sang "Any Way You Want It" and got the job. When I asked Derek about his technique, he said, "Technique? I just get up there and do it." Then he added, "Once, I was standing outside having a smoke before a show when the lead singer from the headlining band, Honeymoon Suite, came up beside me with a scarf wrapped around his throat, humming to himself. I asked what he was doing, and he said, 'Warming up.' Then he asked me what I was doing. I hauled on my smoke and told him, 'Same as you.' We played great that night and left the crowd screaming for more. I looked over and the singer was standing side-stage, making a cut-throat motion with his hand. It was a bad idea. We played five more songs, and most of the crowd left afterwards."

Keith, the sunglassed drummer, told anyone who'd listen that, after eating what turned out to be a plate of duck tongues at the banquet the previous night, he could feel the carpet swaying underneath him. We raised our eyebrows, knowing that Forever had gone deep into the night playing a Chinese drinking game. A few days later, Bernie told us that he'd stashed a bag of twenty-four beers, and that Pete had found them and murdered them, causing the bassist to spend the next day and a half in bed. When Pete finally woke from his stupor, it was three-thirty in the morning, which didn't stop him from pounding on his band-mates' doors in an attempt to wake them. I told Bernie I thought that this was out of bounds considering how hard it is to estab-lish a sleeping routine after a long trip, but he said, "Nah, we all got out of bed, drank some more, and wrote two new songs. It was actually pretty productive."

This revelry might have hamstrung other bands, but it fuelled Forever's Oriental Hall performance, which was as ener-getic as it was unselfconscious. Because of the way they looked, I'd secretly hoped they'd play grimy swamp rock or heathen metal or Celtic shred, but their music sat at the point where Journey meets REO Speedwagon. Before their set, a video was shown on the big screen of the band hanging out in a photo studio surrounded by babes; this was a promising sign, I thought. But then Dennis, who wound the microphone chord around his hands when he sang, opened the set with a song about how he missed his girlfriend. Two tunes later, he asked the crowd a ques-tion that, for a moment, made my heart sink: "Do you guys like Journey?" The audience indicated that they did, and because Forever liked Journey too, they ripped into the mutha (if any Journey power ballad can be considered such a thing). Still, just in case the guy from Honeymoon Suite showed up and "Blinded by the Light" or "Carry on Our Wayward Son" or "Hold Your Head Up" was next, I ducked into the dressing room.

The Sons of Maxwell from Halifax took the stage next, and then the Rheos-Not-Rheos got ready to play. There was some-thing suspenseful about the moments leading up to our perform-ance, not only because we were making our Chinese debut, but because no one in the band had any idea what we would sound like once we started to play, as we'd rehearsed only three times before our departure. We'd rented space in a Toronto rehearsal factory, sonically elbowing our way between metal-tribute acts and indie-kid bands in a room no bigger than a refrigerator box. The songs had come together okay – Al and Dwayne alternated between bass and guitar, and we learned equal measures of one another's tunes – but because of the size of the room and its sound-beaten speakers and monitors, we weren't sure what or who we sounded like, or whether our music would burst alive or shrink away in the presence of strange new listeners on the other side of the world.

Another detail that Andy had overlooked was getting someone – anyone – to introduce the bands. (There were no food or drink riders backstage either.) So we walked out on stage more or less announced by an old Rheostatics video, which glorified a band that no longer existed. Still, when our first song ("The Land Is Wild") started and I turned to face my new bandmates, the peculiar feeling of having different musicians playing alongside me was blotted by my desire to pour into our performance every great song and album and band that China – not Joensuu, nor Hämeenlinna, nor Helsinki, not even St. Petersburg, but *China* – had never heard or, worse, had never been allowed to hear. I certainly wanted to do better than "Take Me Home, Friggin' Country Roads."

We played four songs at full pelt. There were lots of cheers and a few kids danced in the aisles, but what I'll always remember most is what happened when I went over to yowl something to a tier of fans sitting near the stage. They threw up their hands, but instead of clapping on time or punching their fists into the air, they did something I'd never seen done at a rock show before.

They waved.

For the guitar-break in "Horses" (a song I had the crowd introduce, as I'd learned the word *ma* moments earlier), I went into the audience and sat down in the first row between two well-dressed middle-aged women. Farther down, two more women in their mid-sixties if they were a day were sitting together and, behind them, a family with a young son. I hoped I was burning an impression on him of the wonder and beauty of rock 'n' roll, rather than simply of a loud guy with a nose like a bugle. All in all, the audience seemed pretty wholesome and straight: not a single person looked like they listened to Tortoise. I threw myself around the stage, spatscreamed choruses and chewed up all of the heat and energy I could possibly muster. The Pudongese responded with the kind of love and affection usually reserved for the mega-pop star I'd never be, the stadium-filling song god I hadn't become.

After our set, I scaled the auditorium to watch the evening's final set by the Jordan Cook Band (the G.E. Smith of the Prairies). Cook played the guitar with his teeth, behind his back, with a pair of drumsticks. He played drums, joined the drummer during his solo, talked about being in Memphis (implying he was from there), and, before spinning like a flipped turtle on his back during his final song, told the crowd: "China, I'm starting to love you!" It might have been me, but I thought the room answered him with a desultory cheer. Perhaps on a night filled with rock 'n' roll and love, there was just no room left for the blues.

SHANGHAI

THE DAY AFTER OUR SHOW IN PUDONG, DWAYNE SUGGESTED that we test one of Shanghai's massage parlours. Because they were in such great abundance, the offer was hard to resist. In China, there are massage parlours good, and massage parlours bad (if bad in probably the best kind of way). Reputable massage agencies are signified by a huge foot rotating outside – China's version of a barber's pole – with its pressure points illustrated in fine detail. The disreputable ones, by contrast, are signified by lithe women in robes who stand outside and wink at you. After finding a proper bone-cracker just a few steps from our hotel, Dwayne and I approached the little counter inside the shop and gestured to a wall chart illustrating the massagist's various techniques. The proprietor gestured for us to kick off our shoes and slide into a pair of slippers and then led us up a narrow staircase. Dwayne was waved into a dark room with straps hanging from the ceiling, where he lay face down on a gurney. I was ushered into a brightly lit salon and lowered into a reclining chair in front of a flat-screen television.

After a while, a beautiful young woman with full lips like a ripe plum entered the room. She poured me a cup of tea and dragged over a bucket of warm, sloshing water that turned a reddish ochre when she emptied a packet of powder into it. She handed me the television converter, tugged off my socks and placed my feet in the bucket. Then, kneeling between my legs, she started to massage my inner thighs with her powerful kung-fu grip, seductively pushing out a single word every few moments: "*Tong?*" ("Pain?") Stricken with equal measures of delirium and carnal panic, and wishing I'd worn steel-enforced trousers rather than light-fitting jeans, I frantically clicked the converter until – horror of horrors – I came across a match featuring a dozen short-skirted young Dutch field hockey players playing a short-skirted young Spanish team. Things went from bad to worse when she squirted a plug of lilac goo into her hands, rolled up my pantleg, tugged my ankles out of the bucket, and, for the next sixty minutes, masturbated my feet.

During my massage, I could hear howls of "*Tong!*" coming from the adjacent room. Dwayne, he told me later, was being punched in the back of the neck by his masseuse. At one point, she used the straps to hold herself above him and kicked the young Newf until he could no longer weather the assault. While all of this was going on, he drew a small measure of solace knowing that I was being similarly victimized. Afterwards, he dragged himself sore and tired to my room to commiserate over the experience, only to find me slumped in ecstasy, the sound of girls' field hockey chirruping in the sweet-smelling chamber.

By night, Shanghai is one of the world's most visually stunning cities, and by day it's not bad either. In the forty-eight hours following our Oriental Hall gig, we attacked the city with vigour. One afternoon, Jay, Dwayne, and I headed into Shanghai's old town, keeping in mind that "old" in Shanghai means eighty years, not three thousand. After touring the narrow streets of the city's walled enclave, we stopped to drink Tsing Tao beers at a little umbrellaed table in front of the Yua Yuang Gardens, which provided a fine view of everyday Chinese life.

The area around Yua Yuang is typical of any large Chinese city in that there is so much to see you almost don't know where to look. Directly in front of us was a busy indoor market dealing in popular Chinese icons – David Beckham ashtrays, Superman II handbags, and Willie Nelson playing cards – while to our left hundreds of people poured in and out of the enclave. A fellow in a rumpled plaid shirt with tired hair walked past us scooping pulp from a turtle shell, while a toddler wearing the kind of bumless trousers favoured by Chinese parents circled us in a little car, chewing on the plastic nub of a broom handle and gurgling with laughter at the funny Canadians. When an adult thrust a lighter into little dumpling's hands as a plaything – it wasn't clear who the child's mother and father were; a carousel of minders from nearby kiosks took turns engaging him – Jay got out his camera to snap a photo. This prompted a tall man with wrecked-fence teeth to plug a cigarette into the toddler's little mouth. The child immediately affected the look of a toothless centenarian. Jay snapped and snapped, drawing a small crowd at the gates of the garden. The unlit smoke was then extricated – not without a struggle from the young Jean Paul Belmondo – and Jay's camera was spirited away by a fellow who wanted to print the picture at his friend's nearby photomat. I rode the buzz of the afternoon, while Jay wondered whether he'd ever see his camera again.

When you're travelling, even the most pedestrian sounds are exotic: the clink of heavy coins in your pocket, the strange ring of a telephone, the grumble of an old smoke-spitting truck, the clack of a soup spoon against a porcelain bowl. Musically, another country's melodies are tonic to the aural palette, cleaning out whatever domestic cadences and old Jesus Jones melodies might have gummed it up over time. During my last visit to China in 1999, my wife, Janet, and I passed a movie theatre in the southern city of Yangshuo, where a surf-rock anthem was playing out of a speaker near the tiny entrance. Judging from the chorus, the song was called "Batman," but it was nothing like the theme song from the legendary TV show. I desperately wanted to know who the band was so that I could preserve it as a curio for record-collecting friends, but I couldn't figure how to buy a ticket into the theatre, let alone find someone who knew the name of the song. So, we just lingered in front of theatre for a while, absorbing it into memory as best we could.

In another instance, during a World's Strongest Man competition in Dubai, a traditional Arabic treatment of "Kashmir" by Led Zeppelin came over the PA. In the sticky heat of the desert, it sounded like the greatest version ever of the greatest song ever, as if it had been born that moment for me to hear. Another time, I landed in Omsk on an Aeroflot jet to the sound of the craziest swinging synth-jazz I've ever heard. When I asked Yulia if she could somehow acquire the song for our hockey film, she told me that Aeroflot hadn't changed the plane's music in forty years, and that its source was an old reel-to-reel machine bolted onto the plane's chassis, never to be removed.

At my umbrellaed table in old Shanghai, I listened to the cacophony of music: a discount shoe stall playing an electro-beat version of Hank Williams's "Jambalaya" sung in Chinese (I looked for playing cards featuring the honky-tonk master, but they were sorely lacking); a nouveau riche dude with a ponytail driving a sleek black Lexus singing "Gangsta's Paradise" while greasing his car through the impossibly narrow streets; a small yellow bird whistling from the crooked arm of an old tree; an Asian woman modelling a watch on a video loop to a faux Massive Attack treatment that spilled from a speaker hung with rough wire below the awning of a nearby jewellery store – the first few dramatic violin flourishes of a generic Chinese epic repeated to maddening affect over invitations to barter by a woman selling cheap handbags out of a stall no wider than a high-school locker; the beguiling sound of a Xun, an ancient, five-holed, egg-shaped wind instrument of the Sang Dynasty, which a hopeful merchant played while passing out leaflets that read, "The quality of the Xun is of antique and primitive simplicity complete and charming melodious and sweet creates a lot of fancies cross your mind"; and rising above it all, a gutbucket of car, scooter, and motorcycle horns sparring with one another, occasionally goosed by the pling of a bell or the sawing of a rusty bicycle chain.

Our musical trail ended later that night at, appropriately, the Peace Hotel, just north of the Huangpu River. Getting to the hotel meant walking down the eastern section of Nanjing road, Shanghai's pedestrian promenade, which after dark poured more light into space than any thoroughfare this side of the Strip in Las Vegas. Soaking in the hot red glow of a two-hundred-foot electric Coca-Cola bottle, Steve Clarkson looked up and said, "This is China playing a heavy duty game of catch-up." Progress, money, and power could be seen in full flex across the city, from oceans of office towers to a Möbius strip of freeways entangled in the sky and lit purple at night. We saw no small construction projects either. Wherever there was bamboo scaffolding and green canvas cover, it was always sheathing a monstrous rectangle that filled a chunk of cityspace and acres of air.

We drifted through this astonishing swirl of colour and mass to the historic Peace Hotel, which had art deco ceilings, rosewood balustrades, and a venerable jazz bar. The northern tower of the Peace Hotel was originally known as the Cathay, a former mecca of decadence operated by Victor Sassoon, a British-Iraqi opium baron who'd held the hammer in one of Shanghai's most feared crime organizations of the 1940s. It was here, in Room 314, that Noel Coward wrote *Private Lives*, while living among a procession of foreign artistocrats, many of whom spent their debauched evenings in the bar, dancing with concubines and digging the hotel band.

After the Revolution in 1949, jazz was outlawed at the Peace Hotel, and all over China. For the next thirty years, European and Russian bands were no longer sanctioned to tour, so there was very little outside musical influence. Then, in the early 1980s, the members of the original Hotel Cathay band reformed as the Old Jazz Band and played once more inside the bar, which had remained intact despite pressures to destroy it during the Cultural Revolution of the 1960s. On the evening we visited, the group of six men – all over seventy-five and wearing black-and-white tuxedoes – was playing "Smoke Gets in Your Eyes," each musician seated except for the bass player. The drummer, eighty-two-year-old Cheng Yueqiang, played with arthritic candour, thrashing his snare drum with the stiffness of a toy drummer, while the clarinetist squawked and the brass section sighed like old bed springs. Yet each night, every night, they honoured their promise to play seventy songs, pausing occasionally mid-tune to sign napkins, photographs, and playlists for thrilled tourists.

As soon as the Rheos-Not-Rheos parked ourselves at the long wooden bar, Jay ordered whisky and sodas, and Al started to cry. Rubbing his face, he said, "This is it. This is it right here. This is the Russian feeling all over again." Once more, he'd travelled a great distance to a strange city and found himself deeply moved. The more the band played, the more we drank. It was turning into our first great evening in China. And then I mentioned Rush.

In hindsight, I suppose I should have found out whether any of my new bandmates were allergic to Rush when the idea to form our group was first raised. But I figured that anyone who wanted to play in a band with me knew of my devout allegiance to them, if not through my music, then through my books. But right after Jay told me that he thought that Rush's drummer sucked, he told me that he hadn't read my books either, and that he found a lot of the Rheostatics' albums "spotty." I chanced that more whisky might help weaken his stance and ease my apoplexy, but the booze only made it worse.

Watching the Old Jazz Band perform opened deep feelings in all of us. For me, it made me miss my old friends. These feelings were exacerbated by Jay's comments, which were meant playfully yet hurt all the same. Sometimes the simplest things can trigger the heaviest emotions, and in this case what it did was launch a protracted discussion of whether Neil Peart swung. Jay had cited Rush's arcane concept album, *2112*, as proof of the band's leaden feel; I countered with "Tom Sawyer," which innumerable hip-hop bands have sampled for its groove and subtle power. It was a winless argument, of course, but it evoked strong feelings in me because I was certain that, were I sitting around with the Rheostatics in the Peace Hotel in Shanghai, the last thing we would have argued about was whether Neil Peart of Rush had feel.

Jay could have been any musician taking me to task on any subject dear to my heart (Neil, one of my rock 'n' roll heroes, had played on the Rheos' album *Whale Music*). I hated having to defend something I loved to a new bandmate I barely knew. Sitting at the bar pretending for the sake of our tour that my good time wasn't being ruined made me realize how much more than the music is missed when a band breaks up. All of this was driven home while we were arguing by the lively presence of six men who'd overcome revolution and cultural oppression and political hatred and were now playing "Begin the Beguine" in one of the great hotels in the world. Even if the Old Jazz Band only sputtered through their inexhaustible repertoire, they did so together. As I watched this, whether Neil Peart swung was about as important as whether they did.

That evening at the Peace Hotel was just the beginning of a distressing twenty-four hours. The next night, we played at one of the city's only rock 'n' roll clubs – the Shuffle Club – opening for the Wombats, a great young Liverpuddlian pop group. We were originally supposed to play at the Yuyintang Warehouse, which had recently been opened by a group of young Shanghai Nirvana fans. The warehouse was an old toxic dump, and because the purchase of the building had to be kept quiet from Chinese authorities, the kids had cleaned up the space themselves and wired and painted it with friends. I was thrilled at the prospect of visiting this vanguard Chinese rock room, but because organizers hadn't had enough time to promote the gig, they suggested we play the Shuffle Club, which was mostly an expat rock bar. I was mildly disappointed, but at least we had a gig.

I was hoping that the band would come together the more we played, but the gig did more to wrench us apart than tighten us up. After the show, I spotted Al struggling with his equipment at the side of the stage. When I went over to help him, his hair had horned into two horrible peaks, snakes were crawling out of his eyes, and words were flying out of his face like bats through the window of a dark house. Al yelled at me: he yelled long and loud. He yelled and pushed his shoulders at me and turned hot with rage. I stood there yammering whenever he paused to think of other things to yell at me, but it was no use. I absorbed the venom until, fully exasperated, my friend and travelmate threw the rest of his gear into a bag and faced me, waiting to hear what I had to say.

People who play in rock 'n' roll bands get yelled at, sometimes worse. It happens: it's even supposed to happen. Still, this didn't make seeing my bawdy-Christmas-ballad-singing-friend transformed into a storm of anger and frustration any easier. Once the snakes had retreated and the fire had fizzled, I put my hands up and told Al that whatever I'd done to worry him musically, I'd done unthinkingly, having been warped by travel, the collapse of my old band, the learning curve of our new one, not to mention verbal brawls over Rush, and wondering whether I was about to lose my second band in three months. Part of me wanted to vent back, but I quelled the urge. Al's anger had come from the same spot that had triggered his tears at the hotel, and since musicians on the road are, generally, a train wreck waiting to happen, to verbally counter-punch would have shown that I had no understanding of the rock 'n' roll organism. Besides, after sadness and anger, I had to believe that love was in the corridor, chalking its palms.

I cursed my fuckhead ex-bandmates who liked Rush for ending the group just as opportunities were arising for us to tour China and do a million other things we'd always wanted to do. It felt bitter that, just months earlier, I'd *been* in a band that – as the ancient jazzists at the Peace Hotel had reminded me – would never grow old playing together. Sometimes, I'd wondered whether the idea of an eternal Rheos was an idyllic dream, but the Old Jazz Band proved that it was not, and that while most bands break up, there are those who persist because, in the end, it's much harder to do. I'd wanted it to be this way for my old band, but now it would never be. Alas, fighting with my friend only deepened this awful feeling of defeat, and as the Wombats took to the stage – their great performance propelled by the excitement of being in China on the fabulous brink of their musical lives – the end of mine suddenly seemed a lot closer than the beginning.

SUZHOU

MY FALLING-OUT WITH AL WAS NOT THE FIRST TIME I'D been struck with the backing-band blues. In the Rheostatics, we'd never had a problem playing one another's songs, but whenever another musical principle was introduced, it always soured the alchemy.

Our first experience as a backup band came when our friend, West Coast promoter Jay Scott, suggested that we twin forces with a fellow named Carmaig de Forest, a ukulele-playing folk-pop singer from California. The concept was exciting to us – perhaps this would take us down new musical roads, provide a gateway to the United States – until we realized that Carmaig was *a ukulele-playing folk-pop singer from California*. Finding common ground between our burgeoning Etobicoke prog-punk and Carmaig's ironic pop was a trial. During rehearsal, we approached every song like Rod Stewart attacking a crate of Chivas, but no matter how hard we tried infusing his music with polyriffs and counter-melodies to create something grand and beautiful, it all sounded wrong to Carmaig. He wanted no epic splash, no bass lines doubled on the tripleneck; all he wanted was a solid pub band who could coax his songs to the end. Of course, this begat outrage, starting with questions about why

Carmaig hadn't taken to our brilliant, post-rock treatments and ending with doubts about whether he might know a good arrangement if it space-junked him in the head.

Because we were kids, we had no seasoned way of articulating our feelings. Instead, as Carmaig left rehearsal one day, I shouted, "This is fucking impossible!" or something like that, at the top of my lungs. Tim said, "He probably heard you, you know," which only made me feel worse about the fact that, despite our mangled sound and painful rehearsals, we were scheduled to start a cross-Canada tour with him in a matter of days.

We did a tune-up concert at the Silver Dollar Tavern in Toronto. We sabotaged the show, making fun of Carmaig while his back was turned and flinging ourselves across the stage like a bunch of competing apes. Even worse for Carmaig was the fact that we played a full set afterwards, setting the house on fire with the pure freedom of performing our own material however we wanted. The next day, twenty-four hours before we were supposed to leave, Carmaig called us to the Bagel restaurant on College Street and told us that he was going to "drop a bomb." He didn't think the band was working out and would be leaving without us. We told him we were shocked, but that it was okay.

A few years later, a similar deal was brokered for us to back up Jane Siberry, the internationally regarded new wave/New Age singer. We loved and appreciated the Sib's music so much that we'd covered one of her songs, "One More Colour," on *Introducing Happiness*. Like Carmaig, however, Ms. Siberry proved to be an intractable force when it came to adapting her music.

We started daytime rehearsals at the Gas Station studios in Toronto while working on music for a film by night. At first, the sessions were a breeze. I still have recordings of them that reveal big, meaty grooves and wild guitars married to Jane's perfect, fragile singing. But then, things went awry. The Sib, who'd just

released her noted album *Bound by the Beauty*, started to decon-
struct all that we'd done, uncertain that all of the layers we'd
provided were serving her music (at which point, I thought, Here
we go again). It was her prerogative, I suppose, but we found it
hard to support her musical anxiety, mostly because we thought
it was all sounding good. It was also difficult to hear the music
she was hearing in her head, which – because she'd spent the
entire year recording by herself in the isolation of her home –
were lots of simple, electronically programmable parts. Martin
was asked to unplug his effects. Dave Clark – a master of dex-
terous playing – was told to drum as if he were a beatbox, and I
was told, kindly, to keep my foot off the fuzzbox (how Tim got
off the hook, I'll never know). Instead of being outraged, we
were disappointed. The outrage came later.

In attempt to breathe some life into our sessions, one of us
suggested that we cover a song. Since Jane was quiet at the best
of times – she only spoke to tell us what not to play – it was difficult to know whether she thought this was a good or bad idea.
Nonetheless, we adjourned to the studio's listening room, poring
over CDs to find the right song. In some instances, it took only
a single bar of a song for Jane to say, "No. I don't like it," or
"No, not this one." We must have listened to thirty, forty songs.
Finally, I reached for a song that I consider to be the greatest con-
fection in the history of pop music – "Everyday People" by Sly
and the Family Stone – convinced that I'd found a winner.

I first listened to Sly as a ten-year-old in Florida on a family
vacation. It was if everyone in America was stepping to Sly's delicious, low groove. The song's elevated beauty (and genius) can
be found in Larry Graham's single-note bass line, and the way
the verses move from one singer to the next defined for me the
essence of what it is to play in a band. "Everyday People" is a
musical celebration of what happens when a lot of people share

in a common creation, rather than thrusting it inward on a single voice or instrument, all the while keeping it in focus.

Jane hated it. "No, don't like this one," she said, shaking her head, and that was that. We struggled to patch together seven or eight songs – Jane would pad the set by playing "My Mother," a solo piano opus – for a performance at the Hillside Festival in Guelph, Ontario. Three thousand people came to see us on a soft summer night, crowding a long field on the far side of a lake. Before we were about to go on, I stared out the stage entrance at the darkening sky and said, "Boy, the crowd looks really beautiful from here." Then Jane, in a dumb-jock voice, parroted my words: "Boy, the crowd looks really beautiful from here." I stared at her, disbelieving. And then we walked on stage.

It was apparent from the beginning of the set that, while my bandmates and I were familiar with Jane's music, she had very little idea about ours. We did our best to get into the perform-ance, flying around the stage to compensate – and probably overcompensate – for our lack of excitement with the song's arrangements. This startled Jane and threw her off form. She'd never been on stage with an energetic, physical band before, and as a result she stayed tight to her microphone, keeping away from our thrusting headstocks.

It was around the third song that I stepped on my percus-sion egg. I crushed it but didn't realize I had until I reached for it a few songs later and found it destroyed. I quickly grabbed a jangle-stick – a drumstick with tambourine bells – and pro-ceeded to keep time. I can't remember which song we were starting, but I was doing fine until I flourished the jangle-stick over my head, at which point a bunch of people standing directly in front of the stage laughed. Because the beginning of the song was hushed, we could hear the laughter as it rippled through the crowd, found the back of the field, then rippled back toward the stage. Jane stopped singing, stepped back from her microphone, and announced, "I feel like I'm on some kind of stupid game show."

To this day, I don't know why what I did struck so many as funny. I hadn't been goofing around, just unconsciously trying to break the obvious tension that was spilling off the stage. After the show, a friend told me that it was clear to everyone what was happening, and that the audience was also looking for something to break the ice. After Jane made her "game show" remark, there was a moment of uncomfortable silence before drummer Dave Clark told her, "Sister, you're part of the greatest game show of your life, let's go!"

How we ever finished the set, I'll never know.

Two days after our argument – and after coming to terms with the fact that Jay and I could still rock out together without having to retract our positions on the World's Greatest Ever Drummer – a few things became clear. The first was that it was probably unreasonable to think that Al and I could traipse along in our global adventure without falling victim, at least once, to the stress of rock 'n' roll travel. During a post-argument argument in my hotel room in our next city – Suzhou – we realized that we knew how to fix things, and did. Adjustments were made to our set – Al would open the show by playing a few songs by himself – and we resolved to put our worries behind us and push the fun through the shit.

Besides, it was hard to stay darkly concerned over the state of one's rock 'n' roll *chi*, especially when, in Suzhou, I spotted a young girl sitting in the front row holding the spindle of a kite, a paper serpent flying like a skittish dirigible high above the band. At first look, Suzhou didn't suggest that it would be the kind of city to balm our emotional wounds – it was essentially a city-suburb of Shanghai about forty minutes outside of town – but as we bused with Andy from the hotel to the gig, he explained that we'd be among the first Western bands to play there (our Canadian contingent had parted ways to embark on separate mini-tours, and Jordan Cook and Stradio had gigged in Suzhou the day before). Really, if making Sino-rock history wasn't enough to divert our concerns, nothing would be.

Suzhou is one of those many thousand-year-old Chinese cities that looks as if it's been devoured by Bramalea. Driving to the afternoon show, we passed miles of retail shopping promenades and acres of concrete towers – and acres more being poured – before arriving at a sprawling suburban pitch, the Suzhou Industrial Park, where a roofless chipboard stage covered in red carpet and a great black backdrop promising "The Top Six Bands in All of North America (Canada)" were planted. I tested the floorboards by jumping on them and nearly plummeted through the wood. Soon there were busy hammering sounds coming from underneath the stage, which lasted the entire afternoon.

The promoters had supplied us with three twenty-watt guitar amps, only one of which worked. Perhaps as penance for taking the World's Greatest Ever Drummer's name in vain, Jay had to use a white bucket chair as a drum stool, and the kit itself creaked worse than Kenny Rogers's facelift. During sound check – which more or less consisted of Steve Clarkson trying to figure out if there was more to the PA than a few cables plugged into a handful of outputs (there wasn't) – I watched as someone from the local sound crew ran a thick, fifty-foot cable from the sound rig to a power box on the sidewalk, hoping to tap some extra juice for the show. Once he'd done that – or not done that; from his unflappable expression, it was hard to know if he'd succeeded – he walked to the entrance of the park where, with some local policemen, he helped blow up an inflatable red dragon archway.

After testing the sound system, we headed off to a lavish banquet. There we met the local promoters, who were as typical of North American promoters as we were of Van Halen. Mousey and bespectacled, they wore plaid shirts and loafers and looked more suited to run a hardware store or chair a chamber of commerce meeting than promote a rock show. It was refreshing to be part of a rock 'n' roll gathering where nobody had a ponytail, wore a satin jacket with "BRAM TCHAIKOVSKY '78" sewn across the back, or had ever had a sweaty part of themselves pierced. Knowing what I do about the beginnings of rock 'n' roll – and having experienced a nascent scene first-hand in late-1970s, new-wave Toronto – the scene in Suzhou was a bit of a flashback: rock 'n' roll was still everyone's domain, and nobody had figured out that hanging around with somebody's uncle would get you booted out of Cool Camp. One of the first people in Toronto to book the Rheos was a Greek bartender who sold real estate named Jimmy Scopes. Jimmy didn't really know music, but he knew that kids drank beer, and so he booked acts for the bar Monday to Sunday. The men in Suzhou possessed the same unassuming normalcy, and because these were their first experiences promoting rock 'n' roll, we wanted to make a strong, good impression – provided we could get through the day without falling through the stage.

The crowd in Suzhou was seated in rows of white bucket chairs like the one that Jay spent the better part of the afternoon swearing at. With each chair neatly ranked on the green common, the setting was more like a high-school convocation than a rock show. There was also a gaggle of concertgoers huddled to the side in a shaded glen, which stifled the torrid sun and the day's 30°C+ temperature. Sitting next to the girl with the kite was a young boy twirling a pet turtle on his finger (it appeared that the animal was for play, not lunch), giving Al and me yet another reason to forget that we'd almost Gallagher Brother-ed each other the night before. Two green-sheathed apartment towers were going up across the street behind the stage, their facades prettied by a row of fat red lantern balloons tethered to the back of the stage trailing "Music Week" tails. The PA system's CD player, which, Steve groused, had been as much of a concern to the local sound crew as the rest of the rig, played Canto pop hits strung together by the voice of a male narrator that sounded as if it had been recorded on an old answering machine. Between songs, the narrator said things such as, "I must go now, or else I will be late for my flight. Just remember to set your alarm clock, so you get up in time." I'm not sure whether the narrator went on to mention "worker productivity" or "allegiance to the people's state" because, just as I was about to seek further trans- lation, Al climbed the stage and slashed out a few solo acoustic numbers, getting himself where he had to be to rock out with the band.

Reports from Stradio and Jordan Cook were that the Suzhou crowd had been quietly bewildered. Stradio's soundperson told us, "After every one of Jordan's songs: crickets." Jordan Cook wasn't the only one to get an odd reception. A few days earlier, when the Shuffle Demons' drummer, Stitch Winston, started a solo, an elder from the crowd mounted the stage and began making a speech, which is probably the appropriate response to a drum solo. Stitch, to his credit, responded in kind, drumming along to the rhythm of the speaker's voice. To the average Suzhouian, rock 'n' roll performed outdoors must have seemed pretty pointless and absurd. Chinese parks, after all, are used for dragon-boat races, soccer matches, and box-kite derbies, so gathering in a lush field on a beautiful summer's day to sit in a stiff-backed chair under the blazing sun and get your senses razored and cap blown off by loud, wheedling blues rock must have seemed like the kind of cultural torture that only misguided Westerners could have invented. If I hadn't been raised on this sort of entertainment myself, I would have wondered why I'd been drawn to it, and for a moment I feared that our purpose was to dissuade Chinese audiences from ever falling for Western pop. But as I got ready to join Al on stage, Andy came up, grabbed my arm, and said, "Dave, get the crowd excited! It will be good. They will like it better. Have you learned the Beatles yet?" which blew holes in my theory. Having the show come off well was as important to him as it was to us.

In Moscow, we'd drafted Yulia to be our patter-translator at the Chinese Pilot. Because there was an even greater divide between band and crowd in Suzhou (in Pudong, I'd noticed a few Western faces, but here, there were none) I asked Andy if he'd do the same for us. Unlike Yulia, who had been very nervous, Andy proved to be a baked ham, commanding and shouting excitedly at the crowd through a hand-held microphone. He was the perfect ice breaker, and after an introduction that ended with a two-syllable word common to people the world over – "Whoohoo!" – the show took off. For a moment, I wondered whether Western-style crowd-goosing might lead to the kind of bad habits and stadium clichés that would make even Neil Diamond groan, but there was no turning back. If the Chinese were going to learn these things, they might as well learn them right, so I dove in, leading the audience in a series of fist-punching, Bic-flicking choral chants that, in a time before the Rheos-Not-Rheos, would have made me choke.

My first efforts to involve the crowd were ineffectual. Whenever I clapped my hands over my head on the two and four, the audience broke into full applause. So I got Al and Dwayne to clap along with me, and the penny dropped. From that point on, I was able to Freddie Mercury my way to glory. My first task was to teach the Suzhouians how to "OneTwoThreeFour!" at the beginning of a song. Coming back at me, the chant sounded like a drunk being woken in the middle of the night, but it was the perfect outburst, in a birth-of-Chinese-rock-'n'-roll kind of way. Later in the set, during "Legal Age Life at Variety Store," Andy had the crowd count to twelve in Cantonese, with yours truly mangling the numbers. Everyone loved it, because everyone loves hearing a stranger batter their mother tongue. I made it to number eight, but then I started making stuff up, shouting out "Yao Ming!" and "Tsing Tao!" and "Sigisoara!" (the name of a small, medieval town in Transylvania). In the middle of another song, Andy told the crowd what he'd learned during his visit to Canada's East Coast, describing the cultural and geographical nature of St. John's as a way of introducing Dwayne or, rather, Dwayne's solo in "Power Ballad to Ozzy Osbourne." For the first time, the crowd in Suzhou lowered their kites, settled their turtles, looked up to the stage, waited for Andy to finish, then laughed uproariously as Dwayne leaned into his shredderiffic solo. When I asked Andy what he'd told them, he said that he'd told them that in the Newfie springtime, hungry polar bears come down from the hills and terrorize people. I filed away the knowledge that nothing gets a Chinese crowd going like the story of a good old Canadian bear-mauling.

After this, there was no stopping us. I managed to get the crowd to wave their hands in the air like swaying sea anemone, which they did carefully, watching their arms move as if uncertain whether they were going too fast. Near the end of the set, the first sign that the audience was reaching out to us came in the form of a radio-controlled fighter plane, which buzzed overhead as we played. Altogether, it was a delightful scene – balloons,

Teaching bad habits in Suzhuo (*Alun Piggins*)

dragons, turtles, kites, and planes – until during the last verse of "Horses" the Red Baron swooped within a few feet of my head. I reared back as if being attacked from above and saw Al roar with laughter on the other side of the stage. The snakes slithered back into their caverns. We were having fun again.

Near the end of the set, we climbed off stage and walked into the crowd, playing "The Ballad of Wendel Clark." People leaped from their chairs to be photographed with us. We happily accommodated the teenagers and children, but I made one middle-aged punter sing the bridge of the song – "Bambam-diggydiggydam" – before allowing his wife to snap the shutter.

What struck me while ambling through the crowd was that Suzhou had provided the mainstream audience I'd never had at home. The irony wasn't lost on me that I'd had to come this far to play for a general public that, in Canada, had found the Rheos' music too strong. There were no signs of disaffection or angst or fringe poetics in the way the Suzhouians behaved or dressed. Nobody looked like they'd ever heard of Charles Bukowski, had attended a comic-book convention, or studied German theatre. This was both a good and bad thing. While the audience was incapable of the kind of chronic arrogance we'd encountered at Kipsari in Helsinki, there wasn't much chance that any of them would leap out of their chair and reinvent the pogo either. But there was no mistaking them for a mainstream audience at home, who watch bands with a stoned-on-TV gaze. When the Suzhouians participated in the show, they did so excitedly, not by rote, as if they'd done it three hundred times before.

Another feature that distinguished the event was the presence – or lack thereof – of concert security. The guards, dressed in blue, wearing white gloves and white berets, were as nonthreatening as any security force I've seen. The handful of policemen patrolling the backstage area were about as hard-bitten and gun happy as Don Knotts.

One of the reasons we travel is to confirm or deny our ideas about the world, and ever since the tragedy and disgrace of Tiananmen Square, Westerners have been quick to assume the worst about cops at Chinese public gatherings. But this was never an issue at any of our rock shows. Maybe it was because the authorities didn't care enough about rock 'n' roll to think it worthy of policing. Then again, maybe vigilantes from the People's Armed Police were waiting behind every telephone pole: I just couldn't see them. There were far fewer bouncers or security personnel than at rock 'n' roll shows at home. If you put the image of hundreds of listeners sitting on numberless seats and strolling freely around the common at their leisure side by side with one of a tightly policed concert bowl with designated rows and walkways where dancing and lingering are forbidden, you would wonder which was in the police state and which was in Jerry Lee and Elvis's homeland.

After we clambered back for one last song, Andy grabbed the microphone and told the crowd to rush the stage. I was about to comment that a classic stage-rush meant very little unless the crowd did it spontaneously, but before I could, people had raced to filled the space in front of the chipboard stage. The police and security personnel watched with curiosity. At the end of the tune, people clamoured after us – mostly for a photo-op – and one of the bigger security men pushed his way to the front. I feared that the afternoon was about to turn ugly, but instead he waved a handful of yuan in the air and pointed to the stack of CDs at Al's feet. Al reached down and gave him one, and the fellow's eyes lit up. Even the cops had dug the show. Maybe rock 'n' roll was here to stay.

CHANGSHA

TWENTY-FOUR HOURS AFTER PLAYING SUZHOU, WE RETURNED to Shanghai – or at least its airport – then flew to Changsha, in Hunan Province, southern China. Andy had told us earlier that it was a small city. "Just about six million people," he'd said with a straight face. For this part of our tour, Andy handed the reins to Grace, one of Life Fashion's assistants and another rock 'n' roll innocent who'd taken her first-ever flight a few days earlier to arrange things in Changsha. Grace was a friendly, willowy young woman surgically attached to her clipboard. The only time I saw her put it down was to hug us upon our arrival in Changsha, which we took as a sign that things would be different in the south, at least in terms of decorum. In Shanghai, it was considered unacceptable to touch a woman even on the arm or shoulder – unless, of course, they were employed by KTV, the dubious karaoke clubs in hotels that cater to Western clientele; and even then, it was the women who did most of the touching – but in Changsha, people didn't seem to be troubled by physical contact. Another of Andy's assistants, a small owl of a girl named Jesse, held my elbow whenever she had anything to say. In the streets packed with little outdoor restaurants behind our hotel, there was much music and shouting and the kind of lively behaviour that had somehow been missing farther north.

The city itself was gritty and loud, uninfested, for better or worse, by the finance capital that had engorged many of China's other cities. The air was hot, dusty, and yellow, the streets less perfect and finely angled than we'd seen before. Even Changsha's scooters and motorbikes had none of the showroom glare found on Shanghai's people-movers. Much of the chrome had been matted by mud and splatter from the countryside, which stretched just minutes from the city centre in a moist quilt of rice paddies and livestock farms. Coming in from the airport, we noticed an old scooter pulling a pen of four enormous snuffling hogs – a good sign, I thought. Most scooterists drove visorless, riding with their teeth bare to the wind and lacking any of the composed, urban cool affected by big-city drivers. They also flouted whatever laws ostensibly governed them. I saw a young boy sitting on his father's lap while driving through rush-hour traffic and four preteen girls riding sidesaddle on the seat of their mother's scooter, their long black hair tail-finning down the avenue. Lots of drivers wore no headgear whatsoever, but those who did favoured a kind of automotive pith helmet, which came in a rainbow of colours as well as in velvet and straw.

After throwing my bags on the bed in my room, I set out to investigate the streets behind the hotel. There were dozens of nameless restaurants where, since it was late-afternoon, the only patrons were the restauranteurs' children watching television or crayoning or writing in notebooks. Stores hummed with people buying supplies, and one very active haircutting shop blasted indeterminate Sino-pop as a crew of young men coloured and blowdried one another's hair into glazed brown and gold dandelion puffs. They were talking excitedly and mock-dancing and doing the occasional air-guitar kick, and part of me hoped that they were preening for the next day's rock 'n' roll caravan. Later, I walked past the dry goods store across the street from the hotel

– Wacko Mart – and paused curbside to gape at three kids wearing T-shirts that hinted at the possibility that we'd found a little bit of Cleveland after Suzhou's Seattle. They read: FUCK DANCING, LET'S FUCK; KIZZ MY ASS; and YOU'LL DO. It's unlikely they knew what the words meant, but it didn't matter. I could almost smell the rock 'n' roll.

The following morning, I took a taxi to the Changha Amusement Park with Jesse and the local promoter, Cody, who worked for, and deejayed at, Hunan Radio 93.3, co-presenters of the event. Cody was young and handsome, with high cheekbones and vaguely Elvisian sideburns. He shared promoters' responsibilities with a cool Smurf who was introduced to me as Double Fat. The first thing Cody had told me when I first met him was that he'd been playing the Rheos' album *2067* all week on his daily radio show, which excited even the Rheos-Not-Rheos, and shot holes in the notion that all radio programming was regulated by state broadcast authorities. Cody asked if I'd written out a set list for the performance, which I took to be a polite way of asking whether – or at what point – we planned on playing "Hey Jude" or "Let It Be." I told him that I usually composed set lists only minutes before the show, and sometimes never at all. He gave a nervous laugh and said, "Yes, but this is China." Then he added, "Beatles, second set, okay?" I sighed and asked for a pen and a paper – Grace immediately took a pad of foolscap from her clipboard – and scribbled the names of fifteen songs, some of which I invented on the spot. I shared my faux song titles with Al and the guys, reaching for laughs with "Ron is a *Hunda*" ("Ron is a Dickhead") and "Pijo [Beer] Drinking Dance Party." It was only later I discovered that in Changsha it wasn't the state censor who'd demanded the list but the local deejay, who needed it to identify song titles during the event's live broadcast. This made me wish I'd tried harder and not called Ron a *hunda*.

The cab driver blew staccato trumpet shots on his horn as we snaked our way through rumbling traffic to the park. We pulled up outside a set of iron gates and a faded-green facade with ticket windows that reminded me of an entrance to an old minor league baseball park. Jesse squeezed my elbow as she led me through the gates to where a small pond surrounded by deep forest harboured a little pagoda and four traditional musicians plinking and sawing in the cool of the shade. I paused respectfully to absorb the sounds – Jesse pinched me harder, concerned, perhaps, that I was carving my own path – and to right myself. I'd just noticed the absence of Suzhou's manicured lawns and composed citizenry. Here, sunny-faced Hunanese walked over flattened brown grass and matted-mud pathways, passing under wild vines and tall Afroed trees that were blooming in the southern sun.

I could hear in the distance what sounded like a gang of heathens with baseball bats thrashing a row of garbage cans. Getting closer, I saw the noise came from six or seven prehistoric bumper cars slamming into one another in a wrought-iron cage. The only time the pounding of metal ceased was when the ride's operator – a Chinese carny in a straw hat who sat on a perch above the fray – blew his whistle and waved the next group of riders through. Farther up the road, a competing noise came from a dragon's-head cart hurtling down a rusted Popsicle-stick roller coaster. Both rides were the kind of unmaintained amusement-park deathtrap that makes parents shiver, but everyone seemed to be having a great time. As Jesse and I broke away from the path to climb a towering set of stone steps through the forest – Spinal Tap in reverse – we heard the echo of a rock band punching away, the singer's soprano yowl cutting through the bush.

At the top of the steps, we drew level with another road busy with carnival games and vendors selling skewered eel and octopus, watermelon slices and roasted corn on the cob. Beside the road was a plot of concrete as big as a shopping mall's parking lot, and, at the far end of the lot, a huge stage with a great red Hunan Radio 93.3 backdrop, fringed on top with lantern balloons. On either side of the stage were knolls toothpicked with trees, where most of the audience sat listening to the band. No more than ten fans braved the stifling heat to congregate in front of the stage, which had three long runways shooting toward the crowd, as if Naomi Campbell and friends were expected to drop by.

Jesse tried to pull me toward the shade of a little sound tent, but I swerved toward the stage, swelling the number of ardent fans to a Mighty Eleven. It was the least I could do. I'd come to the park early because the band was, technically, opening for us. For some reason, the promoters had decided to put them on at 9:30 a.m., five hours before our scheduled 2:00 p.m. set. When I asked Cody about the timing, he explained that if we were presented in tandem with Hunanese groups, nobody would take the event seriously. "Struggling musicians here are considered failures," he said. "In China, bad students and bad kids play rock 'n' roll. Musicians who persist end up playing for no more than a bowl of rice. Most bands quit after they finish school because of pressure from their parents and friends."

The two local bands who started the day – the E Band and Ice, Fire, and Rain – had never had a proper rehearsal in their lives. Because the concept of the rehearsal factory, to say nothing of rehearsal space, was foreign to China, the bands had practised in their tiny university dorms. This partly explained the small electronic drumkit – a V Kit – that had been provided for all three bands. Because the V Kit is light and portable enough to bend and shape into any space, it's the perfect instrument for the rock 'n' roll pariah. You can strip it down and stuff it into vinyl trap bags without anyone in the streets confusing you with Bill Lord or Vinnie Appice and being forced to take appropriate action. The drawback is that it makes every song sound like it's been highjacked by Kajagoogoo. Later, when Jay saw it sitting at the back of the stage, he rubbed his face in bewilderment, wondering when the rock 'n' roll drumming gods were going to let slide his Neil-can't-swing tirade.

The small peashooter amps from Suzhou had somehow made their way to Changsha. Their size better served the hermetic life of a Chinese rock 'n' roll band, for whom getting the chance to perform was a considerable triumph. Playing in a band in China, it seemed, was as much about survival as anything. For both the E Band and Ice, Fire, and Rain, this would be one of only three gigs they'd play all year.

Ice, Fire, and Rain were the band we'd heard echoing through the forest. They would have been the perfect opening act for Earth, Wind, and Fire, I thought, had they not been about as funky as the state of New Hampshire. Their bassist was like a Hunanese Krist Novoselic – six-foot-six, at least – with stained red teeth and praying mantis arms. For most of the set, he stood at the end of his runway, staring impassively. He didn't move, he didn't groove. He just held his spot, looking down at his picking hand.

Considering China's isolation from Western rock, there was very little chance that Ice, Fire, and Rain would have learned of the wildman antics that North American kids raised on a banquet of concerts, MTV/Much Music, rock films, and videos know by heart. But Krist's bandmates were astonishingly well versed in textbook rockisms. Front and centre, the group's headbanded lead singer pranced, high-stepped, and jubilantly shouted

"Solo!" whenever the band's greasy-haired guitarist engaged his fuzz wah. The guitarist skip-ran to the end of his runway, spread his legs, threw his head back, and lost himself in a loud, wheedling solo. While this was going on, the singer flung his head around like a spinning clock hand, his black hair beating the air. Near the end of each solo, the singer peered out at those of us in front of the stage. Deciding that our enthusiasm had left him short, he put his hand to his ear and tried goading us into cheering even harder – really, the Mighty Eleven could only do so much – as if he'd grown up watching Judas Priest at the Hammersmith Palais.

The rest of the band – a rhythm guitarist and a drummer, each of whom had blue hair – played as if they were gigging at the Hollywood Bowl. They were young and ugly, the musical fulfillment of what that "Fuck Dancing, Let's Fuck" T-shirt had promised. Whenever anyone stepped to the microphone, he shouted, no matter whether he was joining a song's chorus or imploring the Mighty Eleven to "May sam noise!" (a command that sounded all the more genuine coming, as it did, out of speaker towers on a fairground stage in the deep torpor of the day). For a moment, I thought I was watching Foghat at Darien Lake Fun Country.

I am a sucker for summer rock played at a fairground. There's something about the way the sound of an electric guitar slides across the heat-buttered air, or how a drummer's booming fill or singer's scream are mirrored by the scale and noise of amusement park rides and booths where kids fire potato bullets from plastic AK-17s at fifty yuan a pop, by far the most popular concession in Changsha. Summer rock is the sensation of one's sweaty shoulder sliding against a stranger frugging in the hot pit of a football stadium filled with the sound of a band named after a wild animal and performing like a pack of them. Summer rock is shirtless and uninhibited, rising fast against the gluey sun.

After another, then another, hard-rock anthem, Ice, Fire, and Rain's lead singer chugged a bottle of water, put the hand-held microphone back into its clip, draped his arms around the top of the mic stand, slouched his shoulders, and announced (all too defeatedly, I thought) that Ice, Fire, and Rain were about to play an original song. The tree people harrumphed a little, then picked themselves up and walked over to the busiest kiosk in the park, the iced coffee stand, where lattes sipped through krazystraws sold for twenty cents a cup. Hearing a band apologize for its own composition was an eerie echo of the past. It's what the Guess Who or the Stampeders or any of the early CanRock pioneers would have done in the 1960s (and what the Rheos had done in the early 1980s) playing to crowds whose tastes were so imma-ture they couldn't accept something they hadn't heard before.

After their original tune, which featured chunking guitars and a neat little synth riff played on a keyboard, Ice, Fire, and Rain lit into their closing number, made famous, Cody told me, by the legendary Hong Kong band Beyond. He said, making two fists to drive home his point, that it was about "how rock 'n' roll, for a moment, had taken over China in the 1980s."

Beyond were part of the Hong Kong rock boom of the 1980s, which also included Grasshopper and Radias. They were mythologized when thirty-one-year-old lead singer Ka Kui Wong died from head injuries after falling from a poorly constructed stage while appearing on a Japanese game show. Because Beyond were China's rock 'n' roll pioneers, they attracted – and continue to attract – legions of followers around China. So it was no sur-prise when the crowd greeted the song with more enthusiasm than they'd shown for any other tune. Those huddled in the shade of the trees cheered approvingly, but because they were still reluctant to abandon their seats, the Mighty Eleven were left to pump our arms and holler that, as rock 'n' roll hadn't quite taken over China in the 1980s, we hoped that it would very soon.

The band finished the set with leg kicks and windmill chords, as if it might be the last time they'd grace a stage (quite plausible). They thanked the crowd and put down their guitars, then sat down together off to the side of the stage. While walking over with Grace to congratulate them, I told her how much I'd enjoyed the show, but she looked at me as if I was being facetious. "I really liked them!" I said, making things worse. She clutched her clipboard to her chest and said, "David, these bands are not professional bands, not like those in Canada. They are not very good. You are very good. You are a professional musician."

We'd been eager to come to the Hunan for a number of reasons, not the least being its tongue-scorching, throat-howling, chili-fired cuisine popularized by Mao Tse-tung, who was born just a few villages north of Changsha. On our first night in the city, we were taken to a well-regarded three-storey restaurant with a round entrance framed in neon to match a monstrous Ferris wheel that had been raised in an adjacent parking lot for the coming May Day celebrations. Once in the private dining room, with only one bottle of still water and six glasses for all of us, we realized that Cody, Jesse, Double Fat, and Grace had disappeared. We tried to get the attention of the serving staff, but they scattered like pigeons, leaving us in the care of a tall, severe-looking gentleman whom the Shuffle Demons called "Mr. Big." We'd met Mr. Big in Shanghai, but hadn't figured out his responsibilities. Now it became apparent that he was employed to play the glowering governmental heavy to Andy, Cody, and Grace's rock 'n' roll keener. The Demons were convinced that he worked for the Red Guard.

During our two nights in Changsha, Mr. Big devoted his energies to making sure we were kept as far away from ordinary Changshaians as possible. He wouldn't let us talk to the wait staff at restaurants and demanded that we order through him. Our opinion of him that first night only worsened once our table became crowded with plates of celery cubes in gelatinous goop, blues-patio chicken wings, and tofu with peanuts. The next night, Cody and Grace reappeared, but we were still served bowls of spaghetti and a plate of iceberg lettuce covered in gravy. Through Grace, we begged Mr. Big to let us try real Hunanese food, but he was implacable. "Hot food is not good because you are performing tomorrow. It will damage your voices." Eventually, the Demons' saxophonist, Perry White, demanded a meeting with Mr. Big in the backroom of the restaurant. After a thirty-minute tête-à-tête, he emerged to report two things: hot food was on its way, and Mr. Big wanted to meet us in his hotel room after the meal. The waiters promptly brought us chicken and tofu dishes modestly spiked with red and green chilis, but they were a far cry from the steamed fish head with Hunan chili and Chairman Mao's pork that I'd tried on my last visit to China. I expressed my disappointment to Grace, and she said, "From now on, we will bring the musicians real Hunanese food. This is my promise." Grace was true to her to word, for later in the week Stradio were treated to genuine gastronomic fire, which left two of them stooped over a toilet on the eve of their fairground show.

At the end of the meal, we asked to visit a local club. With Mr. Big frowning over his shoulder, Cody told us, "Music clubs are very dangerous places filled with drugs and people with guns. They are very violent, very bad, these people." I suggested that if we went together, these dystopian denizens could be held at bay, but Mr. Big shook his head and grunted, leaving Cody to translate, "If Westerners are seen spending time with groups of Chinese, it will be bad for you, and even worse for the locals. People will get in a great deal of trouble." This only hardened our resolve to go, but once we got outside the restaurant to head to a club, we discovered that our driver was nowhere to be found and that it would take twenty to thirty minutes, and a king's ransom, for a cab ride to the bar district. The driver turned up eventually, and drove us to the hotel for our meeting in Mr. Big's suite, where we were scolded for attempting to visit the city's badder-than-Compton bars. This left us frustrated and exhausted, and we ended up drinking in the hotel bar listening to two women in evening gowns play Carpenters' songs on lute and piano. This was exactly the kind of Changsha that Mr. Big wanted us to see.

Because we'd been smothered so far during our visit to Changsha, our afternoon at the fairground felt all the more liberating. When I finally got to meet Ice, Fire, and Rain, the guitarist insisted I look at his wristband, which was red, green, and gold and emblazoned with a stylized pot leaf. He pointed at the leaf, looked both ways over his shoulder, then made the universal pothead's gesture of toking, "You?" he asked. "Me, yes," I said, then ruined whatever chance I had to commune with him over a ceremonial bong by adding, "But never before I play." Ice, Fire, and Rain laughed, as if I'd just told history's greatest stoner joke. To them, it was like Joe Cocker sending back a tray of beers; Jerry Garcia refusing a joint. "Maybe later," I said, trying to flatten the joke, but they just laughed some more before sneaking into the trees where, I figured, they were doing their part for rock 'n' roll in China.

Al waved me over to introduce a young fellow named Lee who confessed to owning seven Motörhead albums, even though, he boasted, only one of their records had been officially sanctioned. Neatly groomed and wearing pressed blue jeans and horn-rimmed glasses, Lee made the middle-aged Motörhead fans we'd seen walking around Tampere look like brooding orcs. He told us that he had an uncle in Birmingham, Alabama, who sent him records by all of the "important" bands, which he listed for us, pausing to throw appropriate weight behind the names:

"Aerosmith . . . Led Zeppelin . . . Mötley Crüe . . . Poison."

We oooohed over his list, even though I didn't know my Poisons from my Corrosion of Conformities. Still, I'd become so used to a Western metalscape filled with cartoon Ozzys and Rob Zombie horrorschlock, it was refreshing to find out that here heavy metal still represented musical darkness. I hoped this suggested that, unlike the crowd in Suzhou who had been too green to appreciate the charging heaviosity of "Horses" or "The Land Is Wild," the kids in Changsha would rise to the noise.

And rise they did. We flew into our first song, "Pornography," which we played faster and more excitedly than at any other point on tour, and after Jay's first jarring electro-downbeat, the crowd in Changsha did naturally what we'd had to teach the crowd in Suzhou to do: they waved their arms above their heads and screamed. At the centre of the arm-waving mob, which numbered about four hundred across the front of the stage and around the catwalks, a young woman in a tight black dress and dark-framed glasses was dancing with a sidewinding, almost Cuban swang. I was so thrilled to find someone so down in the groove after playing to Suzhou's polite crowd that I slipped off my guitar for the last verse of the song, peeled down one of the runways, and pulled the dancing woman from the mob, ignoring

Mr. Big and the handful of soldiers in red hats and gold epaulets who were policing the event.

After bringing her to the stage, I realized that I wasn't sure what to do next, so I guided her to the end of one of the catwalks where, like Uma Thurman and John Travolta, we approximated her groovy Sino-Cuban twist for eight, twelve, twenty-four bars. The woman had a nose ring and a flower tattooed on her shoulder, neither of which we'd seen on fans around Shanghai. The crowd's faces were ablaze. With the exception of striding out to play the arena of my youth – Maple Leaf Gardens in 1996 – it was the most memorable beginning to any show I've ever played.

Things got wilder from there. We torched the set list, playing whatever came into our heads and causing the engineer at the other end of the radio broadcast – who was required to announce the songs in Chinese – no end of distress. Any one of our songs could have been about Ron being a *hunda*. At one point, my hands shaped themselves into the "Taking Care of Business" chords; the next thing I knew, they were playing them. When the song's chorus came around a second time, the crowd chanted "Taykoo cay oh beeness!" as the members of Ice, Fire, and Rain – and other assorted crowd rats – stormed the catwalks. They leaped across the stage and shouted into whatever microphone was closest. Our joyful riot drew a few more fairground-goers to the show, and if the concrete pitch wasn't filled, it was, at least, less empty. In a swirl of flying arms and legs, we cycled Randy Bachman's chords while Jay bashed away on his strange plastic kit trying to be heard above the din. For Changsha's first taste of CanRock, it wasn't bad at all.

The madness ebbed, if only for a moment, about halfway through the set when we played the quiet Rheostatics song "Fan Letter to Michael Jackson," which features an epistolary lyric

Piggins Rocks China/China Rocks Piggins (*Dave Bidini*)

delivered from a kid to his pop idol. On our *Introducing Happiness* album, we'd recorded the song at a snail's pace, then sped up the tape so that we'd sound like a band playing in a music box.

At one point during "Takin' Care of Business," I'd noticed a small, pigtailed girl my daughter's age dancing alongside the Cuban twister. So, before I started singing "Fan Letter to Michael Jackson," I asked Cody to bring the child on stage, positioning her in front of a microphone lowered to her level. I dropped to my knees and la-la-la'ed the song's opening melody, and had her repeat it until she started singing it for herself. Her voice sounded ever more precious in the wake of our extended rock maelstrom, and it made me shiver. I pictured the little melody slipping down the stone steps, through the forest, across city traffic, and into Changsha's beauty shop stereos before threading into greater Hunan, finding rice-paddy bunkhouses, matchbox homes, tilt-roofed tea rooms, and auto-rickshaw garages crowded with men sleeping on cardboard mattresses. The moment was also heavy and poignant: while Canada would never again hear "Fan Letter to Michael Jackson" performed by the band who'd written it, it was being sung for the first time on the radio to millions of Chinese by a young girl.

By the end of our set, the only thing left to do was play the Beatles. Earlier in the day, we'd used our dressing room – which doubled as sleeping quarters for the park restaurant's kitchen staff – to learn "Let It Be" and "Hey Jude" from lyric cheat sheets that Andy had slipped into my pocket before we left for Changsha. I was reminded of those early years playing in high-school cover bands and taking guitar lessons, where the songs of Lennon and McCartney were the first I'd learned. I wasn't sure whether we'd need, or want, to deploy these tired chestnuts – after all, we had important songs about the Canadian wilderness to share – but because the show had gone so fabulously well, it seemed like the right time to acquiesce.

The crowd started bouncing at the first strains of "Let It Be." By song's end, almost half the audience had joined us on stage. For the third verse, I looked down at my feet to where I'd positioned the words, but some eager fan had swept them up as a keepsake. So I sang whatever came into my head:

"We are not the Rheostatics
We are only a facsimile;
Still we've come to rock you
You will see."

When Tim sat on the edge of the bed in Edmonton and told me he was quitting the band, I never would have envisioned that two months later I'd be singing about the Rheostatics' demise in an ancient Chinese amusement park while singing a Beatles song. But here I was. Dwayne vamped the outro to "Hey Jude," and I circled through the crowd, singing endless "Na-nah-nah-nanananahs" with a hand-held mic, which I passed to concert-goers young and old. At one point, I approached a teenaged soldier, the brim of his hat pulled low over his eyes, and offered him the microphone. He stared straight ahead, shook his head quickly, and grunted. So I lowered the mic for a young boy wearing a Spiderman T-shirt. At that instant, he was bookended by a Red Guardsman with a gun on his hip and a hoser wearing a smile as wide as the Yangtze.

I returned to the stage a final time, where we led the Changshaers in a chant of "Pi-jo! Pi-jo!" (Beer! Beer!). It was a moment of Total Rockdom. The stage jumpers hit, struck, and strummed whatever instrument was at hand, and Jay handed his drumsticks to a stranger, who fought bravely to hold the beat together. During this final glorious sonic assault, I saw four six-foot Slavic women in cut-off shorts, high heels, and florid eye makeup approaching through the crowd. They were flanked by two sunglassed wingmen in dark suits. The women loomed over the compact Changshaers, and their mascara made them look like the kind of girls who beat up other girls in high school. They possessed a man-eating fearsomeness. I couldn't imagine why they'd shown up, but then I was struck by a disturbing thought: the promoters had hired four Occidental prostitutes to service us post-gig.

The Amazons sat on the steps leading up to the stage and gave us long-eyelashed stares as their would-be pimps stood arms-crossed behind them. Coming off stage, I avoided them as best I could, then pulled the band together to share my theory. Dwayne suggested that they were transsexual men, which only freaked me out more. From a terrace outside our dressing room, we watched the girls from on high, wondering what to say when Cody or Double Fat (or worse: Grace) pulled us aside and told us to enjoy the spoils of the rock 'n' roll day. I also wondered how I might react when, later that night, the sunglassed thugs busted down my hotel room door, gaffer-taped me to a chair, and robbed me for all I was worth.

The sixth or seventh time I glanced down at them, I noticed that they had transformed themselves from Volga hookers to technicolour cowgirls, wearing frilly blouses, pink bloomers, and purple cowboy hats. Not only that, but the goons were now wearing red vests and black trousers, and practising ballet twirls behind the stage. I climbed down from the terrace and approached one of the thugs whose name, it turned out, was Valeri. He told me that they were part of a Kazakhstani dance troupe, an aspect of the afternoon's program that Cody and Grace had neglected to mention. Valeri hit the stage, and along- side the troupe's four behemoths, he danced the cancan. I was relieved that Changsha – possibly the epicentre of Chinese rock – was still sweet and innocent enough that rock 'n' roll was about music, music, and music. Maybe, in this dusty southern town, there was hope for the old girl after all.

After the show, Grace scribbled out a few Chinese characters on a square of paper and handed it to the members of Ice, Fire, and Rain. It contained directions to our hotel and the time we were expected to meet before heading out on the town. The van was quiet as we headed back until Grace turned from the front pas- senger seat to tell us that Mr. Big was upset that I'd given out my e-mail address to a fellow I'd met on stage whose wife was plan- ning to go to school in Toronto.

"David, this is not allowed," she said, half-frowning.

"Mr. Big can suck an egg," I told Grace, trying to dent her clipboard look. "I don't mean that *you* can suck an egg, Grace.

But Mr. Big, he can suck a whole friggin' barrel of eggs," I said.

"Man eggs!" echoed Al.

"Tasty man eggs," added Jay.

Grace tried to smile. It didn't work.

"We're meeting at nine o'clock in the lobby, right?" I asked her, confirming our appointment with the local musicians.

"Yes, nine o'clock," she said. But at 9:00 p.m. when we gathered in the lobby, the only person there to meet us was Cody, who told us that he had bad news.

"There has been a change in plans," he said. "The other bands, we have sent them home."

BEIJING

I WAS AMAZED WHEN I FIRST READ OUR CHINESE TOUR itinerary, partly because the venues sounded so exotic, but also because none of them were in Beijing. If I wanted to play in the city with the most active rock 'n' roll scene, I'd have to book the shows myself. (Someone at the Canadian consulate in Shanghai had promised me, "If you think Shanghai is like Los Angeles, then Beijing is Detroit.")

For help, I turned to two expats I knew – Steve Chiu and Ron Skinner. Steve worked in Beijing for the *Economist* and had recently rented a cottage near the Great Wall, shelling out 10,000 yuan (U.S.$1,200) for a seventy-year lease. Ron had just finished a stint teaching inline skating to young Chinese, and was coming off a tour of the country with the electro-rock band Dirt Star, which he'd formed with a bunch of local musicians. Both promised to help set up shows for us during our four-day swing to the capital, our last through the land of the dragon.

On my first afternoon in Beijing, I set out to find a cup of strong coffee, which proved remarkably easy; new latte and espresso bars were plentiful in most busy sections of Beijing. Then I took Ron's advice and headed to the *hutong*, the ancient, narrow-alleyed quarter where the last of the city's traditional homes can be found, at least for the time being. Two million

Chinese lived in the *hutong* as recently as ten years ago, but since then acres of its venerable courtyards have been razed to make room for the tourists expected at the 2008 Olympics. These days, it's not uncommon to find its walls or shop grilles slashed with a single Chinese character – *chai* – which is the sign of eviction or, as the Chinese government likes to call it, relocation.

The surviving *hutong* had become the latest pocket for hip new businesses, but I was struck by its antiquity before I noticed anything else. The way its small courtyard homes were open and laid bare to passersby made the cobblestone villages of Western Europe look positively modern. Because the homes were separated not by doors or fences, but by narrow passageways, you could peer into the interior stone tangle of each building. I tried not to linger too long in front of these abodes, but it was hard to resist gawking a bit at Chinese family life as it played out door to door, shop to shop. In one small dry goods store, a young child played with a limbless plastic doll on the floor, as his mother worried over a pot simmering on a cooker in the corner. In another corner, a muddy-faced teenager was pecking away at the controls of a primitive video game while his father or uncle crouched in the foreground smoking and cracking peanuts, their shells piling over the lip of his slippers. Above them, a child lay sleeping in a loft crowded with supplies, and, in the middle of all this, a young woman sat at a public school desk – the store's counter and cashbox – occasionally rising to sell a bar of soap or bag of rice.

The narrow streets and alleyways of the *hutong* were teeming with life: a phalanx of soldiers marching in formation out of a garrison crowbarred into the old city; a pack of uniformed girls skipping rope and laughing; a huddle of stooped elders throwing dice against the bottom of a stone wall. I paused to watch five or six animated Beijingers crowded around a motorbike build a tower of pink, orange, and red toilet-paper rolls on the pannier of the machine, balancing the monolith of tissue carefully before sending the rider buzzing away.

Hours later, I emerged from the old streets onto a shopping promenade with a handful of record and instrument shops. Where the *hutong* celebrated age and resilience in the face of change, here the westernization of Asian culture was in full bloom. In 1999, when I first visited Beijing, the closest I came to finding any current Western rock 'n' roll was a copy of *Born to Run* at the Friendship Store, which prior to China's economic about-face was the only place a Westerner could buy a withered copy of *Time* or a recent classical or pop recording. By that standard, the shopping promenade's music stores represented an explosion of sorts. On one stretch, my path threaded through at least a half-dozen instrument shops where young mushroom-haired kids dressed in black T-shirts, sitting below wall-sized posters of Ozzy, KISS, Aerosmith, and other hard-rock icons, shredded Metallica out of new Fender amps. In almost every instance, the player lifted his fingers from the fretboard as I entered the store and resumed shredding only once he realized – despite my jeans unmarked by headbangers' blood and new corduroy jacket lacking in the appropriate death-metal patches – that I was there to rock too.

Around one corner, I came upon a small record shop no bigger than a wardrobe trunk. I would have missed it entirely had it not been for a hand-drawn sign outside that read, "Fine Folk Handicrafts and Records of all Classes." I ducked through the low door and almost stepped into a stone bowl on the floor that had goldfish swimming in it. Above the bowl, a black Paiste crash cymbal was studded to the wall. Farther along the wall was a shelf crammed with Mao saddlebags, propaganda posters, lanterns, and red-star paraphernalia, as well as framed posters of

Jean-Michel Basquiat and Glenn Gould. On the other side of the store were racks of CDs by Steel Pulse, Collette, the Dubliners, the Eels, and ZZ Top mixed with various Chinese rock recordings: a sophisticated and eclectic mix by any record-shop standard. At the back of the store, a young man in a baseball cap trawling away on his laptop stole a few disbelieving glances at the big pale goose who'd just walked into his shop and was curiously pawing records by local bands he'd never heard of. I held up one of the discs and pointed to my ear. "Yes," said the young fellow, matter-of-factly. He tore the Cellophane off a half-dozen discs and played bits of them in succession.

The young man's name, as far as I could tell, was Ma (Horse). Perhaps it was his nickname, but more likely it was a case of traveller's ear. In rough, halting English – he made a sound like "Ouch!" every time he stumbled over, or couldn't quite find, the right words – he told me he was a drummer and that the wall cymbal was his. I also discovered that he'd opened the store with his brother, and that his parents had been pretty much against it from the beginning.

For about forty minutes, we played a game in which Ma would crack a CD – playing each one a little louder than the last – and I'd nod or, occasionally, snort. After the song, and sometimes during, I'd shout out who I thought the group sounded like: "Died Pretty!" "Talk Talk!" "Emerson, Lake, and Palmer!" "The Nils!" He'd repeat the band's name after me, and we'd continue.

Ma's shop reminded me of Toronto's nascent rock scene in the 1970s – and other burgeoning rock scenes like it – when the city's best record stores were run by musicians who understood that if they didn't sell their own records, and records like them, no one else would. Matt Kagler, who operates Tag Team Records in Beijing with his wife, Heiki, echoed something Andy had told me when he explained over coffee that independent bands in

China cannot record and distribute their records without government approval. "Even though pretty much everything gets approved," he said, "the process is very slow, and agonizingly bureaucratic. And if a band isn't properly signed to a label, then most record stores won't take them." I asked if he'd ever known, or worked with, a band who'd been denied approval based on political content, but he said he hadn't. "One of our bands, Lonely China Day, was denounced by the government for the controversial nature of four of their songs, but they weren't dissuaded. At last year's pop festival, they started the set by playing them in succession. It was a big step for rock 'n' roll in Beijing."

Another expatriate, Jon Campbell, a drummer and local promoter from Toronto, told me that while rock bands are generally ignored by the masses, there's still a lot of people in China who are into rock music. "There are tons of rock bands and audiences to see them here," he said, "especially in Beijing. There are a few bands who have managed to make a relatively good living. Of course, nobody who is living the high life off of music is playing rock. In fact, most people living the high life off of music didn't write the music they perform, and rarely even employ live musicians, or even actually sing all the time. But my point, really, is that it's frustrating to hear people like Andy and Yu talk about bands struggling, though I get why they do.

"There are more places opening in Beijing and Shanghai – in Beijing, there is a fifteen-hundred-capacity livehouse, and just opening is a five-hundred- to six-hundred-capacity livehouse; another club with capacity somewhere between the two opened in Shanghai, and others are supposed to follow; and then there's the other rock clubs around town. From what I understand of Andy and Yu Fei, they don't have the ability to get shows in Beijing because they haven't got the connections that would enable them to do so. They just pretty much ignore Beijing and focus on the rock hotbeds you've visited."

After shelling out nearly the last of my yuan for albums by bands whose names I couldn't pronounce, I thanked Ma and told him that I'd drop off a Rheos record the following day (alas, when I returned, the shop was closed). Back on the shopping promenade, I thought I heard my name being called from across the street. I walked on, still in a musical trance, but the voice persisted. It was Dwayne. He was walking with a small Chinese man dressed like an aging rude boy in a black fedora and grey blazer. I crossed the street and asked Dwayne how he'd made a friend despite speaking little or no Chinese.

Dwayne, more than the rest of us, was prone to lighting out on his own. Once, in Shanghai, he left the hotel looking for "something Chinese and fishy" for breakfast and was drawn to a restaurant across the street by a huge photograph of seafood stew displayed outside. He explained to the waitress in Chinese that, even though he was a vegetarian, he ate fish, but she just stood there looking confused and uncomfortable. (Later he learned that the phrase, which Andy had tried to teach him, meant "I am sexually jealous" when wrongly intoned.) Ten minutes passed before another waitress brought him a bowl of stewed chicken. Dwayne was trying to get his chopsticks around some bits of green pepper when an old man riding past on a bike caught his eye and waved. Dwayne waved back, and the old man parked his bike and came into the restaurant. He introduced himself as Yu and spoke just enough English to communicate. When Dwayne told him that he was playing music in China, Yu brightened because, he said, surely a musician would understand his "stories of uplifting." Yu retrieved them from his bike and they sat in the booth reading them together. They'd been roughly translated into English, and most involved an American boss going to Japan to set up a new business but becoming so frustrated with the backward and lazy Japanese workers that he packed up and went back to the motherland.

After a while, Yu noticed that Dwayne wasn't eating his chicken and suggested that they go to his friend's restaurant. On the way there, Yu called Dwayne his "brother in the Lord Jesus Christ, Our Saviour," as if they'd made a deep personal connection. The restaurant turned out to be a dirt floor with a few tables under a large awning. Yu's friend, the chef, led them to the back, past the outdoor kitchen, into a living room, and then into a bedroom, where a teenage girl lay on the bed listening to headphones. A woman immediately appeared and set up a table and two chairs a few feet from the bed, and Yu and Dwayne sat down. She then produced the most perfectly cooked fish Dwayne had ever had. The whole time they were eating, people came and went without ever acknowledging them. At the end of the meal, Yu said, "Brother in the Lord Jesus Christ, I have something very important to tell you," and passed a sheet of paper to Dwayne under the table. It read:

On April 19, 1945, General MacArthur of the United States Army insulted the Japanese Emperor. A secret Japanese organization called the Mikado swore revenge, and on April 19, 1995, on the 50th anniversary of the insult, the Mikado took revenge by bombing a landmark of the U.S.A. The Japanese government is aware of the Mikado and supports their efforts.

"He made me memorize what was written," Dwayne said. "He had me repeat the paragraph a few times, and when he was satisfied, he asked me to contact American news programs and share this information. Then he ripped the sheet of paper into small pieces that he distributed around various trash cans in the bedroom and outside. The bill came and I tried to pay, but he wouldn't let me. He told me that we were brothers in the Lord Jesus Christ, and that promising to tell his story to North America was payment enough."

On our second last day in Beijing, Ron Skinner, a.k.a. Dirt Star, phoned to say that he'd booked us a show at the Sculpting in Time café in the northeastern part of Beijing, Xiang Shan, near the emperor's Summer Palace, which is also known as the Fragrant Hill. Getting to the café proved to be an adventure all on its own. We spent thirty minutes in the hotel parking lot as the concierge, a crew of bellboys, and two bewildered taxi drivers tried to determine the whereabouts of the café. They gathered around a map unleafed across one of the taxi's hoods, drew phantom routes with their forefingers, and grunted. They phoned Steve Chiu to confirm that the club existed, then phoned him back to confirm that a road to the club existed too. The rest of us stood around while they argued and scratched their heads and argued some more before we decided that, even though no one really knew where we were going, we might as well go anyway.

Divided between the two cabs, we drove endlessly into nowhere. Night had fallen, and soon the outskirts of the city, which glittered with car dealerships and new factories – a hint of brazen commerce squeezed into the fringes of the old borough – gave way to villages like those we'd seen around Changsha, where men played snooker on weatherbeaten tables, a family dined in a gas station's parking lot, and small children chased a fat hog. I would have appreciated the liveliness of this scene more if the driver hadn't been crooking his neck all the time, looking for village names and obscured road signs. Every now and then, he slowed to a crawl, threw the car into reverse, and drove down a lightless road that stopped at a gaunt field or concrete abutment. It was a small blessing, I suppose, that at least he kept our car moving. Dwayne, who was travelling in the other cab – we'd lost them soon after exiting the city limits – told me that, at one point, his driver stopped the taxi on the narrow shoulder of a country road, got out, and smoked a cigarette.

We drove and drove some more. Eventually, even the villages faded away. The air turned fresh and crisp as the last streetlight disappeared. Our driver held up a single finger – "One more street," said Al, translating the gesture – and blindly steered the taxi up another lane. The road soon turned from the scrub of a country path into a proper boulevard, and, all of a sudden, there were streetlamps and the muted pulse of life. A few minutes later, we stopped directly in front of the Sculpting in Time café. As I got out of the taxi, another car drove up until it rested bumper to bumper against ours: Dwayne's cab.

The dining room offered Italian food cooked by young Chinese – after two weeks of duck tongues and roasted pork marrow, it felt good to lay into an approximation of Western cuisine – but it was the backyard patio that gave Sculpting in Time its real distinction. It had wooden tables, deck chairs, and crooked Chinese pines rising through the floor and, at one end, a low wooden stage facing the Fragrant Hill, which lay like a sleeping colossus beyond the café. Above the patio, a treehouse provided a striking view of the moonlit hill. We could almost smell it better than we could see it: a perfume of fat blossoms pushing against the scent of diesel and cooking oil floating in from the city. On the stage, Dirt Star had taped a microphone to a broomstick handle, which he'd wedged into an old table stand.

There were two small amps at the back of the stage and, in the corner, a table with a laptop. The patio was illuminated only by candles and the soft light of a half-moon, under which thirty or forty people, mostly friends and followers of Dirt Star, were drinking gin and waiting for the show to start.

One of Dirt Star's friends, a man named Airbag, had come up from Beijing for the show along with a friend, Ka Kong, whose name sounded like the first two hits of a tom roll. Dirt Star had played with Airbag's Radiohead cover band in 2002 (most Chinese concerts feature the headliner at 9:30 p.m., followed by a cover band). Airbag had been musically educated in his bedroom, studying whatever records he could get his hands on, downloading music software, and recording through digital trial and error. A few years later, he joined one of China's most successful cover bands, earning as much as fifty dollars an hour, an unprecedented wage for a young Chinese musician playing something close to rock 'n' roll.

China's cover band scene was the polar opposite of North America's where, because there are so many opportunities to play original music, the cover band racket comes across as an exhibition of artistic defeat. But in China, cover bands serve the necessary function of keeping rock 'n' roll alive, as so few Western bands tour there. One evening, Al and I traipsed over to the Sanlitun, Beijing's cover-bar district and home to a row of popular clubs: Boys and Girls, the Red Moon, Swing, and Skyline. We were promptly hounded by greeters asking if we liked girls and sexy kissing and sexy kissing girls, and dodged them by ducking into the closest club. Our plan was to stay for a quick beer, then leave without having our feet masturbated, but the band was so lively and good that we stayed for two sets. Typically, bars on the Sanlitun strip feature Filipino singing trios and pop quartets fronted by beautiful women in low-cut evening gowns, but the band in this club featured two singers: a young fellow who sang Canto pop power ballads with his fist frozen in the air, and a Joan Jett apprentice with stringy hair and torn jeans who thrashed her way through several Bon Jovi standards. The punters were into it, and the band played loud. Fans waved green glow sticks, laughed at the band's between-song jokes, and sang along to every chorus.

Airbag told us that he could take playing other people's music only for so long, despite the comfort and success of being in a top Chinese cover band. Eventually, he forfeited his salary and went to Changsha, where he rented a farmhouse and spent three months writing original material. Then, he took his act on the road, but because the country's rock 'n' roll culture was slow to grow, he played no more than a dozen shows a year, and radio stations stonewalled him. His parents were deeply concerned for their son's future, and he was close to packing it in when the producers of *Supergirls*, a national, Changsha-based, pop-star competition, contracted him to produce a series of CDs featuring the show's contestants. The show became China's highest-rated television program – no fewer than 500 million viewers, weekly – and Airbag's CDs sold well. He'd made it at a time when most rock and pop musicians were struggling to piece together a life.

Airbag was there on the patio when Al, Dwayne, Jay, and I took the stage at around ten o'clock under a long, velvety sky and a ceiling of stars. After two weeks of high sounds and wild colour, it felt strange to be in a pocket of such deep quiet, especially after the madness of Changsha, but it served our music well, and we played a great set. We sat on fold-up chairs so that we could all fit on stage, and Jay played brushes on the top of one of our guitar cases. Al and I took turns singing into the broomstick microphone. The first few tables were occupied by pretty young Chinese girls, student friends of Dirt Star's, who made me feel larger, hairier, and louder than I had all tour. Whenever we segued from one of Al's raucous touring songs into another – "Tonight in Edmonton" into "Drunk in America" – we felt like yargling yetis playing to a gallery of rabbits.

At one point during the instrumental break to "The Land Is Wild," I invited Airbag to the stage – the laptop, it turned out, was his – and asked if he'd create a digital rhythm to our song, on the spot. He shuffled to the stage, strapped on his head-phones, arched over his computer, pushed around his mouse, then released a tight, itchy groove that married perfectly with what we were doing.

We were elated. Not only were we jamming to postmodern laptop beats – a first in Al's musical life, and the first time in a long while in mine – but we were doing it within flinging distance of the Fragrant Hill, so the moment felt wonderfully heavy with cross-cultural and historic weight. The show became stamped even deeper in our memory when, after our set, Airbag and Ka Kong borrowed our acoustic guitars to play two Radiohead songs from *The Bends* ("High and Dry" and "Fake Plastic Trees"). They sang beautifully and quietly, their hair falling across their eyes as their voices curved phonetically around the lyrics. Radiohead gave way to one of Kong's original composi-tions, a cool, riffy instrumental that sounded like bits of Gentle Giant and My Morning Jacket, and then Dirt Star asked the 'Bag to play one of his songs. The young musician obliged, strumming and singing with brooding intensity. As with any fine musical moment, I understood none of it and all of it at the same time.

Coming off stage, I told Airbag and Kong how much I liked their singing, but they were embarrassed by the praise, which they deflected by effusing at length about our performance. His eyes down as he searched for the right words, Airbag said, "Great, great, great," then added, "Very good," as if worried that he hadn't gone far enough.

We were flattered. Still, if Airbag and Kong had found the Rheos-Not-Rheos' set three times great, and very good, I wondered what they would have thought were they suddenly tsunamied with all of the great music they'd never heard: the amphetamine snare shots of "Let Me Stand Next to Your Fire" or the kick drum in "Highway to Hell" or "Layla's" weeping outro or *Rocket to Russia* or John Lennon's headcold vocal in "Twist and Shout," which he sang shirtless after sucking back a pint of milk, or Paul Westerberg's "Can't Hardly Wait," which he sang pasted on his back on the studio floor, or Nazareth's "Love Hurts," which Dan McCafferty howled while sitting wasted in a rolling office chair; or "School" by Supertramp, the Muffs, Joni Mitchell's *Blue*, XTC, GBV, TMBG, BEP, or NRBQ, or Sly and the Family Stone at Woodstock or the gypsy tag of "Baba O'Reilly" or *Jesus: The Missing Years* or Neil Young's "Alabama" solo or Aretha or James Brown's good foot or the Bonzos or Pavement or "Mama Let Him Play" or "Play That Funky Music, White Boy" or "White Man in Hammersmith Palais" or "Pretty Vacant" or "Pretty in Pink" or "All Her Favourite Fruit" or Dave Edmunds or Wreckless Eric or "I can't take another heartache" or *Arthur* or the Slits or No Means No or discovering Loudon Wainwright III on cassette in a church in Edinburgh in 1994 or *A Night at the Opera*'s highway of sound or "goingtoapartymeetmeonafterschool" or Lambchop or Cherry Blossom Clinic (or, ya, even ELO) or the Wilburys or Fairport Convention or the Jam or the Dishes or the Poles or Max Webster or "Tom Sawyer" (for Jay) or the classic New Wave era bass lines of "Every Breath You Take," "Cities," "The Ugly Underneath," and "Peaches," or Mick Waller, Clem Burke,

Bernard Purdie, Sly Dunbar, Lonnie James, Sheila E, and Richie Hayward on the tubs, or the cold pooling intro to "Bad" by U2 or how the American government killed Kurt Cobain because he was the last dangerous rock 'n' roll star or Tonio K or Plastic Bertrand or Vic Chesnutt or the time Yoko crawled out of a bag at Varsity Stadium or *Warm Leatherette* or the Dickies or "Life On Mars?" sung in English and Portuguese or *Beer Cans on the Moon* or the Specials, Madness, Fishbone and the Selector or Cecilia singing Josh Rouse at bedtime or the Polaroids of Billy Bragg in his underwear that Martin took from our English road manager's home in Chiswick and harboured until our last day in the U.K. or watching Jon King get knocked unconscious by a ceiling pipe after jumping five feet off the ground at the Palais Royale during "Anthrax" in 1980 or Rick Danko's bass strings that were given to me after he died or the wonder in Peter Buck's face as I stared up at him from the crowd in Croke Park after he'd struck the opening harmonic to "Feeling Gravity's Pull" looking shaken and overwhelmed by the way it chimed through the stadium's old iron grandstand or the Super Furrys or Eno or the Undertones or the Decemberists or 1910 Fruitgum Company or the Modern Lovers or Jimmy Page's "Hotdog" solo or how, during our last night in Compass Point Studios in Nassau after recording *Introducing Happiness*, we went into town and tried to get drunk but couldn't so we headed back to our oceanside apartment but not before drummer Dave Clark pointed to an old stone pub and said, "Let's try there," so we did, and the first thing that happened was a young woman spun around on a bar stool and asked, "Hey, aren't you guys the Rheostatics?" and, because we were, we stayed and got drunk and karaoked deep into the night before somebody drove us home and I decided to sleep on the beach in my suit only to wake up hot and sweating at ten in the morning hungover realizing that we'd missed our plane so I phoned the airport and they said, "We're sorry, sir, the plane is taxiing down the runway," which gave me the chance to say something that I'd always wanted to say:

"Hold that plane!"

The woman hung up. Dave Clark zombied out of bed and asked what was wrong. I told him that we'd missed our plane, and then he puked. Then I puked.

In my life, rock 'n' roll has meant everything to me.

As we packed up our guitars, we heard giggling coming from one of the tables. Dirt Star was imploring a young woman to sing in Chinese. When I asked what was going on, he said, "Mai is a singer on *Supergirls*. She's one of the final two contestants, and she'll be singing next week to 500 million viewers. I'm trying to get her to sing for you."

I told Mai that the Rheos-Not-Rheos would not leave the Fragrant Hill until she sang. She threw her hands to her face, as if trying to make herself disappear, but eventually we coaxed her to the stage. By now, the stars had become lost in the clouds and the candles extinguished. The lights of the dining area had dimmed too, and as the young singer stood in the middle of the stage, only her pale face and hands were visible. Before starting, she steadied her legs, cocked a hip, pointed out and down with her forefinger, and said, in close-jawed English with a hard Beijinger's accent, "This song is called 'What's Up?'" Those words and the song's lyrics were the only English Mai uttered all night.

She sang a pop song from 1992 by the Four Non Blondes. It was a very Strawbsesque moment: a defunct, all-dyke band from San Francisco having an afterlife in the Chinese pop scene while so much other music had never made it here. As Mai performed for us – her hands butterflying the air, feet rooted to the stage, chest heaving, and eyes squeezed in melodic rapture – I wondered if, once the canon of modern music finds its way into this great and hungry land, it'll be the Baha Men and Sting, Tony Basil and Gwen Stefani who'll survive beyond the rest. Perhaps, in twenty years, Airbag will still be singing songs from *The Bends* to thirty-seven people in a café, while Mai's sold-out European tour will be sponsored by a billion-dollar noodle company. After all, revolution in rock 'n' roll can never be taken for granted.

On our last night in Beijing, I was scheduled to do a reading and acoustic performance at the Beijing Bookworm, an English-language library, bookstore, café, and salon. Steve Chiu, who'd helped organize the event, told me that a few Canadian expats had expressed interest in jamming with me. This seemed like a grand idea, but when I called him, the store's owner, Alex Pearson, told me that a guitar and banjo player, trombonist, mandolin player, accordionist, and bassist were all coming to play. I was immediately apprehensive. It would be our final night in China, and the last thing I wanted to do was grind out memories of the West with Canadians desperate to hear stories of home. Making the situation even more difficult was the fact that I'd have to leave early as our hosts, Andy and Yu Fei, had planned an end-of-tour banquet for the Maple Rhythm Festival bands, giving us a chance to reconnect with them, drink buckets of rice wine, and trade stories.

The Bookworm gig had suddenly become too much for me to handle, so I phoned Al. No answer. He was fast asleep. Then, five minutes before I had to leave, he phoned and agreed to come with me. I collected him from his room before he could change his mind, and we were whisked by taxi through the early-evening traffic to the bookstore.

As it turned out, only two musicians – an American with a double bass and a Canadian guitar player – showed up to jam, which allayed my fears of a sonic car crash. I read for about twenty minutes, and then Al and I traded songs, teaching our guests the chords at the beginning of each number. The room was full and everybody seemed to be having a pretty good time.

During the performance, a small white-haired woman sitting near the front of the room engaged us in lively patter. While some musicians want their crowd to be button-lipped between songs, I've always enjoyed the banter between musician and audience, provided, of course, it enlivens rather than sabotages the show. In a club called Crocks and Rolls in Thunder Bay, a beefy, square-headed man named Fred who sat at the back of the bar would shout, "*Die!*" whenever we finished a song. It's all he ever shouted. He never once elaborated on his command. Fred's shouting eventually got to us, and we started shouting back, which was the worst thing we could have done. Finally, there was a post-gig confrontation, which saw the large scowling man – who'd sat through every three-hour show we'd ever performed in Thunder Bay – shout, "Die!" at us as we loaded our gear into our van in the middle of the horrible winter. A few years later, a friend told me that Fred had suffered a serious heart attack and was convalescing in the hospital. He asked if I'd sign a card for him, which struck me as preposterous, considering that Fred had ensured that we were miserable every time we played Thunder Bay. But my friend said that Fred owned all of our recordings and was a big fan; he just had an awkward way of showing his appreciation.

The white-haired woman was the anti-Fred. Her comments tickled the room and cut through the tension that exists at the beginning of any performance. That she was an older person made her presence all the more memorable since very few sexagenarians had ever attended Rheos' shows. Once we finished our set, I went over to thank her, but Al had got there first. The old woman was in tears.

Yvonne, it turned out, had been Al's father's girlfriend at the time of his death, six years earlier. She'd moved in with Mr. Piggins, but he'd died soon afterward, and she'd escaped to Beijing to forget her sad life in Wales. A few days before our performance, she'd read in a local magazine that a hockey-playing musician from Toronto was coming to the Bookworm. She'd thought that perhaps this person would know Al and she could ask some questions about him. When Al told Yvonne that he had a newborn son – Deklan – she was overcome. That Al possessed his father's mannerisms made it even harder for her to keep it together.

They talked for about an hour, then we taxied to the restaurant where the members and crews of six Canadian bands were crowded into two small banquet rooms, making cellphone movies, toasting one another with rice wine, and singing "O Canada!" like thirteen-year-olds on a bus trip to the States. There was lots of drinking and the kind of sloppy hugging that only twenty-seven men distanced from their homeland could produce.

Forever told us that their best gig had been – as ours had – in Changsha, even though the keyboard player had nosebled over his synthesizer after suffering heat stroke. Pete, the one-eyed bass player, told me that a record company in Shanghai wanted to buy the rights to one of the band's songs, a wedding song, with the purpose of getting a local Canto pop star to record it. Negotiations, he said, were already underway to bring the band back in a year's time, which proved one thing, if it proved anything at all: at least we knew which band among us was the Strawbs.

After we destroyed an enormous sea bass candied red with sweet-and-sour sauce, Andy took us to a nearby KTV disco, where we gathered in a narrow room with blinking lights and a karaoke rig reefed to its limit. Jordan Cook promptly glued himself to the microphone. I'd arrived at KTV feeling nicely tippled from the rice wine's boozy assault, but the idea of spending my final moments in Beijing watching a bunch of musicians I'd probably never see again eviscerate the worst of the Eagles was sobering. Our tour deserved a better send-off. I slapped Al on the knee and suggested that we escape while we could.

We were dropped off by taxi at the top of the *hutong* in an area known as Huo Hai, an old enclave where canals of green water give Beijing the look of Venice among the dragons. We made our way along one canal past great shaggy trees, their branches bejewelled with red lanterns, looking for the No Name Bar, which I'd visited a few days earlier with Dwayne. I stopped to ask directions from a vendor selling chinaware from a wagon, but before he could answer, I dug fifty yuan from my pocket and bought a plastic bag filled with colourful porcelain tea cups. It's fine for revellers to boast of wild evenings spent bellyflopping in city fountains, but you're not really drunk until you've convinced yourself that buying teacups in the middle of the night in the *hutong* is a good idea. The china clacked happily against my hip as we crossed a bridge over the water, and, a few streets later, we found the No Name shouldered against the winding canal like an old houseboat hauled up on the bank.

The No Name was as much like a Hunanese cottage as a tavern: narrow, dark, and wooden. If you stuffed forty people inside, you'd be flouting fire safety regulations (provided such regulations existed) but the place was almost empty. Along with the Shuffle Demons, Steve Chiu, and a few other stragglers from KTV, we sat down and toasted the ascent of Sino-Canadian rock 'n' roll and other booze-fuelled platitudes. At one point, Al caught the attention of the bar's other patrons, and joined them at their table, where a few laughing women started pointing at his nose.

They were twentyish, with radiant faces, and they were singers. One of their friends, a publicist who spoke a kind of fitful English, told us that their party was from Lhasa, and that the girls were a pop group, considered to be the Spice Girls of Tibet. Dressed in cool eveningwear with jewels prettying their hair, they were like four elegant birds next to us. There was one smallish fellow among the Tibetans, with eyes to match the twinkling skies. His face was as round and perfect as a saucer, and he was the table's clown prince, telling stories and waving his arms and making everyone laugh. He did this, I learned, every week as host of Tibet's most popular music video program. I went over to meet him and he rose to greet me – he was only as tall as my armpit. I took my black fedora and placed it on his perfectly round shaved head. He touched his hands to the brim of the hat, which looked as if it were meant to live there.

The fedora had been given to me by my stepmother, Joanne, after her father, Bill Chahley, had passed away a few months before I'd left for China. Bill was the kind of person that you used to find in the taverns, ball fields, and social halls of Canada a generation or two ago: strong-willed, genuine, wise, and tough. Because I'd worn a fedora all of my adult life, as he had, I was given his black Biltmore in memoriam. I was honoured to wear it, but now that hat had left my head.

I told the publicist, "This is my grandfather's hat. He died a few months ago, but I think he should have it." When the smiling man was told what I'd said, he opened his arms and came toward me. "Man, after you gave him your hat, you guys couldn't stop hugging each other," Jay said later.

Word of the hat transfer passed around the room, and, to be certain I'd done the right thing, I canvassed my fellow Canadians, who assured me that it was a good call. The TV host turned his back for a moment and struggled to free something from around his neck. Finally slipping out of a necklace, he pressed a small tin icon into my hand, telling me, through his friend, "This is a Tibetan symbol of love and compassion, a *hung*. I've worn it since I was a child, but I want you to have it." I thought that we were both tempting fate, but I nonetheless accepted the gift. We hugged some more, then he held up the flat of both hands. The room grew quiet. "Your friend here," said the publicist, "he wants very much to sing you a song."

The TV host put one hand to his chest, let the brim of Bill Chahley's fedora fall across his brow, and in a sonorous tenor sang a Tibetan anthem of friendship. He was soon joined by the other Lhashans, and finally by the Spice Girls, whose voices cruised sweet and high above the small, Biltmored man's lead. This song gave way to another, then another, and for forty minutes, the Tibetans stood and sang to us, their voices swimming out of the bar and down the ancient streets until proudly – and maybe a little foolishly – Mike Hiltz of the Sons of Maxwell climbed a chair and led us in a version of "Barrett's Privateers." It was the least we could do.

At around 4:30 a.m., the singing stopped and the barkeep corked the whisky. We said goodbye to the Tibetans and stumbled into the old city looking for a taxi stand. As we made our way down a dark alleyway, we noticed a bright light shining about twenty feet in front of us. It was a record store, open at four-thirty in the morning in the *hutong*. We had to go in.

The first thing we saw was a fully stocked beer fridge. At the back of the store, three young Beijingers lay on two small couches, their legs slung over the arms, drinking tea, smoking

The Greatest Song in the World (*The Diodes/Ralph Alfonso*)

cigarettes, and listening to music. They showed no reaction to our invasion, which is exactly how I would not have responded had the equivalent of four pelted Norsemen walked into my place in the middle of the night.

A modest rack of CDs stood near them, and I passed a finger along a row of spines, before stopping, impossibly, at a record by the Diodes, an obscure Toronto new wave band from the late 1970s. I might have paused a moment to figure out how an album from a minor Canadian band – whose reputation had only spread to two hit songs on a local Toronto radio station – had landed here, but, really, I wasn't surprised at this discovery, considering the kind of night I'd had. "You guys have to hear this," I told the young Chinese, who smiled and nodded like lazing cats. Steve Chiu pulled four cold beers out of the fridge as I evicted whatever music they were listening to on their stereo, pushed in the disc, punched "Tired of Waking Up Tired," and played air-guitar and sang for three minutes and ten seconds as if the Diodes were the greatest and most important band in the world. Because in that moment, in that little record store in the *hutong*, they were.

GANANOQUE

THE SIZE AND NATURE OF CANADA ENSURES THAT NOT
even the most itchy-footed musicians will see all of it over the
course of their lives. Even Stompin' Tom can attest to this. He's
visited pretty much every chunk of sovereign rock, but he never
made it to the Queen Charlotte Islands during his exhaustive
touring years in the 1960s and 1970s. So, after I'd arrived back
in Toronto I decided to seek out the exotic at home, heading
east to the Maritimes, a region less travelled during the Rheos'
twenty years of touring.

My first Eastern gig came ten days after I got back from
China: a weekend jam at an annual fishing trip in Gananoque,
Ontario. For twenty-seven years, my friend Ben Gunning, his
brother, their dad, and thirty friends and relatives had gathered
together to fish, most recently at Dorothy's Fishing Lodge, near
Chaffey's Lock. The lodge's namesake was a gregarious, commanding Ohioan with a voice like diced gravel who operated two
lodges and a restaurant on the grounds, which sloped toward a
bay where an old railway trestle hung over the green-blue water.
It looked like a great place to sit and strum after weeks spent
under dirty Chinese skies amidst the sweat and noise of the
chattering masses.

I collected Ben at his Toronto home on a Friday afternoon in May. We piled into my 1991 grey Ford Mercury Grand Marquis, a car that my wife, Janet, had bought while I'd been away in China with the intent of driving it to Newfoundland. The Grand Marquis proved to be a fine fishing-trip car, if only because it could accommodate two guitars, a few bags of clothes, two cases of beers, and two buckets of gin and whisky, which we'd brought along to ensure that we'd do more singing and drinking than fishing. Hitting the 401 in advance of rush-hour traffic, I pushed a cassette – *The Best of Spike Jones* – into the tapedeck, and we laughed at the music through Oshawa, Whitby, and Port Hope.

Cassettes are one of rock 'n' roll's great, forgotten media. When Janet told me on the phone in Beijing that our mechanic had found us a new car, one of the first things I'd asked her was whether it had a working tape deck. Because tapes have long been usurped by other technologies, they're cheap and plentiful in the junk shops and old clothing depots of North America. They're a great way to acquire lots of music for little money, and they encourage the listener to explore new sounds without having to lay out serious cash. During the Rheos' Scottish tour in 1994, I came away from an Edinburgh record store, Reptile Records (which has since closed), with two cassettes by artists I'd never heard before – Loudon Wainwright III and the Move – and a record by the Kinks, *Preservation: Act I*, which blew my mind as I listened to it while lying across a bench in the milk delivery truck that doubled as our British touring rig. Because cassettes were once considered the iPods of their day, they hold the same portable charm. Unlike the iPod, which requires a certain fiddling, cassettes are hearty and unprecious, encouraging the mobile listener to stuff them into their tapedeck with little worry of damaging a fragile, expensive shuffling machine.

I don't want to sound like too much of an old walrus – ah, what the frig, here goes – but I believe that digital technology has greatly devalued music. This isn't an anti-download tirade; I'm not on the side of someone such as Lars Ulrich of Metallica, who once groused about how downloading was robbing their million-selling band of thousands of dollars in royalties. On the contrary, downloading effectively popularizes new music where most major record companies fail. Still, the delete button has done a lot to reduce albums to single tracks and render them as squiggles on a computer screen. It has also encouraged consumers to regularly dump songs like so much Viagra spam. The great thing about albums or cassettes is that they stick to consumers like birthmarks, and they're wonderfully hard to get rid of. Without having tapes or records staring at you, the listener is less compelled to play them while doing the dishes or firing up the bong. Album covers goad listeners into returning to them, while iPods merely blink from the night-table, or flicker inside the dark recesses of a coat. The cassettes that carpeted the floor of my Grand Marquis were rarely sorted or, for that matter, maintained, but they were a big part of my musical life because they beckoned me daily from the front seat. Only a shovel and a plastic bag stood in the way of consigning them to landfill but, to steal from the campaign that launched the iPod, what modern citizen has time to do that?

Ben and I had been friends for years, ever since the Rheos and the Local Rabbits hooked up for a few national tours. Ben's early pop life had dovetailed with the renaissance – and also, the commodification – of punk rock, and the appropriation of angry-sounding music by the corporate record world. In 1993, the Rabbits had played on a Canadian festival package, Edge-fest, that included Green Day, Foo Fighters, Our Lady Peace, and others. During our drive to Gananoque, Ben told me how

Green Day had torched a drum kit at the end of every show, passing off their manufactured rebellion as passionate and incendiary. My bandmate Martin Tielli called them the Sha-Na-Na of Punk because during every gig, lead singer Billy Joe would grab a kid from the crowd to play guitar with the band. Billy Joe made it seem as if he'd come up with the idea at that very moment, even though it happened at the same time each show. The odious part of all of this, Ben told me, was that while the band gave the impression it was tearing down the wall between performer and audience, the front of the stage was, in fact, patrolled by security monkeys with headsets who made sure that the right kind of kid was chosen. When they weren't doing that, Ben said, they were wrangling no-goodniks and laying their muscle on the crowd.

Every concert kid has their story of conflict with cops or security forces. When I went to see Joe Jackson at Massey Hall on his "Night and Day" tour, an event that plays large in the lyric to "My First Rock Concert" (just so you know), the first song of the show was "On Your Radio," a driving tune from his first album. As Joe's band hit the song's chorus, I leaped to my feet, dancing in the middle aisle of the hall, my legs and arms and feet swinging like pinwheels. I was the only dancer, but like any excited concert kid, I kept pogoing. By the second chorus, still no one had joined me, and a moment later, I discovered why: the room was thick with Toronto cops, their arms crossed, eyes pinched in disdain. One of them grabbed me and lifted me into the air, grinding my spine into the lip of the stage. The cop's face turned red, his teeth were gritted in fury. I leaned my head back and saw Joe stalking the stage, hollering into his microphone as the band kicked harder, his eyes trained on the drama. I drew in my shoulders in an attempt to fall from the cop's grip, and as I did, Joe leaned over and stole the hat from the cop's head, as casually as if he were picking a daisy. He slapped the hat on his head and the cop became apoplectic. With the cherry-top sitting low across his eyes, Joe pulled the mic stand behind him like a caveman dragging a club. The cop made a grab for Joe's feet. I fell from his grasp and stumbled to find my balance. The cop turned to me, then to Joe, then back to me, but before he could react, I was gone, out the door onto Shuter Street. I snuck back in a few songs later and I watched the show from the darkness of the balcony.

Ben had tried to manufacture a similar confrontation with the security throng. During Green Day's performance, he waded through the crowd to the front of the stage. Dressed in grey and black drab, he put his back to the stage, crossed his arms, and affected the look of boredom and menace of the security patrol. Ben planned on turning to the band when the moment came for Billy Joe to pick someone from the crowd, waving his pick and screaming Green Day's name in an attempt to be chosen. Once onstage, he vowed to play relentlessly, at an obnoxious volume, forcing the band to react as they hadn't all tour.

Ben knew that his charade was working when one of the other security guards passed him a set of earplugs. When Billy Joe gestured for his band to settle into a long, instrumental groove – a showband trick that would have been anathema to early punk groups, who played their songs as if as anxious to finish as start them – he rapped about wanting to bust down conventions by getting someone from the crowd to join the band (I'd seen Stevie Wonder execute this same trick on a previous tour using a beautiful confederate with impossibly angelic pipes). At the end of his speech, Billy Joe deferred to one of his handlers standing side-stage, who pointed out the overzealous kid in the crowd waving his red guitar pick at the front of the stage: our Ben.

Ben shouted his love for the band, but as he was about to be lifted on stage, one of the security guards fingered him as another Edgefest performer, and the gig was up. Ben broke from the crowd, and a chase ensued. When they finally managed to catch him, he was taken to one of the tour's organizers office and upbraided for trying to "wreck" the gig. "That was what galled me the most," Ben said as we drove past Sharbot Lake and Kingston, "that this guy, who was supposed to be responsible for this rock 'n' roll event being something real and great and wild, was freaking out because something unexpected might have happened."

At Dorothy's Fishing Lodge, the fishermen had made a tiny jam space on the third-floor loft of the main lodge. It housed a four-piece drum kit, a bass amp, and an army of acoustic guitars. Anticipating a spray of beer suds, cigarette ash, and bug splatter over the weekend's celebrations, I'd brought along my ancient red Yamaha 445 guitar, knowing that the old beast could absorb whatever indignities a bunch of drunken fishermen might inflict upon it. But as day faded into night, and folks collected in the jam space, I saw that everyone else had brought much better instruments than mine – Larivees, Taylors, Gibsons – which worried me a little, because it was obvious that they took their evening jam a little more seriously than I'd expected. Next to these precious instruments, my axe, which was gummed over with old band stickers and saddled with long dead strings, looked a wreck.

Most of the fisherman at the jam had nicknames: Carp, Fat Kenny, the Doctor. This was also true for Ben's dad, a venerable, wiry cat with a beard whom everyone called Dickie Joe. There was one fellow without a nickname – Rob – who made up for his disappointing handle by wearing a hat with a fish stuck through it. Rob was the person to whom everyone turned when nobody could figure out what to play. He reminded me of a kind, folksinging Rick Moranis, and the room came alive whenever he picked up his harmonica, which he played like a scoundrel. Rob, it turned out, had gone to Woodstock, and he told me about it when the bong fell into our laps.

"The thing I remember most," he said, "was how the ham sandwiches looked after being dropped into the crowd by a U.S. Army helicopter. I don't think I saw much of the bands. I heard them, but I don't think I saw them. I also remember that there were naked people everywhere. At one point, a canoe floated past me on the river holding about nine or ten beautiful, naked twenty-three- or twenty-four-year-old girls. I got undressed, sheepishly waded in the water and was just trying to be cool, standing there with everything hanging out. I heard a sound, and when I looked beside me, I saw a huge guy standing behind a naked chick, putting it to her from behind, making sloshing sounds in the water."

One of the great things about trading songs with a group of strangers is that you get to play with as many people in one night as you'll play with the rest of the year, especially if, like me, you're devoted to one band. And gigs like these are a lesson in how other players approach their instruments. I'm always amazed how many different ways there are to hold a pick or finger a chord. You're taught to strum this way or that, but over time your musical personality emerges and your technique changes, no matter what you learned. At the Gan, everyone had their own way of sounding an A chord or barring a G major. This, along with the boozing that had just started, complicated the challenge of figuring out what chord was being played so I could strum along.

The fishermen warmed up with some Dylan, Springsteen, and John Prine, and when the time came for me to play, I was ready. I'd learned the "Green Acres" theme in preparation for the weekend. Because the song only requires three chords, I thought it would be perfect for a bunch of drunken fishermen. I played it up-tempo, probably faster than the TV theme, and after a few verses, everybody started playing along, filling out the musical treatment and making the sound of the room swim as only a bunch of loose-wristed, edge-of-the-couch players could. The song ended with the kind of acoustic crash that the song deserved, but after blunting the last ringing note, there was none of the cheers that had greeted the others' songs. Someone said, "What's next? 'One Hundred Bottles of Beer on the Wall?'"

I was crestfallen. Resorting to desperate measures, I played "This Song Ain't Any Good." Every musician has a few nuggets that they pull out in dire circumstances, and "This Song Ain't Any Good" is mine. I wrote it in forty seconds, on my way along the Georgian Bay shoreline to the front porch of my wife Janet's parents' cottage. It arrived bundled and fully formed from the heavens, and while I would have preferred being delivered a twenty-first-century version of "In the Court of the Crimson King" or "I'm So Bored With the U.S.A.," I'm still grateful for the gift. Because it sounds like the kind of tune that could have been written by anyone – it possesses none of the political subtext or bent rhythms for which the Rheos were known – everybody sang along.

Ben was up next. He played two songs by Michael Smith – "Spoon River" and "Come Away Anita" – and, for the first time all evening, the hosers fell silent and just listened, making me wish that I'd learned something achingly beautiful to pad out my repertoire – maybe "Karma Police" or "Handbags and Gladrags." (Ben also played Van Morrison's "Fair Play," cinching his musical trifecta.) Ben's mini-set gave way to another fisherman named Mike, who played the first verse of "Born to Run" before shouting, "How the fuck does it go?"

After this, the Doctor sang "Simple Twist of Fate," which led to an avalanche of Dylan. It was only a matter of time. In most Canadian summertimes, there's a good chance that, every hour, at least one hoser is playing a song by either Bob Dylan or Neil Young, which may explain why very few wars have ever been waged in this country. I've only recently come to this conclusion, for there was a time when upon hearing either of these artists I'd grouse about their insignificance and abundance of lyrics about parrots and Siamese cats and Indians and wool sweaters. Because my musical awakening happened in the late 1970s, I'd been forced listen to aging hippies extol the greatness of these artists when all that mattered to me, at the time, were songs by young bands about world decay set to screaming power chords.

It wasn't until I went to school in Dublin in 1985 – I was twenty-two – that I connected with the music of Bob and Neil. I'd brought bits of *Highway 61 Revisited* and *Bringing it all Back Home* with me to Ireland on cassette, along with a Walkman, headphones, and little speakers. Still, I'd ignored the tapes until I found myself sitting alone under a canopy during a rainstorm in the seaside hamlet of Bray, looking out at stilled amusement rides and children's swings creaking in the wind. When I clamped my headphones to my ears, I pressed play and heard Dylan singing "Just Like Tom Thumb's Blues," a song about being lost in Europe. The first line of the song is: "When you're lost in the rain in Jaurez, and it's Easter-time, too." The song seemed to have been written for me, at that very moment. All of the snideness and self-absorbtion I usually heard in Dylan's voice had vanished, and he sounded friendly, self-deprecating, and wise, and all that I'd thought about him before fell away as the rain tapped on the canopy and the sea roared at my feet. With a lot of great music, you simply have to wait for it to find you, and that's what "Just Like Tom Thumb's Blues" did, reaching out like a gentle, calloused hand to a young traveller lost in the world.

That year was also the summer of Live Aid. Dylan was part of that too, but his performance with Keith Richards and Ron Wood was messy and tuneless. My friend Mary Keane and I wandered the city – it was raining that day too – and watched parts of the broadcast in different pubs and people's homes. When U2 played – their set was the turning point of their career – Ireland's national broadcaster, RTE, scrolled little inspirational messages at the bottom of the TV screen: "We're proud of you, boys!" and "Well done, lads!" At one point, Mary and I stopped in a tiny pub, and when I looked up, Neil Young was on the television, live from Veteran's Stadium in Philadelphia. Mary and I leaned over the bar, ordered pints, and watched as Neil played "Helpless."

I'd grown cynical about Neil, the Band, and Joni Mitchell because their story – leaving Canada for the promised land of American pop music – had been aped by many of my peers who thought that the only way to achieve any kind of wealth, fame, or notoriety was to abandon their country for the United States. Besides, Neil had come out in support of Ronald Reagan, and, to me, he just seemed like every other old hippie lost in the fog of his own thoughts.

But when Neil sang, his voice – which is both strange and beautiful, masculine and feminine, husky and high, strong and fragile – needled straight into my heart. As he brushed the long hair from his eyes and sang, an old, tweedy Irishman turned on his bar stool and commented, "Great, isn't he, this one?"

"Ya, really good," I responded.

"American, isn't he?"

"No, Canadian."

"Are you sure?"

"Oh, yes," I told him, feeling a shiver climb slowly up my spine. "He comes from where I do."

◖▭───

Ben sang "Barstool Blues," from *Zuma*, his voice twisting around the vocal, climbing just high enough to hit the notes. By this point, everybody was drunk, and the fishermen set into a glorious, sloppy, and uproarious round of song-trading: Bruce Springsteen's "The River," Daniel Lanois's "Jolie Louise," Leonard Cohen's "Chelsea Hotel," some David Wiffen and CCR. Through all of this, Dickie Joe played the drums, a salty old totem at the back of the room, passing his sticks over the toms and smiling. Watching him play, I was affected the way I always am whenever I see anyone older than fifty do their thing. It reminded me that the most any musician should hope for is the opportunity to play. Whether you're playing to thousands of fawning fans or thirty drunk fisherman, at least you're playing; just being able to express noise and melody is all that matters.

By 5:00 a.m., the fishermen and I were exhausted. Ben and I shuffled back to our sleeping quarters, followed by Carp, who was looking to carry on the night. We tried begging off to bed, but before we could, Carp, swaying in our lodge's living area, began to sing "Jersey Girl" by Tom Waits. Halfway through the tune, he lost the words, fell onto a coffee table, and broke a lamp. We picked him up and put him on the couch, leaving the crickets to fill the air.

NEWFOUNDLAND

AFTER RETURNING TO TORONTO TO COLLECT MY FAMILY, I hit the road for a series of Maritime gigs and a summer in Newfoundland, where I'd hook up with Dwayne. I'd strung together the gigs to ease travel costs and ensure that the Solo Me didn't stay dormant for too long. It was probably the first sign that while I still didn't love performing solo, I'd finally stopped hating it.

Before I went on stage for my first official Canadian solo appearance, at the Capital Bar in Fredericton, New Brunswick, when I overheard two patrons talk about what they expected of the evening's performance. One fellow said, "I don't expect much musically. I mean, he really doesn't have the greatest voice. The other guys, Martin and Tim, are better singers, especially Tielli. Maybe he'll tell some stories about China. Maybe he'll talk about the time he saved Gord Downie's life. That'd be cool."

I wasn't sure what to do. It's not often that a performer hears directly from his detractors, although it's happened to me before. Once, I was sitting in Morrison's diner in Kingston when I overheard a group of people talking about that evening's show at the Toucan, a local club. Someone said, "I'm thinking of going to the show, but I hate Dave Bidini." After a moment of deep shock and embarrassment, I walked over to the group, put my hands flat on the table, and told my critic, "I'm really not such a bad guy once you get to know me." The poor fellow's jaw dropped and his body folded like a melting soldier at the end of *Raiders of the Lost Ark*. Everyone else froze in disbelief. "*Hate* is pretty strong word," I continued. "Are you sure I'm worthy of it?" And then I walked away. Later, I received a letter from the fellow apologizing for what he'd said and saying that he'd ended up going to the show and was now a big fan.

The difference between what had happened in Kingston and what was happening in New Brunswick was that I knew that the Rheos were a good band, and that I was pretty good in the Rheos, but I had no idea whether the Solo Me was terrible or great – despite what Airbag and his friend had thought. Being in Canada playing to veteran fans who could compare the mightiest and most important Rheostatic moments to my performance made me doubt myself in a way I hadn't since our debut in 1980. And now, some dickhead in a rock club toilet was saying that he'd rather listen to Tielli or Vesely, and that maybe I'd reward his time by telling a few humorous stories, like I was Stuart Friggin' McLean.

After they left, I headed straight for the dressing room, which wasn't a room at all but a small basement crowded with shelves of pickle jars and tubs of ketchup and mustard. A lot of people imagine backstage as a place lively with wisecracking road managers and drummers wearing salami slices for aviator goggles, but you're more likely to find condiment tins, paper towel rolls, and boxes of beer glasses, especially in clubs where food is served. The Capital's dressing room wasn't the worst I'd seen – the Rheos had been forced to change in a backstage toilet at AJ's Hangar in Kingston – but the whining hydraulic beer lines pumping draft to the bar overhead made it impossible to do anything other than sit solemnly on an empty milk crate and write my set list on a napkin.

The Capital's dark wood tables and chairs and old photos of early settlements made it indistinguishable from a lot of bars. In fact, it was almost a duplicate of the club in Hämeenlinna, minus the West Ireland watercolours. Because the stage area was tucked into a corner near the front of the room, you could tell that the place had been designed as a beer den first, a live venue second. I shuffled over, plugged in my tuner and gestured to the soundperson that I was ready to begin. Almost immediately a whole pile of people filled the small space directly in front of me, transforming the room into a club that was as good as any other. It felt reassuring to have so many bodies so close to me after the distance of the audiences in China, so, despite what I'd heard in the bathroom, I played confidently and well and everyone had a good time, even my detractor, who told me later that he was mortified after seeing me leave the washroom behind him. I assured him that it was fine and that he was entitled to his opinion – had the gig gone horribly, I might not have been so gracious. Then he asked if I'd really saved Gord Downie's life. I told him that I had, and he wondered if I could retell the story. I said that it would cost him, so he grabbed some beers as I started into one of those mildly humorous stories for which I am, apparently, well regarded.

A group of fans gathered on the patio behind the club to hear the story, which goes: In 2001, while the Rheos were gigging at the Canmore Hotel, we were treated to a tray of dips and black and red corn chips in our dressing room. The chips had crisp star-points and a jagged texture, and I remarked to one of my bandmates that they looked beautiful, "almost deadly." After the gig, we poured the remaining chips into six-pack cases and then drove two hours to the Delta Calgary, where we put our luggage, instruments, and precious corn chips on a baggage cart, which we wheeled into the lobby. Gord Downie wandered out of a festival party and greeted us – both his solo band and the Rheos were performing at that year's Calgary folk festival – and then Martin asked politely if he'd like to try a corn chip.

We talked for a while. Then Gord fell silent. Then he turned blue. Then he pointed to his throat. I got behind him in one stride and squeezed. Because my knowledge of the Heimlich manoeuvre was foggy at best, I squeezed him like a giant tube of toothpaste to dislodge the deadly snack from Canada's most acclaimed rock 'n' roll windpipe. It did the trick; the killer chip jolted upward, and Gord's colour and voice returned. A few weeks later, a large cardboard box the size of a refrigerator was left on my front porch. Inside was a seat from old Maple Leaf Gardens. The Gordfather had sent it in appreciation of my impulsive squeeze.

The fans loved the story, but then they started asking other questions: What's up with the Rheos? Are you guys really breaking up? Do you hate each other? Is this really the end? For a moment I pined for the wilds of Jyväskylä, where the Rheos hadn't mattered, and in the end, I dodged the truth and never gave them the straight answer they deserved. I told them that maybe our breakup would turn out to be nothing more than a glorified hiatus, and that somewhere down the line we would get back together and play for the sake of playing, without getting hurt by the emotional weight that falls on every artistic endeavour. I disappointed myself for not being honest.

Driving back to the motel, I remembered a story told to me by my friend Johnny Sinclair, who plays bass in the Toronto pop group Universal Honey. In Hoboken, New Jersey, after they opened for Sweet 75, the band formed by bassist Krist Novoselic after the demise of Nirvana, Johnny was hauling his gear out of the club when Krist walked past. Putting down his amp, Johnny told him, "Hey, man, I just wanted to say good luck." Krist turned on his heels, and said, "What do you mean?"

"I just mean, you know, good luck."

Krist looked at him suspiciously, then walked away.

The death of every band is fraught with varying degrees of pain and sadness, but it's hard to imagine what it must have been like for Nirvana's bassist, especially in light of the smooth and successful post-Nirvana emergence of drummer Dave Grohl's solo band, the Foo Fighters. Novoselic had been kicked so far into orbit after Kurt Cobain's suicide that Johnny's best wishes sounded cursed and complicated. After Sweet 75 failed to find an audience, Novoselic formed Eyes Adrift with the Meat Puppets' Curt Kirkwood, but in August 2003, he announced on the group's website, "I can't deal. I can't read the magazines, listen to the radio or watch music television without feeling like I've just come from outer space. I just don't get it and I probably never did. People walk up to me and ask me about Sweet 69 or Sweet 76 or whatever tortured recollection of that musical triumph they can muster. My lot in life is that every band I've ever been in just falls apart."

When I got back to the motel, Janet was awake and sitting up in bed. She'd stirred around 3:00 a.m. after hearing a voice outside the room, saying, "C'mon, Dave. C'mon, buddy. All right, buddy, you'll be okay. All you have to do is stand up." She'd thought that I was so drunk and disconsolate that the promoter had driven me home. But it wasn't me who'd passed out in the cab outside; it was another Dave, an electrician from Truro, who was living with his coworkers in the room above us. Dave, it turned out, had got himself hammered with the money he'd earned from installing fuel pumps in a gas station up the road. He probably had a better reason to get drunk than I did. I might have lost my band, but at least it didn't mean that I'd have to spend the rest of my days digging the cold Maritime earth. But then again, I didn't know where it would lead.

We drove east to Sydney, Cape Breton, where we boarded the morning ferry for Port aux Basques, Newfoundland, on the southwestern tip of the island. When we arrived six hours later, the port was frosted with fog and it was spitting rain, as it is pretty much every day. We'd wandered into a Lemony Snicket dreadscape of dark fields shrouded in fog and spiky rocks that promised angry Celtic ogres and grotesque mammals that time had forgotten. But as we moved north along the Trans-Canada Highway – our Grand Marquis packed to the roof with children's games and books, guitars, and bags of Maritime-related travel dreck – the fog thinned and pretty soon the sun was glossing the tips of the mountains.

Western Newfoundland is one of the few places where Canadian travellers feel they've been dropped into a completely different cultural and geographic landscape. Unlike eastern Newfoundland – with its familiar fishing coves and gumboot fiddlers, craggy shoreline and weather-scratched churches – the island's unpopulated west coast has looked the same since early settlers first scaled the island's blunt edge. Perhaps because of this the land has an aura of mystery. As we drove past furry, green mountains, fields of spilled rock, and crooked-armed trees dotted with bald eagles along the island's main highway, it was all I could do not to feverishly preach the virtues of a country where you can put most of the land at your back and still be engulfed by it. Instead, I drove in silence, which was as good a tribute as any.

Heading north toward South Branch – Dwayne's hometown, just two hours from Port aux Basques – we drove a stretch of the TCH (which, of course, we renamed the THC) known as Wreck

House, where gale-force winds were reputed to have thrown tractor trailers off the highway like brontosauri hoofed by the force of God's bootheel. My hands gripped the wheel tighter than a strongman bending a tire iron, but the wind was unusually calm, which only served as a reminder that in Newfoundland myth and reality are often equal parts of the same fuzzy truth. Before coming here, we'd heard lots of stories – most of them about the weather – from people who'd lived on, or visited, the Rock. One fellow, a Toronto artist named Mike Hansen, who summered in a saltbox cottage in Fermeuse, on the island's south shore, suggested that we pack winter clothes for our visit, telling us that a friend of his spent every July dressed in a parka sitting in front of a roaring fire because of the fog that clung to the shore-line. He also told us that in NewfieSpeak, steak meant bologna, a chainsaw was called a Newfie steak-knife, and you couldn't wander twenty feet in any direction in most towns before running into ten accordionists, twenty fiddlers, and an army of acoustic guitar players and voices singing deep into the night.

After Wreck House, we turned onto a small winding road and, a few minutes later, were in South Branch, a town (though calling South Branch a town is a bit hyperbolic) nestled between two mountain ranges, the Long Range and the Anguille. The demise of the CN railyard – the result of Tory downsizing in the 1980s – meant that there were very few jobs in town, short of occasional salmon fishing and forestry work. Most young people had left to work in Sydney, Halifax, Toronto, or Fort McMurray. St. John's – the island's eastern civic jewel – boasted a growing population and housing boom, but South Branch, like a lot of west coast communities, seemed to be shrivelling. The Goliathian mountains, the emptiness of the land, and the mature age of the townsfolk left me with the initial impression that South Branch was a speck soon to be swept off the map.

But despite its size and relative economic insignificance – or maybe because of it – the South Branch community was strong, and, on most weekends, the community hall thrummed with music. It had become even busier after the area's main dancehall – the Chignik, which once hosted Stompin' Tom – was destroyed by fire. Not that its destruction had stopped the South Branchers from partying at the Chignik. Before embarking on a recent pub crawl by bus to other West Coast watering holes, the townspeople had gathered on the burnt front steps, which are all that remains of the dance hall, and toasted the memory of a place where their forebears had brought life to the quiet emptiness of the region.

Dwayne's mom, Genita, one of South Branch's social convenors, programmed our short visit there. On our first full day in town, she marched us deep into the woods to a glorious clearing near a mountain stream; later, she took us to Winter's Pool, an idyllic swimming hole with a gilded bottom and pure water. I ended up spending a lot of time at Winter's Pool, mostly on purpose, but sometimes not. One of things I'd told myself before coming to the Rock was that I wouldn't fall prey to the trap of getting Screeched In or having to Kiss the Cod or whatever other colourful ceremony Newfoundlanders have invented to punish visiting mainlanders with great quantities of potent liquor. Because I'd drunk liquid bacon in Joensuu, I considered myself well prepared to resist any South Branch attempt to lure me into its boozy grip. So, when Dwayne announced on our first evening in South Branch that he was going on a beer-and-liquor run, I suggested that he stick to the suds, and because he'd become part of my immediate family, having recently become affianced to Janet's sister Melanie, he had to heed my request.

Dwayne returned from his trip with eighteen bottles of India beer, an unthreatening amount. The label showed a small black dog wagging its tongue, so I assumed the beer was just as benign. Had the bottle been stamped with the image of a great bearded ruffian waving an axe and wobbling atop a mountain, I might've paused before cracking my first ale, but I drank two bottles, then three. After Janet and Melanie headed to bed, Dwayne and I made for the Grand Marquis, where I rolled hash joints on the children's toy tray. We finished the last of our beer while listening to a beatup cassette of the Beatles' uproarious Christmas 45. An ocean of stars stretched above us. It was a perfect night in South Branch.

Then I had to walk five steps from the car to the house where we were staying, and I showed my appreciation to Dwayne's Uncle Brian and Aunt Jessie for lending us their beautiful home by yakking all over their bedroom floor. The next day, Dwayne told me that he'd bought the beer with the little dog on it even though he knew that not even the bravest Newfoundlander ever went near the stuff. Genita advised me that a swim in Winter's Pool would soften my hangover better than anything else. I took her advice and survived to continue the tour.

After a short trip up the coast to Woody Point – a fishing enclave in Gros Morne Provincial Park, where I performed a set in an old, haunted Orangeman's Hall – I returned to South Branch for one of the summer's weekend socials at the community hall. I didn't get there till 8:00 p.m., narrowly missing a dinner of salt beef, cabbage, carrots, turnip, dumplings, and pease pudding – Dwayne, who'd been raised on this island staple, suggested that I was lucky to have avoided it – but because Newfoundland crowds typically gather late, the music wasn't expected to start until well after 10:00 p.m.

I lingered on the terrace outside the hall and watched a procession of dark clouds ride the peaks of the Long Range mountains. One of Dwayne's uncles brought me a Labatt Blue before apologizing – and feigning deep regret – that they were out of bottles of India. I acted disappointed and raised my bottle as a tall, weedy gentleman in his sixties named Ben Brake joined me on the terrace. Ben was a veteran musician who'd played in bands around St. John's in the 1970s. He claimed he'd discovered how to play four sets seven nights a week, drink copiously, and hold down a steady day job. "At the show, I could drink eight or ten beers easy," he said. "But sometimes it would catch up to me. I worked during the days too, and shows back then wouldn't finish until midnight or one o'clock. As you can imagine, this wore me out pretty good, so I learned how to sleep while I played. I could nap right there in the middle of whatever song we were doing, and when I'd wake up, I'd be right on the money. All I needed was two or three of these little naps, and I'd be fine."

I asked Ben if he'd seen a big change in music throughout Newfoundland, and he said that "a lot of it has come down to using MIDI files"; the basic tracks of a song preprogrammed on a computer. "A lot of guys don't have to worry about getting a band together any more. You just carry around your keyboards and MIDI files and you've got your show." When I told him that I found the notion of computers replacing musicians depressing, Ben argued, "It's still good music. I write my own MIDI files, and I'll tell you, they're good files."

To avoid an argument, I asked Ben if he'd introduce me to some of the evening's performers. He brought me inside the hall and beckoned over a local singer named Billy Walsh, who promptly asked if I'd join him for his set.

Long tables ran the length of the hall, and its walls were filled with plaques honouring the town's darts champions and the shuttered dart boards upon which these titles had been won. The stage sat low at the far end of the room, as if in retreat. A small Canadian flag was taped on the wall behind it and the light from a single blue bulb painted the scene. Forty or fifty older people were sitting around the tables quietly murmuring to one another, which made me wonder whether quiet conversation was yet another western Newfoundland characteristic; perhaps because it had been settled by the Scots, its people possessed a certain propriety and reserve. Any travellers wanting yargling pirates breaking rum bottles over their heads would have to go to the east.

I joined Billy Walsh when he took to the stage just after ten, sitting beside him in a bridge-table chair with my guitar across my lap. I'd hoped that rumours of my struggles with the infamous dog beer had established me as a brave and hearty Ontarian, and that the audience would shower me with the sympathetic applause before I'd strummed my first chord. Instead, when Walsh stepped to the mic and looked down at me, the crowd's murmur turned to deep grumble. Walsh drew a long breath, arched his eyebrows worryingly, and introduced me, but it quickly became apparent that he'd forgotten my name. "We've got a fellow over here, folks. A good fellow. Yes! A guitarist! From Toronto! Yes! Please give a warm South Branch welcome to this here fellow! From Toronto!" The crowd stopped grumbling and offered yours truly some muted applause, before hardening into a cold, unyielding silence as Billy Walsh started his first song.

When I told Dwayne the next day that I'd played with Billy Walsh, he was surprised I'd survived the ordeal, not because of any musical mishap, but because the previous week, Walsh had fired his band, all of whom were from South Branch. Walsh had probably intended to extend the hand of musical diplomacy by inviting me to jam, but it was also true that nobody else in South Branch would play with him.

We might've won over the crowd had I played like Mick

Ronson to Billy's David Bowie, but, as we've seen, it's not often that two musicians can be thrown together and gel. It didn't help matters that Billy's repertoire leaned toward modern, proto-country. I confess to disliking a handful of musical genres but I consider new country to be one of the most bone-chilling musical confections since Mungo Jerry. The recent corporate scourge of country music has forever disfigured what was once one of America's noble musical inventions. An art form born from six family musicians gathered around a single microphone singing a fifty-year-old song about cornfields and tornadoes taught to them by their grandpappy is now the domain of telegenic cowboy bands invented at marketing meetings who perform songs pregnant with bum-slapping sexual innuendo and the worst elements of hip hop and grunge light. The nadir of this – "Honky Tonk Badonkadonk," an elegy for the cultural apocalypse performed by Trace Adkins – is what happens when musicians take advice from marketers, some of whom apparently decided, in the mid-1990s, that what American music needed to get back on track was a deadeyed army of goateed bumpkins in tight jeans and reversed baseball caps playing red, white, and blue fiddles to funk grooves written by guys named Topal.

Billy started with a song called "Back When," which was popularized by the creaseless Nashville hunk Tim McGraw. Like a lot of new country, it preys on America's rose-tinted nostalgia for a time of "family" values and black-and-white wars, larding its jingoistic retro-drive with phrases like "peanuts in a bottle," "a fried bologna sandwich with mayo and tomato," and corn-pone puns – "back when a hoe was a hoe" and "Coke was a coke." Not that I hold Billy Walsh solely responsible for this musical travesty, but if he'd chosen to play "Guns of Brixton" or "Bastards of Young," I might have done more than just dutifully follow the chords and get through it as quickly as possible.

After our set, it became clear that Billy had been asked to play first so that no one would have to pause later to give him the cold shoulder. As soon as we left the stage, we were replaced by an accordionist named Neil MacCarthur and four or five other players – a bassist, a few guitarists, a fiddler – whose music brought the room to life. During the third tune, someone crept to the stage and jammed a pair of pale-blue underpants on Neil's head, and soon the dance floor was filled with couples waltzing to "The Wild Rover." I thought this might have been part of an old South Branch ritual, but when I tried to get confirmation from another of Dwayne uncles – Uncle Hector, I think – he chose, instead, to tell me which person was, or wasn't, a good fighter, saying, "Oh, that one over there could take a good punch before he had his triple bypass last year," and "In the old days, you'd have to knock this one unconsciousness before he'd stop swinging, but he had a stroke and then he really slowed down." He finished his treatise by gesturing toward the small, slump-shouldered man playing the accordion with the bloomies on his head. "Before Neil's heart attack, he was a terrible, mean fighter. You'd give him a couple of drinks and, boy, he'd go to town on ya."

Neil's band gave way to an entirely white-haired group called the Joe James Crowd ("We couldn't come up with a better name," Joe told me later), who were introduced as being from Winter's Pool, which immediately endeared them to me. None of the musicians were under fifty, and their songs were mostly fatalistic – "All Good Things Are Passing On," "It's Time for Us to Leave," and "Leave Her, Johnny." After Joe's set, a group from Port aux Basques took the stage, and after that, Neil and his band returned for a second set. Considering the size of South Branch, and its greying population, it was a remarkable ratio of musical activity to people. It supported the notion that, in

Canada's poorest and emptiest province, music is a beacon of life, particularly in disappearing towns such as South Branch.

After Neil's group played, it was time for me to do my thing. Much of my evening had been spent listening to Uncle Hector tell stories about South Branch, and I wouldn't have minded not opening my guitar case at all. I tried to recruit some of the evening's players to join me, but they all demurred. The musicians treated me as if I were David Clayton Thomas blowing in from the big city, expressing almost to a man that it would be wrong for an amateur island player to get in the way of my "professional" set. But because I was left to play solo, the liveliness of the evening was temporarily dimmed. Even though I was blessed with a crowd that, like the one in Hämeenlinna, respectfully hung on my every word, no couples waltzed during "This Song Ain't Any Good," beer sales flattened through "The Land Is Wild," and the prankster's underwear crown was stuffed back into his pocket as I ploughed my way through six or seven other tunes. All of Dwayne's uncles – and few of his aunts – came over and slapped me on the back, but their attention was diverted once the next act – local singer Terry Harvey – rigged his hulking MIDI keyboard into the small PA, strapped on his acoustic guitar, and clicked a button on his keyboard that triggered an electronic arrangement of "Bad Moon Rising," which had the crowd dancing long after I wandered into the night.

Our journey across Newfoundland to St. John's was as breathtaking as it was wet. Rain fell hard from the sky before being chammied by the sun, leaving radiant green hills, shimmering lakes, and deep, smoky valleys to fill the scene: the *Land of the Lost* Tablelands at Gros Morne; the looping, tree-thick Codroy Valley; the nearly tropical overgrowth of the hills around Green

Bay; and the jagged coast of the Bonavista Peninsula, with slouched fishing villages and monolithic rock outcroppings fraying the surf. When we weren't being pelted by rain on our drive, our faces were pressed against the windows, absorbing the staggering and diverse beauty of a province that, because of its coordinates in the middle of the ocean, remains largely ignored by the rest of Canada. No measure of tourist bumper stickers or pamphlet prose can do justice to the island's dizzying power. It would require an epic poem or triple-gatefold concept album, which I made a note to start composing as we wheeled south around the Irish Loop, then on to St. John's, and finally to Foxtrap, the home of my friend, Haddon Strong, and his wife, Karen.

Tim Mech – the Rheos' former guitar technician – had introduced me to Haddon after meeting him in an airplane on a runway at Toronto Pearson International Airport. Because Haddon uses phrases such as "Yes, me son" and "Oh, I'd say that's true, boy" the way you and I use "uh" and "duh," Tim heard him clearly over the grumbling of the taxiing aircraft as he opined to his seatmate that, while he'd had a good time in Toronto, he'd wished he'd seen his favourite band, the Rheostatics, play. Tim traced the voice to a tall, suspendered gentleman in thick glasses with a scrabbly grey-white beard and introduced himself. A few weeks later, Haddon wrote me a letter about meeting Tim, and that's how we became friends. When I told him about our plan to visit South Branch, he insisted that we cross the island to play a house party in Foxtrap.

The evening before Haddon's shindig, I was booked to play at the Ship Inn in downtown St. John's. Along with the Hotel Jokela, the Chinese Pilot, and the No-Name, the Ship is one of the world's great taverns. Pocketed against a stairway that ascends the hill from the harbour, the Ship's atmosphere evokes men and women in wool sweaters and gumboots smoking pipes, eating chowder, and singing shanties. Being a people's tavern, however, it's exclusive to no one, and its proximity to the sea gives it the distinction of being the last great club before Europe. This connection to the far side of the ocean works the other way too. In the mid-1960s, clubs in downtown St. John's were the first places in North America where Merseybeat and other British and European records were heard, brought west to Canada by sailors whose vessels docked in the harbour.

Before the show, I warmed up in the Ship's kitchen, which had closed a few hours before my set. In between exercises in howling, I peered between the kitchen's shutters to see if any bodies had wandered into the club. With the exception of Janet and the Strongs, the Ship remained empty for the better part of the evening, the result of a nearby performance by Newfoundland heroes Buddy Wasisname and the Other Fellers. After a while, I snuck out of the kitchen to Duckworth Street, where, just as I had done as a nervous and bewildered seventeen-year-old playing the Edge for the first time in 1980, I sized up pedestrians approaching the Ship's laneway – too elderly, too hip, on holidays, possibly drunk and staggering home, doofus in a Michael Bublé tour T-shirt, and so on – and was disappointed when they walked past. I suppose there was something charming about a CanRock warhorse suffering pre-gig anxiety, but I grew even more anxious when people who looked like they might attend my show – they were preposterously beautiful and radiated intellect, of course – kept on walking. Even more discouraged, I retreated to the club.

The Ship's promoter, Tony Murray, found me in the kitchen looking distressed and tried to rally my spirits, telling me to wait until about eleven thirty before hitting the stage. He said that St. John's crowds were notoriously late-arriving and that people would be coming over to the club after Buddy's show. At around eleven fifteen, I chanced a look into the main room and, to my delight, found the Ship to be not completely empty, which seemed good enough to start.

The show, and the crowd, ended up being perfectly decent. The solo musician's life is one of small triumphs, and "decent" is sometimes good enough when you are fighting through the musical ranks on your lonesome. In a rock 'n' roll band, it's hard to be satisfied with your performance until you've scaled the heights of sonic beauty, then brought it down with your own fists. But solo shows can be buoyed simply by the enthusiasm of a small voice in a quiet crowd, a difficult song delivered with as much musicality as emotional intensity, and a warm PA or monitor mix that makes you sound as if your strumming hand is tied to God's gentle puppet strings. Successful solo gigs are less of a grand conquest and more like an able journey across a tightrope, with both player and audience precariously balanced. My gig at the Ship was like that, and I was relieved. Going a long way around the world and tanking was one thing. Going a long way in your country to suck was another.

On the evening of Haddon's party, a huge pot of chowder sat bubbling on the stove, which Karen told me was for consumption only after I'd dented the beer supply and reeled off the better part of my repertoire. Haddon had set up speakers on his back-yard deck and wheeled a tiny old trailer behind the house, which would harbour those guests for whom Haddon's living room wasn't large enough. The Strong's teenaged son, Mark, set up the PA and helped arrange the pre-show soundtrack: a snippet of an Edmonton versus St. Louis game, which the Oilers tied with last-minute heroics. As evening approached, the Strongs'

friends showed up with tickets that Haddon had designed and printed. One by one, they took me aside and said, "For Haddon, this is his Woodstock" and "We're all Rheostatics fans because he wouldn't stop playing your music until we admitted that we liked it." A few minutes after ten o'clock, I squeezed into the living room, stepped to the microphone, and started playing.

Before coming east, I was hoping that I'd experience something similar to the events of one day in the summer of 1993, during the Rheos' first performance in the Maritimes. On the evening of our gig, at Club Flamingo in Halifax, we were invited by our lawyer, Chip Sutherland, to his cottage nestled in St. Margaret's Bay. We bought a dozen lobsters and ate them while listening to Stan Rogers. On the van ride back into the city in the dimming blue light of the day, we listened to "Carefree Highway" by Gordon Lightfoot, and I was struck by how the road could be beautiful and comforting too, delivering us, as it did, into the heart of Halifax.

Our gig at the Flamingo was unlike any other. Every song we played was roiling and huge, sweet and strong, smart and tender. At one point, we heard the cheering inside the club echoed by a chorus of voices outside, and I stopped the band to trace its source. There were underaged kids sitting in the stairwell behind the club, listening to the show through the doors. We carried on an animated conversation with them, then had them count in the next song – "Rain, Rain, Rain" – with handclaps. It was a joyous moment, and from then on, I never again felt inhibited talking to a crowd. Halifax helped me secure my voice and confidence as a Rheostatic and as a performer. I hoped St. John's would do the same for the Solo Me.

At Haddon's, I was joined by three nomadic musicians I'd met the previous night at the Ship: a guitar player from Toronto named Tariq, his drummer friend, Keith, and their bassist,

Grant. The four of us had never played together before, but I'd invited them to the party, figuring that I could use some help covering what promised to be an epic evening. The communal spirit of Newfoundland music made performing with a bunch of strangers in someone's living room seem just about right.

Playing whatever song came into my head – every one of them untried by my new bandmates – the living-room dance floor filled with twisting Newfoundlanders, most of them middle-aged, perhaps older. Their glasses of beer and whisky swished in their hands as they spun on the small dance area in front of the stage. At one point, after we'd got three-quarters of the way through "Folsom Prison Blues," only to forget the fourth verse, Janet walked to the microphone, pulled it down to her height, and finished the song. The crowd cheered and raised their glasses. Later, we moved the party – and the concert – inside Haddon's trailer, which was filled with people smoking and shouting in an accent so thick that everything sounded like an exhortation to play more. At one point, Grant lowered his double bass into the trailer and Keith set up his kick and snare inside, making us the very image of a movable rock 'n' roll feast. I imagined the trailer tipping back and forth on its haunches as we all got drunker, louder, and happier. There was something about the combination of great sloppy playing, off-key singing, the scent of chowder and cigarette smoke, and the taste of the salt sea air drifting in from the bay that made me feel as unconcerned and relaxed about my music as I'd ever been. It was my Flamingo moment all over again.

The next morning, we peeled ourselves off the beds, couches, carpets, trailer benches, and wherever else we'd collapsed on after the last chord had been strummed. I was sitting bleary-eyed on the patio when Haddon appeared with a cup of coffee for me and sat down in the lawnchair next to mine. Knowing that it would be best if he learned it first-hand, I told him that the Rheos were probably going to break up. Keeping with the spirit of the weekend – and the spirit of Newfoundlanders altogether – Haddon sighed and said, "Well, if you don't break up, then you can't have a reunion, right?"

ACCRA

I TRAVELLED ALONE TO AFRICA. IT SEEMED TIME THAT I got to the essence of this lonesome troubadour business and leave my bandmates and family behind for a genuine leap into the solo artist's life. Going to Africa hadn't been at the top of my list of musical destinations, but after a year of playing, I felt confident enough to go somewhere truly different, and difficult.

A lot of noted musicians, such as the Grateful Dead's Mickey Hart and Rush's Neil Peart – two drummers who've written books about Africa – have been drawn to the continent for its root-of-all-music-and-culture allure, searching for the purity of whatever heartbeat begat every genre of popular music known to humanity (though only the Swiss could have given us lite jazz). But as a new wave kid, I was oblivious to the genesis of music. My sense of pop history reached only as far back as the Kinks, the Who, the Beatles, and other British bands that played the sounds I loved best. That Pete Townshend had invented the guitar wind-mill, Ringo Starr, the pop drum fill, and Dave Davies, the fuzz tone, was good enough for me. Besides, in the 1980s, when African music was becoming better known and more widely toured in the West – largely thanks to pop giants Peter Gabriel, Paul Simon, and David Byrne – it no longer seemed mysterious as

224

it was when Ginger Baker brought his drum kit to Nigeria in 1970 to play with Fela Kuti, or when Paul McCartney flummoxed the pop world by announcing that he would record *Band on the Run* in a studio in Lagos.

Still, Africa is so big, and Africans so preposterously musical, that not even Angelina Jolie and Madonna's paparazzi trail can reveal all of its micro-cultures. And because a lot of Africa is still not navigable – it lacks a continental railway, so few Africans are able to visit even their neighbouring countries – many of these micro-cultures have proved hermetic to the rest of the world, despite the developed world's notion of a contemporary musical global village.

I first explored the idea of going to Africa with War Child Canada, an organization that tries to bring balm to the war-torn lives of children, principally through music. A few years ago, War Child sent the suburban punk band Sum 41 to the Congo, where they were held captive in their hotel, while fighting raged on either side of them. It took some diplomatic brinkmanship to get them out safely. From a distance, this seemed like a wonderfully bookworthy adventure as I was not actually plunked into the middle of it (the Rascalz and Raine Maida from Our Lady Peace had gone with War Child to Africa too). Two of War Child's directors – Samantha Nutt and Anne Game – told me about their programs in Uganda, the Congo, and southern Sudan, but they said that if the power of music and the resuscitation of culture in the face of extreme hardship were what interested me, two projects – the Liberian Dance Troupe, located in the Buduburam (Boo-doo-boo-rom) Refugee Camp outside Accra, Ghana, and the Artists United for Children and Youth Development (AUCAYD) music program in Freetown, Sierra Leone – would provide endless illumination. The more I learned about the Africans involved in these projects, the more I realized that not including Africa in my *Around the World* project would be irresponsible and probably more than a little negligent.

War Child planned to send a few of its staff to West Africa to evaluate these programs, and told me told that I could go along – its office in Toronto would facilitate my trip. This sounded good to me, not only because I'd have company in Africa, but because, after telling a handful of friends where I was going, my imagination had become polluted with thoughts of disease-fuelled bugs, stomach-wrenching sicknesses, and rebel junkie insurgents whom one friend insisted were "walking around in nightdresses and slippers carrying Kalashnikovs." Someone else told me, "Watch out for bacteria. Use hand sanitizer constantly and keep your hands to yourself, which, on second thought, is pretty next to impossible, since Africans are very physical." It wasn't long before my paranoia produced visions of man-eating fish, baby-stealing jungle birds, and impoverished scoundrels who fed on touring white rhythm guitarists. I was gripped with the notion that this was a trip from which I might not return, which was as good a reason for going as any.

War Child tried to allay my fears, but they only made them worse. Naomi Johnson, War Child's director of the Africa program, said that she'd meet me at my second destination, Freetown, Sierra Leone. She also said that while Freetown had the world's poorest urban economy, ran mostly on generators, and was only a decade removed from one of Africa's most horrendous civil wars, it also had beautiful beaches and good beer, which I thought would be fine were I spending my time drinking and tanning instead of following young hip-hoppers around town, which was the plan. I wasn't any more encouraged, either, when the travel agent who was booking my plane ticket, a fellow named Abraham, asked if I'd ever been to Africa. When I told him that I hadn't, he laughed nervously as he handed me my itinerary. I asked him if there was anything that I needed to know before I left, but he answered a phone call, gestured for me to see the clerk at the front of the agency, and never answered the question.

Before leaving Toronto on my KLM flight to Amsterdam – then another, to Accra, in Ghana, West Africa – the only thing that made me feel confident about the trip was my guitar case, which no longer looked like it had been pulled out of a factory show-room. It was in perfectly terrible shape, its top bowed and warped, its handle barely hanging from the rivets. Like Al's case, it was now also mummified in duct tape, which had feathered and collected gobs of worldly gunk on its underside, and one punt from a surly baggage handler could send it – and the guitar – into a flurry of splinters. For me, it was proof that, in a small way, I'd achieved something as a wandering, road-beaten tune-smith. I thought that, if I showed up in Ghana with a wrecked guitar crate, I might fit in better with local musicians than if I arrived with an intact, velvet-lined roadcase.

When I arrived in Accra, I stood at the baggage carousel at the Kotoka International Airport wondering whether my guitar had made it. Truthfully, I was just as concerned that my tubes of sunblock and cans of DEET spray had made it too, imagining that a cloud of insatiable mosquitoes was waiting outside the building to prey on me. I had been so preoccupied with all of this that I had barely noticed the enormous, star-specked sky above me as I'd walked across the tarmac from the plane to the termi-nal, or the great wooden storks and large black star – Ghana's emblem – that hung in the arrivals corridor of the dark, shop-worn airport.

After happily gathering my intact luggage, I found War Child's Jen Roynon and our driver, Kofi, waiting for me outside behind a set of barricades meant to slow the press of taxi drivers hustling for business. The air was hot and wet – Accra is an equatorial city pressed against the edge of the Atlantic Ocean – and our late-evening drive to the hotel readied me for fourteen consecutive days of *swass*, as Jen called it, referring to one's posterior, which in the sticky heat of Africa is almost always rude and slippery with sweat. Our hotel – the Hillview, where no hill was in sight – was small and friendly and located in a section of town called Dworzulu, a name that always reminded me which country I was visiting. At first, the room at the Hillview did nothing to ease my fear of bugs or guns or bacteria, for it was clearly penetrable by dangerous flying things and skulking thugs. The drapes barely covered my two windows – both of which looked out onto a darkened hallway – and a cluster of wiggling red spots – ants, not maggots – was gathered around a bit of hardened goop atop the desk. For a moment, I sat on my bed, which sloped like a four-legged animal bending a knee, and tried to gather my wits about where I was and what the next two weeks would bring. Then Jen tapped on my door and suggested that we hit the town. Dragging our *swass*es out of the Hillview – which, in the end, proved safe and clean and secure – we hailed a taxi and headed through the African night, my mind good and twisted after thirteen hours of travel.

The driver brought us to the Osu, Accra's famous strip of nightclubs and restaurants. We ended up at Frankie's, a twin-level restaurant that was, apparently, quite famous, though I wondered whether its reputation had been fostered by homesick Westerners, for its menu featured colour-saturated Polaroids of hot dogs and double cheeseburgers and not a single mention of palm wine or grass-cutter, a large rodentlike creature favoured by locals. There was also a popcorn maker humming on Frankie's first-floor terrace and a few Accrans sitting on stools eating ice cream above the street.

After dinner, we went to a club that Jen had heard about, a place called the Biwell, or, alternately, Bywell's, or the Bywel, for it was spelled every conceivable way on signs posted around the venue. The club was roofless except for a small canopy in the corner, and it felt good to be sitting outside listening to music in the evening's heat. Because it was Thursday night, the Biwell was loud and busy with Ghanaians seizing the opportunity to enjoy live music on the only night offered by the club. The band was called the Alpha Waves, which I learned after studying an enormous yellow bedsheet with black letters hanging beside the stage. They were, ostensibly, a highlife outfit – highlife being Ghana's musical gift to the world – but they took more right turns than the Bush administration. One minute they'd play an eight-minute highlife standard with lots of melodic shouting and the obligatory trumpet solo, the next they'd play a slow North American standard – "What a Wonderful World" or "Bésame Mucho." After a while, I began to suspect that these slower numbers were an attempt to curry favour with the one-fifth white crowd, whom Jen fingered as fellow non-governmental organization (NGO) workers. The lone exception was a pale, walrus-shaped, middle-aged fellow who spent most of the night entwined in the arms of two concubines wearing purple hot pants. When he wasn't slow dancing with them, he was being pawed over by his gold-braided rentals while sitting in a large wicker chair. In many ways, he made every other white person in attendance look bad, but in some ways, his behaviour flattered us all. Before coming here, I was concerned that I'd stand out as a white man in Africa, but next to the walrus, I looked like Cedric the Entertainer.

The crowd sat simmering in the heat at small tables and benches gathered closely together. Jen and I ordered two quart-sized beers to toast my arrival, and after easily killing those, I headed to the bar for more. The bar was covered in a thatch awning, and behind it were hand-painted wooden signs advertising a variety of local businesses: Ghana Fire Service, Mariners at Large, Rumours Casino, and the Pepper Steak Chop House. At the bar, two Accran women in silk partywear asked me, "So, you are alone here?" perhaps taking me for one of the walrus's younger cousins. I told her that I wasn't, then headed back to our table where a similarly dressed woman – or undressed, considering the low cut of her blouse – sat down at my elbow and argued loudly into her cellphone with her boyfriend. She hung up, answered another riotous call from him, hung up again, then continued her argument with the fellow in person when he showed up a few minutes later.

The scene was all very lively and excellent. The branches of a large jacaranda tree rooted in the middle of the club swayed with the breeze as the Alpha Band invited audience members and local hangers-on to join their set. One elderly fellow, who was announced only as La La La, slowly made his way to the stage. La La La – who later refuted his nickname, telling me that I should call him Nat – wore a black fedora, a black dress shirt with gold lightning bolts, and sunglasses, and moved with the urgency of a highway abutment. When we'd first spotted him ambling around the club, Jen said, "Hey, Dave there goes your double." After reminding her that I was only forty-two, and that La La La looked older than the *Farmers' Almanac*, I had to admit that the singer and I shared a certain stylistic affinity, crowned, as he was, with the type of haberdashery near to my heart.

La La La faced the band, counted in the tune with four bony fingers lowered successively, then sang "My Way." Hearing this old Ghanaian gentleman croak his way through the Frank Sinatra chestnut – by way of Paul Anka – in the heart of West Africa was both beautiful and strange. Not only did La La La spirit his way through the song without collapsing, but he proved to be the consummate showman, wandering into the audience to sing for those very Accran beauties – and a crowd of others – who'd tried to tease me out of fidelity within my few first hours on the continent. When I asked around about La La La's musical history, one fellow told me, "If you are having a party, La La La will be there to sing. If you are having a cookout, he will be there to sing. If you are standing around on the corner of your street with your friends talking football, he will sing too. Wherever there is any gathering, there will be La La La. He sings, and we love him for it. But he has pneumonia, you know, and he is not well."

Near the end of the song, La La La sauntered back to the stage and faced the band, all of whom were grinning. For the tune's rousing coda, he turned to the crowd and sang, "I did it myyyyyyy wayyyy," tipping his chin, closing his eyes, and shaking his head back and forth. A great cheer rose as the band played him out. When the song ended, La La La flashed a smile, righted his sunglasses, then handed the microphone to the person sitting closest to him. A few people stood and extended their hands, but he shuffled past them out of the club, headed, I imagined, to a cookout or anniversary party to sustain his musical prowl.

The following morning, I awoke to the sounds of the Hillview's staff shouting at one another in one of Ghana's two native languages – Ga – and the deep-throated warble of what sounded like a very large bird. At breakfast, I drank Nescafé and watched a 1980s skateboard movie starring Randy Quaid. Striding out of the hotel with my guitar to meet Jen and Kofi, I was slowed by the steady push of the morning's heat for a few minutes before finding comfort in the cool backseat of the car, which lasted only until the car started moving. Because it was any day other than Sunday, navigating across Accra to the Buduburam Refugee Camp – located about two hours on the other side of town – meant an automotive crawl slowed by malfunctioning stop lights, fuel-less gas bars, herds of goats, and random power outages.

Still, leaving Accra would prove to be as exciting as arriving there. The city's main motorway was a fine and well-maintained asphalt strip, but what surrounded it was pure madness. The road snaked through an endless curbside marketplace splashed with the teeming sound and colour and dirt and diesel of hundreds of merchants hustling the motorway's wheeled patrons. The edges of the pavement were lined with men and women of all ages – some in florid traditional gowns; some in bright Muslim robes; and some, like one young man, in a Jonathan Richman and the Modern Lovers T-shirt – selling every kind of dry good, and some wet goods too. These were invariably carried high on their heads beneath a ring of cloth used to steady baskets, barrels, trays, and jerry cans containing everything from tiger nuts to Michael Essien keychains to small green mangoes stacked to within an inch of collapse. One man was carrying seven patio chairs on his head. Some sections of the motorway featured a sinuous snack procession: plantain chips, tins of Milo, peeled green oranges, pineapple slices in bags, half-moon coconut shards, and plastic pyramids of water and synthetic-tasting juice drinks that everyone sucked to staunch the fiery heat of the day. This was followed by a conga line of young men selling Mentos packs from plastic trays held at their waist. Other sections of the motorway offered household products piled on high – wooden spoons, drainage trays, toilet paper rolls, whisks – and, farther down the road, a floating parade of grilled mud-fish, yams, potato leaves, cassava, dandelion greens, and hunks of chicken and goat. It was thus possible for the motorist to purchase lunch while heading out of town, then dinner upon his return, because it took no less than four hours to navigate the world's longest natural drivethrough.

Beyond the front line of commerce was more action: wide, sloping red-dirt boulevards on both sides of the road were crammed with businesses housed in cinder-block shops, clapboard closets, and Popsicle-stick constructs built straight and crooked and every degree in between. We passed a shoe merchant sitting under a canvas pillared by six two-by-fours, his footware dangling from ropes like perch on the line. Other shops, such as the Been-To market, spilled out of great, unfinished concrete squares as if the builders near completion of the project had been ordered off by impatient merchants eager to load in their goods and start selling. Every shop, it seemed, was missing part of a wall or roof, but this only facilitated the Ghanaians style of selling, which was to push everything into the boulevard anyway and cry out the name of whatever they were selling. It seemed that there was no less than 700 of anything: 700 wooden bed frames rising up a grassy ramp to the road; 700 dog collars; 700 patio flagstones; 700 enormous iron gates laid flat; 700 old tires stacked to the heavens; 700 brightly painted vases and pots; 700 green and yellow sugarloafs; 700 chicken coops; 700 all-purpose foldout stadium seats; and so on. Tiny barbershop and massage and religious counselling and tilapia huts were tucked in among the shops, each of them announced with a large, hand-painted wooden sign, one more colourful than the next: the Moustache Place, the Bigot Pub, God Is Good Fast Food, Benji's Sexy and Hot Tilapia Hut, Be Strong and Wait

Upon the Lord Tire Services, Chevy Chase Kids Shop, In the Name of Jesus Real Estate, All-Gay Saint Enterprise, Don't Mind Your Wife Chop Bar, Flexico Haircut, God Is One Battery Centre, Dr. Jesus Prayer Ministry, Peemen's Guest House, and, in the middle of this dusty ruckus, the Toronto by Night Motel, whose name was written across a sign that looked like it had been used as the target of a rock-throwing contest. There was also a constant chatter among the shopkeepers and procession-aires, which, laid against the growling diesel of cars, trucks, and Ghanaian *tros tros* – small, low-ceilinged vans that shuttle people from place to place – created a high roar that, for the first time, made sitting in mind-numbing traffic seem deliciously fun.

The sounds of the streets were different here than anywhere else I've visited. There were more people and cars in Shanghai or Beijing, but they weren't half as vibrant or loud. Every bar's sound system was broadcast at tweeter-splitting volume, as was every distorted car stereo and shopkeeper's radio trying be heard over the din. Wherever there was music in Ghana, it was played as if waging sonic combat with what was being reefed beside, behind, above, or below it. The previous night, Jen and I had been drinking at Duncan's bar on the Osu, where we were sere-naded for ten thousand cedi (one dollar) by a dizzy-eyed Rasta named Frank, who played bass lines on his nylon string guitar, and his partner, Jessica, who sang and strummed a steel string. They did two Bob Marley songs: "Waiting in Vain" and "Turn Your Lights Down Low." Jessica sang like a Marianne Faithfull of the tropics. Her voice, I suspected, was ravaged from years of trying to sing over Ghana's roaring musical storm. During their streetside performance, Duncan's sound system blasted a Beyoncé CD – or that's what Jen told me it was – forcing Jessica to strain her voice even more, forsaking "Waiting in Vain's" tender vulnerability for a weary melodic defeat.

Another time, I drove with Kofi to Buduburam while listening to a broadcast of a local soccer game – Hearts of Oak versus Liberty International – for which the announcer called the action by screaming without pause into his cellphone. I am a fan of what people who are bigger fans call "the beautiful game," so I know that, even though soccer is exciting, it's not the kind of sport where every play is worthy of breathless and frenetic description. Nonetheless, the announcer's voice – he was calling the game in Twi, Ghana's other native language – left a profound impression on me not only because of his unique play-calling, but because I could hear it echoing through every preposterously loud stereo rig that we passed on our drive.

The motorway's barrage of life eventually dimmed, with the processionaires giving way to patches of green and then to a large man-made lake – Weija Lake – created by a nearby hydro-electric dam. (One of the reasons for the area's power outages had been attributed to the lessened capacity of the dam, from lack of rainfall.) Still, Accra wasn't lush or overgrown, which is how I imagined Africa would be. Many of the displaced Africans from Liberia, Sierra Leone, or Guinea that I met in Accra mentioned the city's lack of foliage with a measure of disappointment and a trace of cynicism. "The first thing Ghanaians do when they build a city," one Liberian immigrant told me, "is take down all the trees and replace them with bits of pavement." It wasn't until he pointed this out that I noticed how parts of the city – like the Osu – were quite bare, and as we inched toward Buduburam, the landscape didn't look so different from sections north of Toronto, almost as if the terrain was being prepped for further expansion of this sprawling – and, in African terms, economically vibrant – city of four million.

Eventually the motorway started to wind a little, and we caught a strong, cool breeze after being expunged from the worst of the traffic. Farther down the road, a signpost announced Buduburam – or, rather, half-announced it, as part of its metal facade had fallen away. Beyond the sign, I saw the bottom of a village sliding toward the road and a parking lot filled with *tros tros* and a few old cars in front of a low-roofed market selling Liberian grains, rice, and other goods, which, every now and then, I was told, were spirited back to Ghana on trucks from a country that some of the young residents of Buduburam had never seen, and their elders might never see again.

BUDUBURAM

THERE ARE PLACES THAT MOST OF US HOPE WE NEVER END up in. A refugee camp is probably one of those places, even if you're there to play Canadian folk-rock with a bunch of Liberian drummers. Sleepless the night before this excursion, I conjured up the worst images on late-night TV charity appeals and in documentaries about uprooted communities – footage of people distraught by the utter helplessness of their lives. So it was with some sadness and not a little trepidation that I climbed from the taxi at the lip of Africa's largest Liberian refugee camp.

My first instinct was to look for the wire fence, for small, frail hands thrust through the links, and for the fly-dotted faces of children and their hollow-eyed parents staring at the world's oblivion. But, with the exception of a low blue concrete wall that bordered the highway – which, it turned out, was the south end of the camp's basketball court – Buduburam was a camp without boundaries. The refugees are encouraged to come and go, which is why there were several *tros tros* in the parking lot, waiting to shuttle them to the city. The camp has never been fenced, not since it was established in 1990, and as a result, Buduburam has evolved into something resembling a small, busy town.

The second thing I noticed after the blue wall was a storage shed next to the basketball court. My eye was caught by the enormous red and white maple leaf painted on its door. That wasn't the camp's only Canadian connection; its most popular hot spot was the Toronto Blues bar. These places were in keeping with other Canadianisms I'd spotted while exploring Accra – a shop grille with *Toronto* painted across in lightning bolt lettering, and two tiny motorway restaurants advertising "Canadian Food" – which made me feel impossibly at home in the most faraway kind of environment.

Inside the camp's entrance was a small orange building that housed the camp's offices, as well as its single, lightless jail cell. A few days into my visit, I heard a panicked voice calling me from the jail. A shirtless man, gripping the window's iron bars, was imploring me to convince the camp manager to set him free. "You must help me, sir!" he cried, dripping with sweat and shaking the bars. "They said that I am a criminal, but I only stole one raspberry! One! Is that any reason to put a man in prison?"

Beyond the jail, a few young men sat under a bare tree hammering nails into slats of wood, each strike scattering a cluster of chickens pecking at bits of garbage. Because it was weeks before the start of the rainy season, the clay grounds were parched, and dust perpetually dirtied the sunlight with a thin red mist.

There were several points of entry into the heart of the camp, most of them winding paths and narrow streets between colourfully painted cinder-block homes that keened one into the other and housed Buduburam's twenty-five thousand refugees. During my four-day visit, I found it impossible to maintain my bearings, not only because the streets had been dug as if following the scribblings of an unhinged draughtsman, but because they sometimes lurched vertically. At night, the streets were lit by sellers grilling meat and fish over small fires and the occasional glow of a television set blinking outside a bar or sports club, where fans stood arms crossed watching English premier league soccer. The broken-stem streets, I learned, were the result of each expansion being built as if it were the last – dredging a road with an eye to filling it soon, or putting up a row of homes with the intention of disassembling them, like a film set or a carnival midway. But the number of Liberians in Buduburam – most of whom fled the rebel uprising in 1991 or the violence following the collapse of the 1996 ceasefire, which had increased fivefold from the original five thousand refugees – was now holding steady. If residents wanted a glimpse into the camp's future, all they had to do was look south to Kasoa, Buduburam's neighbouring community. Originally a Nigerian camp, Kasoa is now a town that stretches untidily twenty kilometres to the sea. Most Liberians nursed the dream of returning to their native county, but in Buduburam they have established a relatively strong and stable community.

The Liberian Dance Troupe's director, William Jacobs – Uncle Jake to everyone at the camp – was our guide and facilitator while at Buduburam. Tall, bespectacled, and serious-minded, Jake had a quick smile and hands that were always ready with a wave. One of the first things I learned about him was that he and I were the same age. The next thing I learned was that he'd not celebrated a birthday since arriving at the camp in 1991. After a few years at Buduburam, Jake had found work as a journalist for the *Ghanaian Times*, a remarkable achievement for someone who grew up in one of the poorest neighbourhoods in Monrovia, Liberia's capital city. He had a twenty-one-year-old son living with him in camp – "He's into science and stuff, and he's not around that much," Jake said – and neither of them had seen Jake's wife since she fled Africa for the United States. ("She is a very bad woman," Jake admitted.) They lived together in a small home with a yard that had been commandeered by a tree. "I should probably have more house," he told us. "But I can't bring myself to chop the darned thing down."

Jake started the Liberian Dance Troupe as a way of keeping Liberian culture alive in the camp while it was being lost at home by a citizenry preoccupied by surviving war. The troupe was also a way of educating Liberians born in the camp. "They have no idea what Liberian drumming sounds like," Jake said, "or what the dances are. We want to keep these things alive and to teach the children that they don't come from nowhere. Of course, we have a dream beyond the camp, but this dream starts here."

Jake met us at the camp's entrance and immediately took us to the troupe's cultural centre, built by camp residents in 2004 with funds provided by War Child. The early days of the centre weren't easy. "People were suspicious at first," said Jake. "We were demonized because they thought we were going to take away the children and transform them. Parents didn't even really know why we existed. People would come and do their toilet in the centre, but we chased them out. Then, before we had a roof, people would do their toilet in bags and throw them over the wall. We had no choice but to collect the bags and throw them back. It wasn't long before people stopped and we were able to do what we wanted."

Outside the centre hung a large canvas of a ship and the words *Go East, Go West, But Home Is Best*. Inside, the long, rectangular room, which would have been a grim bunker in the wrong hands, was painted pink and had a bright, welcoming glow. A low concrete stage sat at one end, its backdrop a painting of a Liberian plain, featuring two grass huts whose entrances framed the doors to the backstage. Above the backdrop was War Child's logo and a list of the issues that the troupe addressed: cultural awareness, teenaged pregnancy, drug abuse, AIDS/HIV, and payment of fees. On the wall near the door, children had painted the words to Liberia's Pledge of Allegiance, which they inherited from their American colonizers of freed slaves and the country's national anthem, which, like every African song ever written, was four times longer than "MacArthur Park" and ten times better. While the passing of time had made their connection to America tenuous – they'd kept their stars-and-stripes flag, albeit with a single star – Liberians possessed a Yankee forthrightness that I hadn't found among the Ghanaians, who had a British reticence. Jake explained, "Liberians talk back, and we talk a lot. Our country might be underdeveloped, but our minds are independent. When you drive around Accra, you'll see people sitting down having drinks and quietly talking, very genteel-like. This would never happen with a group of Liberians. We'd be standing up, dancing and moving around to the music. Someone would be playing a drum and singing, and there would be more life than you could imagine."

Before settling into what would, more or less, be our home base at the camp, Jake suggested that we visit the camp's Harmony Centre for disabled children, whose organizers had asked if we'd join them for their afternoon music program. We made our way across Buduburam's dry, tilted streets to a small yellow building where the Harmony Centre shared space with the Adolescent Friendly Club. We were joined in the dusty courtyard by the centre's director, a tall, radiant, gap-toothed woman named Elizabeth Deddeh Carter, who found us seats under a canvas canopy shading thirty or so Buduburams and a few aid workers. Before the performance began, Elizabeth talked about the centre's crafts and music program for the physically challenged (they also ran lessons to help young people develop computer, printing, and dressmaking skills). Then an a cappella trio, Harmony Rocks, skulked out of the office as if trying not to be noticed and gathered in a horseshoe to sing: "Welcome to/The Harmon-eee/Cent-er/The place where weee/Exhi-bit/Our skills!" The singers voices rose and fell with the song's gospel melody, which, they told me later, their grandparents had learned from American missionaries. The tallest member of the group, who called himself Joshua the Bishop, sang in the middle register, while the voice of his bandmate, Herbert Collins, soared above, and Stephen Lewis, who was also Elizabeth's assistant, rooted the song with a sonorous growl. Joshua used crutches to get around, and both Herbert and Stephen's ankles bent against the ground as they walked, but it wasn't until the song had ended that I noticed they were disabled. I was too busy listening to their sweet voices.

Next, a group of physically and mentally challenged children were steered into the courtyard by a few adults, their hands on the kids' shoulders. Elizabeth led them in a song that they'd been practising for six weeks: the alphabet sung to the tune of "Auld Lang Syne." The tune reduced Jen and Jake to tears and struck me hard too because of the Rheos' song "Saskatchewan, Part 2," the story of a shipwrecked sailor who, after getting washed ashore in the tropics, teaches island dwellers to sing the old chestnut. In the studio, we'd sung it as part of the song's backing vocal, slowing down the tape, then speeding it up to affect the same high, giddy timbre as the Harmony kids' voices. Hearing the song in a Liberian refugee camp was surreal. Near the end of the tune, a few camp residents drifted into the courtyard to listen, but they were immediately distracted by the presence of yours truly sitting in the front row. The children launched into the next number – a song about Liberian folklore's most devious totem: the incorrigible fly – during which I watched the Liberians watch me as I watched the choir. Then, halfway through the tune, a small woman in red and gold robes walked into the courtyard carrying a box filled with Liberian pastries on her head.

After the performance, Joshua the Bishop told me that there were 250 churches in the camp, which, he said, meant that more and more children were being exposed to music. When I told Jake this, he scoffed. "I don't go to church any more," he said. "The only time I go is to spy. A lot of preachers tell their parishioners that everything's going to be all right and that it won't be long before they are resettled or repatriated. You know, a lot of false hope." I asked Joshua what he thought about the promise of repatriation and resettlement – a June 30 deadline for the refugees to move home or to some other country was looming, and it was uppermost in people's minds. He folded his hands and said, "Some will say goodbye, some will stay, but the Harmony Centre will always be here." Jake countered, "People are too afraid to return. Those who do are given five dollars and told to make a go of it."

Back at the cultural centre, Buduburam's musical society soon found us. Jake pulled out a few chairs and we sat talking with Eddie Amilcar, Terry Williams, Francis Wesseh, and Richard Neufville, whose group, King's Jubilee, had formed in the camp. They were all young men in their twenties from Grand Bassa county who earned money singing gospel every Sunday at a church in Accra: the Living Streams International Ministry. Eddie, the band's most effusive member, told me that fans had recognized him on the street and that, despite a dubious beginning, Ghanaians had warmed to the notion of Liberians singing Mass in one of their biggest churches. King's Jubilee had recorded one CD and were working on another, but since they had no access to guitars, keyboards, or basses, they had to rehearse, arrange, and record in one fell swoop. The band's leader, Terry, who had a keen and steady gaze, said, "We record songs with one eye on the clock. When we write, we have the instrumental parts in our heads, but it isn't until we get into the studio that we put them on tape. The process can be slow, and since we have very little money, it takes us a long, frustrating time before we make any new music."

However difficult it had been to record, the CD was getting played. Jake told them that the last time he'd visited Monrovia – Jake was one of only a handful of refugees who dared to visit home – he'd heard a few of their songs played on the radio. Their reaction to this news was mixed. The band was excited about getting airplay, but their enthusiasm flattened under the realization that the most obvious audience for their albums was the one for whom they could not perform. Still, they held out the hope that, one day, they'd enjoy a successful musical life in their homeland. When I suggested that perhaps Ghanaian radio would open up to them before this happened, Eddie laughed and said, half-joking, that it would only be right considering what Ghanaian music had taken from Liberia. According to him, highlife, Ghana's national pop music, wasn't Ghanaian at all but Liberian. When I raised my eyebrows at this, Eddie (whose real name was Zaroe) clutched my shoulders and said, "No, Dave, really! The Liberian fishermen invented this rhythm to give them energy to go out on the seas and keep working. Without it, they would have fallen asleep. In Liberia, this music was played with drums and a bunch of singers. But the Ghanaian fishermen who came down the Gold Coast heard it, and when they got back to Accra, they added lots of musicians and formed big bands, which is how it's done here. This ended up becoming the kind of the highlife that everybody knows, but it's not the real highlife. The real highlife is drums and singing, not trumpets and guitars and bass. But the Ghanaians are good instrumentalists, good players. Still, they can't really sing. Liberians are much better singers."

While Eddie was talking, he'd walked over to a map painted on a wall to the side of the stage and pointed to the exact place on the coast where highlife was born. Then his hand drifted to the northern part of the country – the Liberian interior, the bush –

The author with King's Jubilee at the Liberian
Dance Troupe's cultural centre (*Olivier Asselin*)

where, like so many others, he'd hidden from the rebels. During
his time in the interior, he said, "I learned how to fix a trap, fell
a tree, make a fire, and write a song. Being in the countryside listening to the birds, watching the moon, and hearing the old men
sing was the first time that I realized that I could sing too and
make music. In the beginning, there were funerals for those who
died in the war, and there was always lots of music around."

"The war came slowly to our village," Eddie continued. "It
crept upon us. First, the power went, then the water. It happened
bit by bit, step by step. I was able to escape into the country, but
other families weren't so lucky. People were rounded up by the
rebels and told to march out of the village, where, one by one,
they were shot. In some cases, the gunmen were neighbours of
mine – people I'd grown up with – and sometimes they were children who'd joined the rebels and come to savage our village."

"I was taken by the rebels," said Terry, who'd joined us onstage. "I was put in a room and told to strip off my clothes. They pressed a gun to my head, and I thought I would die. Before the rebels came to my village, I'd been instructed that if I showed any emotion, I'd be killed immediately, so I suppressed my emotions, even when I saw friends killed before my eyes. A lot worse happened to younger children. When they weren't being taken by the rebels and turned into child soldiers, they were watching as their parents, aunts, cousins, brothers, and sisters were butchered. One family I know was marched out of our village by the rebels. They pulled the father out of the procession and put three bullets into his head without any discussion or announcement. They killed him in front of his children and his wife. People who saw this said that the children didn't cry, didn't say anything, even though they were very young. The father's body lay crumpled at the side of the road, but for the rebels, this was not enough. They pulled the wife out of the procession and made her haul her husband's body onto the beach, where it was left to be devoured by the animals and the birds."

"A lot of the rebel soldiers were very young," said Eddie, shaking his head at the memory, "and this made it bad for all of us. Wherever I went, people were afraid that I would hurt them, even though I wouldn't hurt anyone, ever. There were kids who were nine or ten years old, given drugs and brainwashed to kill. There was one boy in my village. He was eight years old when he disappeared, taken by the rebels. When he eventually returned, he came looking for his family. I remember that his mouth was dry and chalky, and that when he spoke, he didn't sound right. He brought his mother and father out of the house, and they had an argument, right there in the streets. His father asked him, 'What has happened to you? Why have you become so violent?' The young boy said nothing. Instead, he took out a knife, ran it across the flat of his palm, and cut himself. He pressed his hand to his face and started licking the blood. He took his parents away and, eventually, his mother returned, but not his father. This is what happened in our home. This is what happened to a great many Liberian boys."

"One of the strange things about the war," Terry said, "was that there was no real enemy. Because the conflict started between two tribes – the Krahn and the Gio – other tribes took sides, and, even then, there were divisions within those tribes." He gestured at the list of tribes painted on the wall. "It was hard to keep track of who was fighting against whom, and why. We were one another's allies and enemies, fighting for reasons that became very confused. For so many years, Liberia had been happy and peaceful, and all of the tribes were content. Like Sierra Leone, we had no history of conflict or civil war."

"The war made people act crazy too," said Eddie. "There was one woman in my village whose husband was killed by rebels. They stuck his head on a pike and left it in front of the woman's house. It decomposed until the skin had shrunken and fallen away and there was nothing left but the skull. This women went insane. For her, the war became not about the rebels versus the army, one side versus another. It was only about revenge. One day, she set out on the road looking for the soldier who'd decapitated her husband. When she found him – these soldiers were never too far from our area, it seemed – she took out a cutlass and sliced him from near his heart to the top of his waist."

Eddie and Terry related their stories without any of the shock or sadness that overwhelmed me as I scribbled down their words. They spoke with an unwavering calm, proud that they'd come through it all to tell their tales. Terry explained, "One of the most difficult aspects of the war was how muted we became, because Liberians love to talk and to speak their minds. We are independent, free, and alive, and this spirit was taken away. Music is one of the ways we can sustain our voices, no matter what's happening at home. It's important that as many people sing and play music as possible. Thankfully, this is not a problem. As you know, Liberians are all excellent singers." He tipped back on his chair and smiled. "I am not boasting. This is just a fact."

It seemed like a good moment to pull out my guitar, which had lain in its case at my feet during our discussion. The wood felt warm from the heat, and it was easy and pleasant to play. I passed it first to Terry, who strummed it a moment before passing it back. I offered it to the others, but Eddie told me that, while they all played a little, they hadn't practised in ages because nobody in the camp owned a guitar. Before leaving Toronto, two music stores had given me guitar strings, tuners, plectrums, and an armful of drumsticks to pass around, but it was only the sticks that would be used. I pushed a dozen sets of guitar strings on them, which Eddie politely said would come in handy the next time they recorded, though they couldn't be sure when that would be.

I started to play "Horses" because it was the closest thing in my repertoire to a singalong. I taught them the chorus – "Holy Mackinaw, Joe" – and soon they were swaying in their chairs, leaning into the rhythm of the song. Children were drawn to the sound, peeking inside, scampering away, then returning with more children. Jake gave them a wave and they burst through the doors. They started dancing, jumping around, chasing flies, and wrestling one another to the ground, which seemed like an appropriate response to our moment of Gold Coast rock 'n' roll hoser unity.

Once we'd exhausted "Horses" – which we extended to African proportions – I insisted that the boys play something, despite Terry's reluctant strumming. They relented, and within a few moments, the King's Jubilee was in full ensemble form. They sang four-part harmony to an African spiritual written in their mother tongue, Bassa, before singing one Zulu hymn, then another, and then another, and closing with a piece by Ladysmith Black Mambazo that lacked none of original version's depth or richness. I felt like a child swept into the eye of a hurricane, and a little embarrassed that I'd asked such gifted singers to voice what was, essentially, a Gang of Four chant in my CanRock anthem. Eddie passed the guitar back to me, but it seemed sacrilegious to play another Rheos song. Still, they were as curious about my music as I was about theirs, so I gave them my only quasi-spiritual piece, "Jesus Was Once a Teenager, Too." They applauded it warmly, but I thought that my voice sounded like Pee Wee Herman's in comparison with their deep, mellifluous tones.

Just as King's Jubilee was about to excuse themselves – the day had drifted on, and it was already late afternoon – a robust, round-faced fellow named Wilfred Brown (who was Jake's friend and confidante, and the troupe's administrator and part-time adviser) took the guitar out of my hands and joked, "These boys say that most Liberians can sing, but they're an exception. This is how a real Liberian sounds." He sang a verse from a song called "You've No Right to Crush God's People," which was quick and bluesy, and his husky voice wouldn't have been out of place on Dylan's *Modern Times*, or a mid-1970s album by Taj Mahal.

Before the war, Wilfred had been the pianist/composer in a local Monrovian group: the Survival Singing Group (SSG). They were popular at the onset of the conflict, but Wilfred was soon forced to decide between fleeing Liberia or continuing to play and accepting whatever fate had in store for him. He decided to go to Côte d'Ivoire, but only made it as far as the countryside, where he encountered a Liberian priest and an Irish missionary who offered to harbour him in their ministry if he could teach their congregation how to play guitar. "My area of expertise wasn't necessarily guitar playing," admitted Wilfred, "but, of course, I accepted their offer. After a few months, I taught them what they needed to know, but, in the interim, word had spread about my whereabouts. I was asked to reform SSG, and we ended up singing for the war victims in Gbarnga, where Mr. Charles Taylor had his foothold. [Taylor's trial for war crimes was scheduled for the summer of 2007.] Soon, we were sent to play in towns at the heart of the conflict. There were times on stage when we didn't know whether the town was going to be attacked or not, but music was our means of survival."

Other Liberian musicians weren't as lucky as Wilfred. One story I'd heard was about the singer Zake Roberts, who charted two wartime hits, "To Be a Man Is Not Easy" and "Sweet Liberia," in which he sang about the conflict using innuendo and parable. Because Roberts was a member of the rebel Krahn tribe, he was spared no quarter and killed. Tecumseh Roberts, considered the Liberian Michael Jackson, suffered a similar fate. His life was taken by the notorious Prince Johnson, the former rebel leader and current senator of Nimba County, who was also rumoured to have killed the father of one of the King's Jubilee – Richard, a government worker.

During the ceasefire-that-wasn't in 1996, Wilfred once played at the Sacred Heart Cathedral in Monrovia for the country's interim political leaders. "The meeting was attended by a famous Italian cardinal who brought with him a message from the Pope," he said. "The temporary leader, Dr. Amos Sawyer, was there too, as well as other members of the government. Because I was also a local choir master, they asked me to perform, and this is what I played them." He placed his hand on the guitar's fretboard and continued with "You've No Right to Crush God's

People." The song sounded as honest and righteous as I imagined it did in Monrovia. After he'd performed it in 1996, there wasn't a single mention in newspapers or on television the next day, but at the troupe's centre in Buduburam, we rewarded him with lots of whooping and foot-stomping approval. If the message had been lost on the Liberian heads of state, it was clear to us. Even though Wilfred and the King's Jubilee were exiled in a strange land, the musicians of Buduburam were freer than ever.

The following day, Jen and I returned to the centre for the Liberian Dance Troupe's performance. We sat beside Jake and Wilfred and the chairman of the Liberian Refugee Welfare Council, a large, imposing man who wore dark sunglasses, a straw fedora, and a gold watch. Jake said that there would be two new elements to the troupe's show: a sound system and an emcee. The speakers and mixer were run off a generator, which War Child had helped Jake rent for the event. It also powered a single bulb that served as both the show's lighting and illumination for a Québécois photographer, Olivier Asselin, who accompanied Jen and I to the camp. The emcee was a twelve-year-old girl called Abbie Kamara, who had recently been named best student in her class. It didn't surprise me at all that Jake had rewarded her for this achievement. The troupe had formed thanks to Jake's knowledge of the camp's residents, and he favoured bright, committed students whose mothers, most of them single, were still coping with the trauma of war. One mother told me that Jake borrowed from his own pocket whenever a child had trouble coming up with the three dollars required for school supplies. Another praised Jake's "sociological eye" and talked about how her understanding of Liberia had been strengthened by what she'd learned from her daughter.

When the elders themselves were growing up, they'd been taught mostly American history, and few of them knew the words to the national anthem.

Besides learning music and dance, the troupe's children, and some who weren't troupe kids – Jake's policy was never to turn anyone away, whether they were officially enrolled in the program or not – also attended classes meant to raise their cultural awareness and teach them about the traps and opportunities of camp life. At the end of the previous day's visit, I'd watched as the hall transformed into a makeshift classroom. The troupe's prefect – a fellow named Mathias Kamara, who had a bulldog's frame and an expression that changed from soft to savage depending on what he was saying – challenged his students to answer questions that, to my ears, sounded unusual for a group of public-school-aged kids:

"Who are you?"

"When you are in Liberia, *who are you?*"

"When you are in America, *who are you?*"

"When you are in Korea, *who are you?*"

"Why don't people know who they are?"

"Why don't *Liberians* know who they are?"

"What makes you a Liberian?"

He repeated his last question a few times before a young boy named Francis in the back row raised his hand and answered, "The way of my culture makes me Liberian?"

Francis's response was exactly what you'd want to hear from young people with the future of their nation cradled in their hands. I can't imagine how I would have answered the question if it had been posed to me as a kid. Then again, no teacher ever discussed such issues with me, and so I didn't know who I was, as a Canadian, until I was twenty-four and the Rheos first toured the country. Mathias's – and the troupe's – approach raised all kinds of questions about life at home: Was Canada reluctant to protect its culture because it had never been directly threatened? Were Liberians better at teaching their culture with very few resources than we were with an embarrassment of tools? If the essence of our nationhood was ever challenged, would we react in the same way as Jake, Wilfred, Elizabeth, and Mathias, or was our habit of ignoring our culture so deep that we'd forgotten what it was in the first place?

At the beginning, the crowd for the troupe's performance was thin, but after a few acts all eighty or so chairs – which the children had arranged into auditorium rows after class – were occupied, with more people standing at the back of the room. I turned to see Joshua, Stephen, and Herbert sitting behind me, along with the troupe's parents and a number of faces I recognized from my previous day at the camp. Abbie, the emcee, proved to have an excellent microphone technique, and she easily carried the day as toastmaster. First, she introduced her aunt, who asked us to close our eyes while she intoned a Liberian prayer. Next, Abbie called out a few young dancers to help sing the national anthem, and then she introduced the drummers. They settled on a bench at one end of the stage, positioned their drums between their legs, and started playing what the single-sheet photocopied program – entitled "Costume Performance To Welcome W.C.C. Team" – said would be a traditional "drum introduction."

The introduction was nearly twenty minutes long, about one-quarter of the performance. To fans of spartan British punk, or to fans of the Residents' *Commercial Album*, which consists of sixty minute-long songs, the introduction would have been an exercise in percussive torture. I too dislike drum jams – at least those done by white, dreadlocked, middle-class hempists in outdoor parks – but by the seventh minute of the troupe's piece, I was hooked.

The performance was as conceptual as any exhaustive Hawkwind workout. In turn, every few minutes, each of the four drummers – Thomas, Sam, Samuel, and Lavelah – rose from the bench and, with a drum slung on a strap around his neck, skid-stepped across the stage to where the Liberian map was painted. Each pointed to a county – Grand Bassa, River Cess, Bong, Lofa – then quoted that region's indigenous rhythm. The rest of the players hollered, laughed, cheered, or occasionally groaned, depending where they were from, then steered their goatskin symphony toward the rhythm he'd quoted. I couldn't discern the subtleties of the piece, but whenever there was a dramatic time change – from 5/4 to 7/8 and everything in between – my sonic equilibrium reacted as if I were in an airplane diving or tipping its wings.

It wasn't only the sudden time shifts or the musical unity of the piece that gave it its power. The drummers' stamina was awesome, their concentration unwavering. It was as unlike "In-A-Gadda-da-Vida" as it was possible to be. They played hard and relentlessly even when moving, paddling their *sinbas* and *killes* and *sasas* and *fangas* with their forearms greased in sweat, eyes pinched. For most of the performance, their faces were frozen in the painful smile that comes from pushing every ounce of strength and energy out of one's body. The drumming was athletic as it was musical, and evoked a physical response that isn't found in other kinds of music. Eventually, my adrenalin became engaged the way it does watching a marathon runner or long-track speed skater over their final few laps. My blood rose to match the tempo and power of the beats, and, for the rest of the jam, my pulse fought to stay close to the changing pitch. With the drummers' last, towering crescendo, I'd probably found what every other Afro-pop admirer strives for: the pure, exultant connection of body and beat.

Young Liberian dancers take to the stage (*Olivier Asselin*)

I was soaked in sweat by the end of it, even though my *swass* hadn't moved out my seat. No sooner had I blotted the sweat moustache that I wore during my entire stay in Africa than the drummers started again. Abbie called out the first set of young troupe dancers, who sprang onto the stage.

They were dressed in full performance splendour. The young girls wore orange and white dresses and moved as if they were enormous, spinning creamsicles, and the young boys wore sleeveless shirts and shorts that looked like Monopoly boards. Most of the children had shark teeth braided into their hair. At one point, the stage was washed with pink and red as a crew of older girl dancers in bright elegant robes performed a series of dances: the feet-on-hot-coals-while-flagging-a-passing-motorist dance; the pushing-someone-from-behind-while-crossing-the-falls-on-a-tightrope dance; the paddling-up-the-rapids-while-trying-to-avoid-getting-hit-in-the-head-with-a-soccer-ball dance;

the constipated-chicken-shaking-unwanted-gunk-from-its-feet
dance; and so on. They were accompanied by the busy sound of
feet slapping concrete, arms whooshing the air, and a lot of
clucking, whooping, squealing, and hooting, which carried like
birdsong over the drummers' wild percussion.

When the older boys took over, they worked closer to the
ground, falling heavy and hard on the concrete stage on a leg or
knee or tailbone, then bounding up to fly in a set pose. Dressed
in baggy navy blue pyjamas patterned with orange and yellow
tire tracks, they swirled in a supernova of colour when airborne,
beads of sweat exploding off their brows. All of this was done
with astonishing speed and dexterity, as if the dancers had studied
a pirated acrobatics tape accidentally dubbed at fast-forward.

To recover their energy, the young men lined up against the
backdrop and slowly shook like they were being nibbled by
bugs. A few minutes passed where nothing else happened, and
then a horrifying figure emerged from the wings wearing a white
rubber mask with grotesque lips and greasy hair and resembling
Joan Rivers. The program told me that this part of the dance was
called "Forbidden Creek." It consisted of Joan rattling her
bracelets and thrusting herself at the dancers, who waved their
hands in panic. Finally, they crept to the middle of the stage and
drove Joan back into the wings. I wasn't sure how I felt about
this caricature of the white race until I realized that it would be
hard to look much worse than Joan. When the dance ended and
Abbie introduced me as "Selection from Dave," I felt positive
about my role as the anti-plastic-surgery-Botox nightmare token
of the West.

I started playing my first song – "Little Bird, Little Bird," a
folk elegy about a Second World War soldier. I stood at the front
of the stage but stepped down on the floor after sensing that the
lyrics couldn't be heard at the back of the hall. Before I got too

deeply into the song, however, I borrowed a trick from our old drummer, Dave Clark, and divided the audience in half, getting the right side of the room to whisper *Zzzzz-Zzzzz-Zzzzzz* on the first three beats, and the left side to shout *Ha!* on the fourth. After I demonstrated this to the audience, Wilfred bounded out of his chair and began conducting the crowd on my behalf, swinging out both arms and counting in the air to show them where the beat fell. The Finns and the Chinese – with the exception of crowds in Joensuu and the Hunan – had been perplexed by this kind of razzmatazz, but the Liberians grabbed it by the neck. Soon their chanting had grown louder than my vocal, polyrhythmically transforming the song. The hall rang with voices, and I was free to take it all in, experiencing one of those rare instances when the musician feels both *inside* and *outside* the performance, as conscious of how the song is being perceived as it is being played.

Then I played "Horses." I went over to where the drummers were sitting and repeated the song's opening riff until they started thumping along. I sang a verse, then a chorus, and Wilfred sprang to his feet once again, waving his arms through the "Holy Mackinaw, Joes!" and getting the crowd to sing along as the King's Jubilee had done the day before. My eyes fell on Stephen from Harmony Rocks, who was singing "The glory of God will take you over!" at the top of his lungs. Wilfred was quick to him too, and within moments, Stephen was on stage standing over Abbie as she held the microphone in the air as if putting distance between herself and a foul-smelling sock. Meanwhile, a tall, willowy woman dressed in a long African gown with her hair bundled in a cloth turban stood up, tightened her fists above her head, and wailed along with Stephen. Others in the crowd followed her lead, and, once again, the Liberians gloriously wrested my song from me and made it their own.

I've played "Horses" at outdoor rock festivals over enormous speaker towers wired through mighty guitar cabinets
juiced to fill stadiums and speedways, and the version at
Buduburam sounded just as big without any kind of amplifica-
tion, Abbie's microphone notwithstanding. The song was driven
by the cries of the crowd, the pounding of drumskins, my strumming hand slashing down on my guitar, and the whoops and
screams of a pack of small children Wilfred had organized into
a choir near the front of the stage. This natural accompaniment
sounded intense in the same way that the wind hammering at a
houseface is intense, or an axe thunking into cordwood, or a
freight train shaking a quiet neighbourhood. It was all the more
visceral for having been created out of nothing by the crowd.
Because of this, the Buduburams were reluctant to let it go easily,
and as the chorus looped and looped, I thought that "Horses"
might never end.

When the song finally began to lose steam, I turned to the
drummers and shouted the song's final bar – "*One! Two! Three!
Four!*" They took this as a metronomical command, and played
loudly and more frenetically in an attempt to straighten the
groove into the tepid Western time signature I'd requested. I
shook my head at them and counted out the song a second time,
but my voice couldn't be heard above the drums. I looked at the
front row and saw Wilfred slapping his hands together and
laughing at me, at which point I realized that it wasn't that the
drummers didn't understand my signal to conclude the song.
They just didn't want to.

I put down my guitar and walked over to where they were
drumming. I fell to my knees and joined them, pounding one of
their *fangas* with the flat of my palms. But they were too fast for
me, and I soon picked up my guitar again. I strummed hard for

a few more bars, stared gravely at the crowd, then did the only thing possible: I leaped off the stage, scissoring my legs and landing in a groin-stretching Townshendian pose at the feet of the crowd. The song tumbled to rest in a hail of laughter.

It took me a moment to rappel back to Earth after the show's giddy heights. I passed around hockey cards to the kids and talked with a few people in the crowd. Then, Jake, who was thrilled with how the afternoon had played out, asked Jen and I if we'd meet with a group of the troupe's parents, who'd waited around after the show. The dancers came out once again and rearranged the chairs in a circle near the front of the stage.

The parents first thanked Jen for War Child's support of the troupe. They told her how much her sponsorship of the organization had meant to camp life. Because Jen was an inveterate listener, she absorbed all of this before probing the residents for more, trying to get them to discuss serious camp issues. This was Jake's cue to speak. He folded his hands in his lap and said, "Jen and Dave, I don't know if you realize it, but we are going through hell here."

Having spent three days jamming, hanging out, and trading stories with the Liberians, my experience of the camp was everything that I hadn't expected it to be. I'd had a great time, met lots of astonishing people, and learned more about the Liberian soul than I ever thought I'd know. But I wasn't sure how much of my reaction was traveller's romance, and whether, because of my limited stay, I'd been left with a slanted view of camp life.

Because of this, I appreciated Jake's candour. Perhaps he was also concerned that my impression of the camp had been coloured by the troupe's performance. While the parents were thanking Jen for War Child's support, he'd sat quietly in his chair, occasionally sighing and wringing his hands. As a longstanding beneficiary of NGOs, he'd heard these violins before. He knew that painting an unrealistic picture of camp life did no one any good, because while the troupe had indeed saved kids from oblivion, the Buduburams still faced limited educational opportunities, less-than-basic health care, medicine they couldn't afford, a lack of energy, clean water, camp sanitation and sewage disposal, bathrooms that had fallen into disrepair, few job opportunities, and a myriad of social problems with drugs, teenage prostitution, drinking, and depression at the top of the list.

After Jake spoke, the parents opened up. One woman, Willomena, talked about returning to Monrovia with five children during the 1996 ceasefire, and losing two of them before coming back to the camp. Another older woman, whose wan face reminded me of my grandmother – who never got over the death of her daughters – had seen her entire family killed: her parents, brothers and sisters, husband, and four of her children. Like the old woman, many of the camp residents were there alone, and while the troupe tried to fill the great empty space where the war had clawed out their hearts, it only blotted the edges of their pain.

One of the troupe's drummers, Sam Taylor, stayed after the show ended and listened to the elders speak. Sam was young and handsome, with gentle eyes and a voice weighted in thoughtfulness. After the discussion finished, I wanted to find out how he'd ended up at Buduburam, but because the day was getting late, Kofi, our driver, suggested that we head back to Accra shortly, lest we spend four hours fighting through the motorway's evening crush. Sam and I made plans to meet the next day, where a soccer game was scheduled on a dirt field behind the camp.

That afternoon, he gave me a CD that he'd recorded. It was a plain white disc with his stage name – Sam E – written in blue marker. He apologized for the lack of a cover, but I told him that, at home, demos weren't required to have artwork. He was encouraged to hear this, but told me: "The cost of printing two hundred demo CD covers in Ghana is very expensive, six-hundred dollars. I'm also worried that my finished product won't have a cover either."

Sam was alone in Buduburam. Of his family, he was the only one who'd escaped the war. He'd scrabbled together enough money to record his CD, which, like the one recorded by King's Jubilee, had been done in haste over a few days. He'd shown up at the studio with a bunch of songs in his head, and had taught them to the studio band who, thankfully, liked what they heard. When I asked Sam if he regretted not being able to establish himself as an artist in his homeland, he looked at it two ways. "Because I'm so close to Accra," he said, "I can try and take things from Ghanaian music and apply it to what I'm doing. It can be a mix. Even though the war forced me to come here, I'm not sure there's a musical system in place at home anyway."

Sam was a prodigy, and had performed on stage since he was a child. He was one of the best young dancers in Liberia, and toured with the Liberian National Cultural Dance Troupe. He was also a natural drummer – he'd stayed with the Liberian Dance Troupe players without dropping a beat – and his CD was legitimate and good. The more I got to know Sam, the more I thought that, if the war hadn't eviscerated his country, he'd have been a sensation at home.

We strolled to the soccer game along a ragged dirt path flanked by hillocks of garbage – Sam said that the sanitation trucks had failed to arrive that week – which gave way to a field surrounded by five thousand young refugees dressed like B-boys and watching the players run like leopards under the heavy after-noon sun. During our walk, Sam told me his story.

"Even when the war was happening at home, we had com-plete faith that the government would prevail, and that it would end soon. My parents always tried to keep our minds focused on what we were doing. They told us that the rebels would not come for us, and that we'd soon be able to return to our normal lives." The Taylors fled into the countryside at the outbreak of war, only to return to Monrovia with news of the ceasefire. "Things were getting better," said Sam, "until, one day, we were alerted that the rebels were looking for my father [a government soldier] and that they were poised to take Monrovia.

"The instant we heard this, my parents told us to run. There were hundreds of others who'd heard the same thing, and they joined us as we ran down the streets toward the American embassy, which, we'd heard, would provide safety from the rebels. I ran without looking around me, and then, in the middle of it all, I lost my parents, brothers, and sisters. We became sep-arated in the crowd and never found one another. That was the last I saw of them. A few days later, I heard that there was a boat coming from Ghana to take the refugees, so I ran to the dock. I was hoping my family would be there, but they weren't. I got on the ship. As it pulled away, my last impression of Liberia was the people drowning in the water trying to reach the ship, and others lined up across the dock and crying."

Because Sam's father had been a high-ranking government official, it's unlikely he'd survived the rebels' seige. When Sam said, "I hold out hope that, one day, I'll see my mother, brothers, and sisters," it sounded as if he'd resigned himself to never seeing his father again. When I asked him if he had any other dreams, he told me, "Yes. To one day return to Liberia as a pop star." We watched the game in silence, then he asked me, "Dave, do you know of anyone back in Canada who could help me? You know, someone I might talk to as if they were a mother or a father?"

Later that night, Jake, Wilfred, and I sat drinking three large, sweating Star beers at the Toronto Blues bar. We talked about Sam, and discussed other refugee stories I'd heard during my stay. A few weeks later, Jake wrote to me in Toronto to say, "I don't know if you know, but Sam did not come to the camp by boat. He came to Ghana through Côte d'Ivoire, overland with the Liberian National Cultural Dance Troupe. His mother is alive, as well. I know this. Sam has told me." Jake went on to say that camp residents often embellish their stories so that visitors will pity them and help them resettle in the United States, Europe, or Canada, though he wasn't necessarily suggesting that this was what Sam had done. If anything, the young singer's need to darken what was already an unbearable situation – living in a refugee camp, having little or no money to achieve his dreams – only proved how desperate he was to change it.

Jake had one other note: Zack Roberts's life had been spared in the war. He'd heard one of his new gospel tracks the last time he was in Monrovia, and reports were that he was alive and well.

Which was certainly a good thing.

FREETOWN

AFTER THE RELATIVE IDYLL OF ACCRA I BOARDED A PLANE
for Freetown, the capital of Sierra Leone, where, for two
decades, chaos had pinned idyll to the mat as if they were WWE
combatants. On the plane there, I met two nuns – Sister Teresa
and Sister Amy – who, after learning why I was headed to
Freetown, lamented that nobody in their abbey played the guitar
any more because it was missing two strings. I offered them a
set from my stash and, after disembarking, I zipped open my
luggage in the arrivals corridor. We were immediately horse-
shoed by Leoneans, who knelt around my exposed suitcase and
peered in as if I were an explorer returning with treasures. It
took me a moment to realize that the Leoneans were just being
curious, possibly about my shirts and underwear. After I'd said
goodbye to the sisters, a young man who'd been tending to the
nuns chased after me to tell me that the sisters would pray for me.

I was looking for a man named Sosay, and found him just
beyond the terminal doors. He took me from the airport proper
to a holding area, where he helped me check my luggage for the
helicopter ride into Freetown.

The helicopter was piloted by two enormous Russian men,
their bellies punching through the jackets of their uniforms. One
of them looked like a friend of mine, which made me both

hopeful and fearful as the copter shook and rattled through take off. Most of the Africans on board crossed themselves, and one fellow threw his head into his hands. It briefly occurred to me that I'd merit the headline MODERATELY WELL KNOWN ROCK MUSICIAN DIES IN SPECTACULAR CRASH OF AFRICAN HELICOPTER PILOTED BY DRUNK RUSSIANS until I was distracted by the sight of the beautiful waters below me and the sinuous shoreline of Freetown, which tickles the ocean like a woman's elegant fingers.

We landed with a thud at Mammy Yoko Heliport, a name that reminded me that I was in Africa and nowhere else. I was met by Cathy O'Grady and Naomi Johnson, the War Child officers whose trip had dovetailed with mine. After years trooping around with male hockey squads and musicians, the prospect of spending a few days in their company cheered me, and I was happy to discover that Naomi's knowledge of rock 'n' roll occasionally allowed us to talk about something other than where we were and what we were seeing. Cathy, an Irishwoman, had spent time in Mercurea-Cuic in Transylvania, a town dear to my heart where friends had planted a wild cherry tree for my daughter, born in the summer of 2000. The two of them also proved tireless in their role as go-betweens with the two teenaged musicians, Barmmy Boy and Lustinjay (*Loose-tin-jay*), I was in Freetown to meet. Together, the two boys had harnessed local hip hop to rap about drug abuse, teenaged pregnancy, prostitution, and AIDS/HIV with the rebelliousness and passion of true musical trailblazers.

Naomi, Cathy, and I took up residence at the Cape Sierra Hotel, which loomed over a ribbon of golden beach tight to the ocean. The hotel was vast and sprawling – its grounds were as opulent as any you'd find in Palm Springs or Monaco – and if you squinted, it was possible to see what it was like before falling into disrepair. Each night, we were entertained by the loud, hiccuping song of lustful bullfrogs, and, in the morning, great black and white magpies swooped through the trees. Because it was the end of the dry season, the trees were Seussian, their branches scarecrowing over lawns of brown grass.

Cape Sierra's faded grandeur was a strange introduction to a land that, just five years earlier, had been embroiled in an inhumane civil conflict. What started in 1991 as an attempt by a former army corporal, Foday Sankoh, in alliance with Charles Taylor – who was also responsible for the war in Liberia – to gain control of the rich Kono diamond region grew into a hip-hop war waged against the army by Taylor's rebel forces – the RUF, or Revolutionary United Front – whose ranks were filled by children and young men stoned on *brown brown* (heroin and gunpowder) and bloodlust. The RUF was out to destroy the government, savage the countryside, and get rid of its ruling chiefs, kidnap children wherever they went, and take control of the diamond industry. When they weren't conscripting villagers as slave labourers, they were raping and torturing them. Both sides recruited common prisoners to fill their ranks, and with the emergence of the Armed Forces Revolutionary Council (AFRC) – a dissident military organization that seized governmental authority in 1997 – Freetown saw two violent and unstable factions wrestling for control of the city. They torched it and almost completely destroyed it. Every day of the war brought new horrors, including the RUF's "Operation No Living Thing," where civilians were mutilated and massacred in great numbers. In 2002, a West African force, Ecomog, intervened on the heels of a successful British military operation and order eventually returned to the capital. When all was said and done, fifty thousand people had died and twenty thousand were mutilated, most of whom lived in amputee camps on the outskirts of the city.

The morning after we arrived, we were whisked by Isa, one of War Child's two drivers, by truck to a Lebanese bakery – the Bliss Patisserie – where we met Barmmy Boy and Lus over croissants and café au laits. Both kids were eighteen, but there was very little teenaged about them. The war had matured them quickly, and they had sacrificed their hanging-out years trying to create a musical impression of one of Africa's most suffering cities. When I asked Lus, somewhat naively, about working to supplement the income they didn't make as musicians, he said, "There are no jobs. As a young person, if you go to an interview for a job, people laugh at you because you have no experience. If you tell them that you have experience, they tell you that it's not enough experience. A lot of colleagues are affected by this. They drink and take drugs. We grew up the hard way too, but we are still progressing."

Barmmy and Lus were part of a former youth collective called the iEARN Music Club, who released one CD, "Salone for Go Befo" ("Sierra Leone Must Progress"), including the songs "HIV Dangerous" and "Freeze." Barmmy was the club's youth music director and, together with Lus, he'd travelled to schools around Sierra Leone rhyming about social issues. War Child had supported iEARN, but the collective had lost the capacity to be effective. Discouraged but not defeated, the kids formed a new collective, Artists United for Children and Youth Development (AUCAYD) to keep their crusade going. One of the reasons for Naomi and Cathy's visit was to figure out a way to get AUCAYD off the ground. There was talk that the guitar maker Gibson was prepared to invest, but nothing had yet come of it.

Barmmy Boy and Lus were opposites both physically and in other ways. Barmmy was small, soft-faced, and careful with his words. He got his nickname when he was a boy fishing for

Barmmy and Lus in Lumley (*War Child Canada*)

tilapia, known locally as barmmy. He had a knack for catching them by swimming below the surface and pinning hooks in underwater caverns. When Barmmy told me about his childhood, he talked about a carefree life of swimming and fishing that ended at age eleven when his father was blinded during an explosion triggered by the rebel forces. Barmmy had left home to ease the burden on his mother, a small-time vendor, and had moved in with a friend. Both he and Lus gave the impression that music was a full-time concern for them, but I learned that Barmmy still relied on fishing to earn money, rising early to catch his aquatic namesake, which he sold at the market.

Barmmy was earnest and bright and appeared to be more studied than Lustinjay, though they were both smart kids. He had made a handful of short films – he was partly supported by the intrepid British NGO, Café Society, who were trying to get him to Hull, England, on an aspiring filmmakers' exchange –

and I'd found one of his movies, about his younger brother, while trolling YouTube. (A video of "HIV Dangerous" is posted on boomrevolution.com.) At times, he was elusive and meditative, but then, he was forever standing beside the taller Lus, who jangled when standing still, busting moves and affecting a rappers' pose at the drop of a hat. Sometimes, instead of explaining the theme behind a song, Lus would sing the theme or, even better, the song. It was hard to finish a sentence without Lus shooting out an arm to grip your shoulder, as if trying to stop your thoughts so that he could take them over. Except for a deep scar below his left eye that he'd suffered in a soccer collision, he had the high-cheekboned face of a pop star. As charming as he was loquacious, he spoke quickly and used words like *travelistic* and *conscientize*, as if creating a new hipspeak born out of English and Krio, the Leonians' native tongue. Each time I saw him, he was dressed differently and within an inch of cool, sometimes strapped head to toe in Rasta gear, sometimes done up like a retro-homeboy, and once in a white Ottawa Senators T-shirt. In contrast to Barmmy, who thought deeply about the world and his work, Lus used his energy to hustle, trying to get himself and the other members of AUCAYD booked at beach bars, which were the only venues regularly available to young players. The night before I arrived, Lus and another AUCAYD singer, Vickie, had won what was basically an American Idolesque sing off at the Village Beach Bar with a song called "Well Done," about how their parents' generation had messed up the future for their children. Naomi, who'd seen the show, said that the song was a duet, but Lus never once mentioned his singing partner. Perhaps being self-absorbed wasn't a bad thing for a young rapper. I saw a reflection of my aspiring rock 'n' roll self in both kids, but in Lus, I saw the part of me that had called club owners unannounced and somehow convinced them to book my band. His

Lus takes his message into a Freetown classroom (*War Child Canada*)

friendship with Barmmy, and the way they finished each other's sentences, reminded me of my relationship with my old and now ex-bandmate Tim, with whom I'd once shared the dream of stamping our musical imprint on the world.

Lus also lived on his own as his family's home was too small and because his father, on old man, required a lot of care. He'd moved in with friends, drifting nomadically around the city. Both kids timed their lives, it seemed, by gigs and sessions, which was really no different from my own rock 'n' roll adolescence, except that I always knew where my next meal was coming from and where there was a bed for me.

After finishing our coffees, we drove to the War Child Canada offices in Lumley. The first thing the boys did when we arrived was bring me into their temporary music room, where they stored the equipment bought for them by War Child: a few old speakers, a CD player, receiver, Yamaha synthesizer, and a bass amp. In the middle of the room a sixteen-channel mixing board and a set of small stereo speakers sat on a desk. This was where they rehearsed, wrote, and recorded, although not in the conventional sense. Rather, Barmmy loomed over his laptop, which he won in a contest, and wrote beats while Lus scribbled rhymes onto foolscap. In the next few days there were times when, because the room's availability was limited to office hours, they became so swallowed in their work, craning over their keyboard and mixing console they forgot they'd planned to take me around the city. I couldn't begrudge them the opportunity to get things done, so I bided my time hanging out on the balcony of the offices, drinking tea and watching Freetown at work and play.

The whitewashed office building was rooted in a steep hill. At the base of the grounds was a brown corrugated shed that housed the building's generator, whose constant grrrrr could be heard inside and outside of the offices. The generator was the responsibility of the building's superintendent, a thin, friendly, and perpetually baseball-capped man named Joseph, who made it his goal to sell me pirated DVDs about the war in Sierra Leone. (I eventually relented, purchasing a copy of a Discovery Channel special about British forces liberating hostages from a jungle rebel enclave, which the kids and I watched during a break in their sessions.) When I asked Joseph if he lived near the offices, he told me that he had a place on the grounds. A few days later, when he opened up the door to the generator's shed to show me the hulking machine, I noticed a small weathered mat on the floor: Joseph's bed.

The office's second-floor balcony looked over a river valley, where on the far side ramshackle homes veered over a slope littered with garbage. A few palms lined the river, their fronds hanging over the tepid, green-brown water. The river looked like a Club Med for the most worrisome kinds of parasites, but there was always someone in the water. Most days, a group of boys splashed about with a plastic jug, trying to catch fish or amphibians or whatever else survived in the river's rank depths.

Above this fetid swimming hole was an old bridge and, on the far side, a clay road led to a wall of trees. Everyone walking along the road – men and women dressed in African robes and groups of schoolchildren in uniforms of deep blues and wild pinks – was swallowed by the trees. On the office's side of the bridge was a carpentry shop with a blanket for a roof where a young man spent hours grinding out a bluebeat rhythm on a handsaw. At one point, a small boy in red swimming trunks marched up and down the road blowing into a whistle and chasing orange dragonflies. Farther along the riverbank, two young women were selling a small basket of green Liberian mangoes, one of them while nursing a young child.

Despite its gouged landscape and hard living conditions, much about Lumley played upon the eye, from the *poda poda*s – Sierra Leone's version of the *tros tros* – that occasionally charged along the road with messages including "Dem Surprise You!" and "The Downfall of a Man Is Not the End of His Life" bannered across them, to the enormous hand-painted billboards that loomed over most street corners. My favourites were the ad for Bell mayonnaise, which featured an upside-down hamburger, and one for Zwan luncheon meat, which depicted two small children looking with pained expressions at their plates.

Dancing beyond these paintings were clouds of black and yellow palm birds that flew from tree to tree pulling out leaves to strengthen their nests – fat, hairy orbs that hung in the palms. Every now and then, a royal blue *yuba* – an African stork – cruised down the river valley; other times, vultures, turacos, grey herons. The dirt roads were busy with *kudu* lizards skittering here and there, then hiking themselves up on their forearms and puffing up their brilliant red neck pouches. At one point an eerie, humanoid figure walked at a somnambulant's pace through the deep, sweltering heat, its body encased, neck to toe, in rough black straw. It wore a stark and frightening mask over its face, which reminded me of the harrowing figure in Edvard Munch's *The Scream*, although it was more uniquely African. The way the creature moved sent a slow cold shiver up my spine.

I called the boys out of the music room and pointed at the straw person. "Oh, this is the genital mutilation woman," said Barmmy Boy, matter-of-factly, "from one of the secret societies." He said that the creature's job was to recruit young girls into its fold. There'd been a movement to abolish the practice of genital mutilation – many girls died from the procedure, which was too often conducted with a rusty blade – but politicians were slow to react, fearing the loss of voter support in the provinces. "Witch-craft and secret societies have a long history in Sierra Leone," Barmmy said. "To this day, they'll sew up young women, then take the stitches out on their wedding night before parading the stained sheets through the villages. A long time ago, when Christianity came to Sierra Leone, these villagers told the church that they could build in the jungle, where they thought that witchcraft would bring them down. But, of course, this didn't happen. As a result, the church was seen as being more power-ful than ever, which is why these societies try to hang on to what they have left."

Before the fellows returned to their work, Barmmy played some songs by Jamaican dancehall and Afro–hip hop artists that he'd downloaded. He liked Sean Paul, Ragamuffin, and Beenie Man, to name just a few. The only thing I knew about the former was that, in one of his videos, he drove the earth's most obnoxious motor vehicle – a flame-throwing Hummer – and that his music – a dirty stew of hip hop, reggae, and dancehall – encompassed all that I despised of current pop music: coke-happy, *Attack of the Robots* digital grooves, and blustery, hyper-sexist lyrics. Once Barmmy realized that I wasn't about to throw one hand on my belt buckle, another behind my head and thrust, he tried a different tack: clicking on a song called "Pussy Clean" by Vybz Kartel.

The name "Vybz Kartel" should make the average music fan approach his records the way you'd approach an old, dead thing at the bottom of a garbage can. Rock 'n' roll has yielded some pretty absurd monickers over the years – names such as Sam Sham and Philthy Animal and Ari Up promised a lot less than their respective bands delivered – but "Vybz Kartel" is just stupid: a cheap cobbling together of two trendy words badly spelled to posit the singer as some sort of "playah," though if you have to say you are, you aren't. The message of "Pussy Clean" didn't sound like some brilliant safe-sex dogma; the song was just ear candy for goofy teenagers looking for a cheap, lascivious larf. All it did for me was to show me that, for all of their political songs, Barmmy and Lus were goofy teenagers too. The world had made them wise beyond their years, but they still liked stupid shit, and I was glad that they'd taken me for a comrade who liked stupid shit too.

Before coming to Africa, I'd thrown together a bag of CDs to play for the boys in Freetown, remembering how I wished I'd had the motherlode of recorded works with me in China when I

met Airbag. The discs included *The Gift of Gab* by Blackalicious, *Rings Around the World* by Super Furry Animals, *The
Private Press* by DJ Shadow, the Clash's *London Calling*, and,
as a shot in the dark, *Rust Never Sleeps* by Neil Young. After
Vybz Kartel, it seemed like a good time to open the bag, but after
playing a few tracks using Barmmy's computer, it was apparent
that the boys were not interested. It didn't help that I stood over
them like an old crone waving a handful of CDs and declaring
them works of pure genius. Not even the funk of Lupe Fiasco
turned them on, which disappointed me. My grand design to
revolutionize their young minds had failed. They were too
absorbed in their own revolution to make room for mine. Just
because they possessed the same heart and conviction as the
Clash, didn't mean they had to know who they were.

Barmmy and Lus eventually called me into the music room
and told me that their song was ready for playback. I brought
out my guitar and stood over Barmmy's shoulder, listening to
the tune. It was a thundering track, thick and busy with jumpy
rhythms and hard electronic percussion, if a little undynamic,
which is often the young songwriter's pitfall. It was easy to find
a place for my guitar part in the song's digital construction, as
it was the only organic sound save for the rapping that would
come later. I strummed and riffed a little, and as soon as Lus
sprung up beside me, churning his arms and swaying his head
and humming a melody, I figured that we were in business. All
the while, Barmmy sat with his arms crossed over the console,
smiling a delighted smile. People gathered outside the music
room's window – the slope beside the building brought folks
level to the second floor – one of them carrying a yellow
bucket of water on his head. Satisfied with what I'd come up
with – but more likely playing to the audience outside – Lus
started rapping:

The youth dem stand alone; they need employment
AUCAYD for all; for the youth dem and the children
I see the children begging by the streetside
I see the children sleeping by the streetside
It's hard to believe what we see now
It's hard to believe.

Barmmy cranked the speakers as if trying to draw the entire population of Lumley to the room, then joined in. Barmmy had a name for his style of rapping – *funkdoc* – in which he rhymed in a deep croak that belied his small size. Lus's approach was the opposite, of course, and he rapped with energy and brightness, machine-gunning his rhymes over the beat.

"We will record this at Studio D!" proclaimed Lus after we'd gone through it a few times.

"So, what I'm doing is okay?" I asked, fishing for a compliment.

"Great, man, it is great! You're *e day inside*," said Lus.

"I'm what?"

"*Day inside*. You're sitting up for yourself, man!" he added, stringing together a set of Krio exhortations.

"You play like your name," Barmmy said. Then he gave me a West African gift that was better than any painted mask, hand-dyed batik, or basket of chickens, which is what Naomi and Cathy were given during their last trip to the country. I was given a nickname:

"You play like Super D!" shouted Barmmy Boy.

"Super D!" echoed Lus.

With that, we were ready to wax it.

We spent the next few days in the city trying to book studio time to record the song. Barmmy and Lus wanted to do it at Studio D – in Freetown, the studios were known by letter, not by name – even though Barmmy's laptop possessed enough software to record, produce, and master the song. Freetown sessions were a social thing, and so they held out for a proper studio. It was the opposite of the trend in North America, where people are turning away from studios in favour of digitally equipped bedroom Montserrats. In the rappers' case – and because most Freetown musicians were in the same boat economically – recording in a studio was as much about people supporting one another as anything else.

Each day, we travelled from Lumley into Freetown with five people crammed into Isa's truck (a rapper in a do-rag named Hopesman often accompanied us), listening to a tape by the roots rock singer Joseph Hills. The town's badly potholed roads we travelled made me long for the Grand Marquis's soft, upholstered bench. But once we hit the main route, driving into Freetown was a panoramic delight.

From the road's peak, the town looked like a jumble of bent sticks and tilted rooftops woven with bright flora and keening toward the sea. Because they were terraced on a steep hillside, it seemed impossible that the houses and buildings had not been swept airborne into the surf by some storm. The glassy blue of the ocean and bursts of jungle green brightened the grey palette of these enclaves, soaking Freetown with colour. It looked like San Francisco built by Africans: a long, snaking coastline and the surrounding hills looming over the city like green velvet party hats.

Once we'd descended into Freetown, we parked, then hoofed our way through the streets. The city teemed with life – a basin of fish being marched up a hill, a busy used T-shirt stall, a lively barbershop, a group of shouting men gathered around the raised hood of an automobile – but everywhere there were reminders of the war. Barmmy pointed out the city prison – Pademba, located in the centre of town – where, he said, prisoners escaped all the time. This immediately overlaid my fear of bugs and sunstroke with a new phobia. One of the first things the rebels had done on their march into Freetown was to liberate the thieves, rapists, and murderers, and simply being near the scene of this horrific episode gave me chills. We moved quickly past it toward the edge of a bay. I found myself tramping across parts of town that I'd read about in Ishmael Beah's excellent and harrowing memoir, *Long Way Gone*, walking, at one point, along a stretch of road where the author hid in the sewers to avoid the rebels. In the same chapter, he describes running past the city's enormous and venerated seven-hundred-year-old cotton tree to avoid being massacred. When I finally saw the great, sinewy tree up close, its long branches were hung with heavy gobs of plump red bats that writhed in the daylight.

The boys brought me to a market where slaves had been kept before being put on boats bound for the New World. At midday, it was as full of people selling African art, necklaces, trinkets, and clothes as it was empty of tourists buying them. The first vendor we encountered held up a bag of dried stems and told me, "This is good for your pee-pee. It makes you have sex a long time." After explaining that my pee-pee was doing okay on its own, I bought a painting of Thomas Peters, the founder of Freetown, then left the market. Across the street was the old city hall – still blackened from being torched by the rebels – where teenaged prostitutes did their business. Barmmy seemed especially heartbroken by this. He pointed to a young black girl leaning out one of the punched-out windows. "It's terrible that young women in this country have to turn to this. As young people, it's hard to get our message across when so many people are resorting to desperate measures." I asked whether he, like a lot of politically motivated artists, was concerned that his message was falling on deaf ears. He said, "No, people are charged up that we're singing about these things. We'll turn up at a show and because very few people are doing what we do, the crowd will get excited. People in Freetown, I think, are open to embracing these issues. It's just that not many people are talking about them, at least not on a wide scale."

"It's hard, as well, when a lot of youth video shows like Channel O are playing British and Jamaican artists and not so many from Sierra Leone," Lus said. "And when they do play music from here, it's all 'Shake Your Body, Shake Your Body' or 'Jiggy-Jiggy Shai, Jiggy-Jiggy Shai.' People don't love these songs for the message, they love it because of the repetition, hearing it over and over and over. And because this music comes from big companies, it's what deejays like Foxy [a local announcer] will play."

"If you don't have money, they won't play you," added Barmmy. "It's more about what you put in their pocket than what you put on your CD, even though they'd never ask R. Kelly or 50 Cent to pay. Only Sierra Leonean artists. It's unfair."

We headed downhill from the market, for a part of the city known as King Jimmy's, where slave boats once docked before hauling away West Africa's best and strongest. Our route took us through a riot of bamboo huts, straw-roofed shacks, creaking wooden ramps, rotten bridges crossing oily green sluices, deeply cracked concrete pathways, and a cement labyrinth of half-built walls and floors crowded with the poorest of Freetown's poor: men and women in rags, naked children with distended bellies, and dogs curled up and waiting to die. This shanty, Barmmy told me, was swept away every year on the high tides of the rainy season. It was a dark and rank place, possessing none of Freetown's trademark bright colours.

At one point, we approached an ancient stone tunnel where I had to stoop to pass under. Inside, it stank of ganja and was lined with thirty or forty young men crouched on either side who, Lus told me later, spent their days hanging out and planning crimes. Had I wandered into this tunnel myself, I'm not certain what would have resulted, but because I was with musicians, the sad, stoned, and angry faces of the men softened, and one by one, they held out their fists, which I tapped with my knuckles. Barmmy told them, "This is Super D. Canadian writer," which, for some reason, was good enough for them.

We made our way back into the heart of the city, where we rested a while in Victoria Park, Freetown's sprawling – if seasonally arid – civic gardens. We found a stoop under a tree where we sat and talked, surrounded by a dozen or so sleeping men. For me, it was pleasant respite after a week driving back and forth from Accra to the camp. Like staring out the window of a city café or sitting on the balcony of a strange apartment, hanging out in the park gave me a feel for the city.

The fellows bought suspicious beef spears from a processionaire for three thousand leones (one dollar) and talked about the state of Africa. Like all worthy musicians from Woody Guthrie to the Pogues, they were acutely aware of their past. "How can the world expect Africa to be more than it is when an entire generation was taken away by the slave trade, only to return to be colonized?" Lus wondered aloud. "And then came many, many wars. Africa has had a very slow and painful start, and it's not hard to see why." Whenever the subject of war came up – as it did now – I talked about how conflict had affected my country too; how thousands of young Canadians were handed their fate in two world wars. This was partly a reflex motion, and partly a way of discussing the wounds of Africa in something other than a pitying manner: poor Africa, shit on by the rest of the world. After hearing my thoughts about war and humanity, Lus put up his hands and recited "The Second Coming" by W.B. Yeats, repeating the line "The falcon cannot hear the falconer" to emphasize its comment on the universal state of the human condition.

"You know that poem?" I asked him, astonished.

"Of course. We read it many times in school," he said.

"Many times?"

"Yes, many, many times. We might not have had a lot of schooling, but we were taught very well. *Julius Caesar*, *King Lear* too," he said and proceeded to fight his way through a soliloquy from each. I said, "I don't know a lot of kids at home who'd pull out the 'The Second Coming' as a way of discussing the condition of the world." Perhaps feeling a little self-conscious, Barmmy reminded me, "Bob Marley sings about these things too. Some Sierra Leone artists as well."

When I told Naomi later that night about Lus's recitation, she gave me a copy of the Truth and Reconciliation report that had been handed out to secondary-school students in Sierra Leone to teach them about the war. It is as chilling a text as I've ever read, and helped explain the boys' emotional and intellectual maturity. The Truth and Reconciliation Commission had started as a way of letting Sierra Leoneans tell their personal stories of the conflict, and their accounts had been collected in the report. This meant that high-school students in Freetown were able to read a section called "Cannibalism and Forced Cannibalism," in which one woman describes how her son was tortured and eviscerated alive before she was forced to eat his heart. The book is an unflinching portrait of the horrors that consumed the country and it showed me why Lus and Barmmy were as enlightened and engaged as they were.

After we left the park, the boys took me to Music Makers, a new local promotion and event management company that booked shows and duplicated CDs on a small scale. Until it set up shop, Freetown musicians were at the mercy of an operation known locally as the Lebanese (or Super Sounds or the Indians, depending on who was talking), the only manufacturers in town. Music Makers was run by a tall, dark-skinned man named Alasan who'd moved with his family to the United States during the war, joined the U.S. Navy, then returned to Freetown despite having settled into middle-classdom with his mother and brothers in Chicago. The boys admired Alasan because he'd traded the affluence of Western life to make a difference at home. The company rented out a top-rank PA system, charged a reasonable rate for copying CDs, and had partly broken the stranglehold on live music in Freetown by staging independent shows – Alasan had brought the pop star Emerson to the city's football stadium – and splitting the profits with performers. Otherwise, it was standard for promoters to "buy" artists: paying them a flat fee without any opportunity to share in the profits if the show did well. Because there were very few musicians with the money to pay these fees – because they seldom made decent cash at their shows – most bands were forced to accept whatever offer was pushed across the table. In many cases, the promoters had no interest in the music. They were Freetown businessmen looking to make a quick buck, so they rarely paid for decent sound or lighting, let alone a good rider or posters to advertise the show.

In its own way, Music Makers was like a tropical Brill Building. Off an alley beside the office was a narrow rehearsal room occupied by local rappers most hours of the day. On the after-noon we were there, a rapper named Paps was getting ready for his CD release show on the weekend at the Young Sportsmen Club of Freetown, where he promised to do something that only a handful of Sierra Leonean pop musicians had done before: sing live, and not lip-synch to backing tracks. This was largely at the insistence of Paps's friend, manager, and financier, a shaggy-haired white student researcher from the United Kingdom named Ed Sawyer. Ed had originally come to Freetown to do his masters in education, but he had fallen in love with the local sounds. "When I got back to England the first time," he told me, "I was loaded down with tapes and CDs I'd bought here. Some-times after you travel, you never play what you bring home, but I found myself constantly going back to these records. So, when the opportunity arose to make a record here, I jumped at the chance." Ed had met Paps on his first stay in Sierra Leone and, so far, he'd invested more than five thousand dollars of his own money in the project because he was convinced that Sierra Leonean music was ready to break out worldwide. "I became friends with Paps and we ended up sharing a place together," he told me. "We live in a palm-wall home, and sleep under a mos-quito net. Actually," he admitted, with a self-effacing grin, "our place is so small that we sleep in the same bed."

Like Ed's digs, the Music Makers' rehearsal space was not much more than a dim cardboard closet with sweat dripping off the walls, one of which was postered with Nubian models wearing nothing but toenail polish. I felt bad about crowding Paps and his crew, but our presence, I think, helped him rise to the occasion, freestyling for twenty minutes straight as the room grew hotter and more airless, partly as a result of the week's record high temperature outside, and partly because of the CD copying machines that were firing on the other side of the wall.

Still, there probably wasn't a more appropriate environment in which to experience Sierra Leonean hip hop close up. Paps passed the microphone to Barmmy, who freestyled to a run of beats triggered on an old sampler. I was buoyed by the deep, heavy electronic rhythms despite the heat and, as at Buduburam, let the groove support my body as it fell loose.

The following morning, I showed up at the War Child offices, where, after a series of cellphone calls in Krio, Barmmy and Lus announced that we had a date at Studio D, named after the studio's in-house label, Dynamic Records. In the early afternoon we made our way to the studio, which was recessed off the main road in a courtyard behind a few houses. I climbed out of the truck and two young kids glued themselves to my legs and held on until I reached the studio. It had started in 1997 as a squatter's space in the hallway of a compound and its first set of equipment consisted of an out-dated Toshiba amplifier purchased from a local mechanic, an old microphone from a nearby church, two eight-ohm speakers, and a 2.5 KVA generator. In those days, nobody knew how to mix or produce, but because of the studio's inexpensive rates, young musicians flocked to it. Just as they were starting to find their way around their equipment, the rebel incursion happened, and Studio D was forced to suspend operation. Café Society has made a short film about the place, and in it, one of the studio's pioneers, Samuel Luke, says, "One Sunday night, we were watching movies, staying inside, keeping off the streets and trying to be safe, when we heard gunshots and crying and wailing in the streets. We made phone calls trying to figure out what was happening, but the next thing we knew the rebels were in the compound and on the top floor in our neighbours' house, which was on fire. The rebels kicked down the front doors and busted in looking for our money. We fled to the National Stadium, seeking refuge. The whole of Freetown was on fire. The rebels stole our belongings and burned our house down. We felt our dream had ended. For five years, we had nothing. Then, in December 2002, we picked up zeal and with help of others collected equipment and gadgets that we used to rebuild the studio."

Most of the compound was still charcoal black and burned out from the fire, but the studio itself, a space that probably wasn't wide enough to accommodate a full drum kit, was fine, painted a faded eggshell blue. Still, a vocal booth had been built in the corner and there was plenty of room for me to play my guitar. For our session, a fellow named James – a Liberian pianist, guitar player, and engineer – sat behind a modest six-channel board staring at an old Compaq computer. Behind him was a young woman – another AUCAYD member – named Jane who, after we were done our session, borrowed my guitar and played a song she'd written called "Precious Love," because, she said, "I think Mariah Carey is great." Another engineer, Sam, who wore a Buck the Fuckeyes NCAA T-shirt, fed my guitar cable into the mixing console while telling me that the studio's recording schedule was often dictated by the region's weather patterns. The walls and roof were leaky and water pooled a few inches deep around the building, so it was hazardous to operate studio gear and run microphones in the rainy season. He also said that the studio only opened when there was money to buy fuel to run their small generator, at which point I gave him eighty-five thousand leones – about thirty dollars – which bought us two hours of recording time.

Barmmy handed James a CD of the basic tracks, which he popped into the computer. Having watched the boys write these beats in the War Child office, and seeing Studio D operate as it did, I could see how valuable digital technology was for music in the Third World. I'd been cynical about how digital home recording wedged musicians apart, giving everybody their own performance and recording space when, before, we were pushed together in the same room. I believe that the Rheos' downfall started during the recording of our last record, *2067*, for which Tim recorded all of his vocal tracks at home, by himself. Recording is a different experience for everyone, but I believe that bands should make music together, and that home studios can foster narcissism and divisiveness. Tim's private recordings showed him that he could do it without our input, which, I think, made it easier for him to leave.

But in the Third World, digital technology makes music affordable for those who have very little. Even though Barmmy and Lus owned no instruments and had no rehearsal space, they were still able to write and produce music. Barmmy could close up his computer and carry around his life's work, laying down sounds in a studio through common music software. How this technology had affected musical culture is a matter of debate. Already, the aesthetic of global reggae has been changed by the proliferation of electronic drums and bass – once unshaking organic tenets – while the sheer, unyielding mass of rap and hip hop has sounded the death knell for less adaptable genres, like ska and soca. And while modern technology meant that more Sierra Leonean records were being made than ever before, none of this music was *bu bu* or *zuck*. This made some people wonder whether these traditional forms will also be lost, not because the sounds are outdated or hard to play, but because *ximbeis* and *wanjuis* and *balangis* can't be captured by mouse clicks.

James fired up the CD that Barmmy had given him, but what I heard coming from speakers didn't sound anything like what I'd jammed to the day before. I asked the boys whether they'd brought the wrong track to the studio, but Lus said, "No, D, we like this one better. It is much more interesting." I wasn't sure whether they'd switched tracks right before our session because they thought I'd have no problem adapting, or whether it didn't matter what I played. Then I remembered a phrase that a friend had used for this sort of eventuality, AWA – Africa Wins Again – meaning that whatever happens in Africa, happens on Africa's terms. I decided not to stamp my feet in protest and tell them that it was impossible for me to write a guitar part for a song I'd only just heard. Instead, I affected a steely professionalism that, I hoped, they appreciated.

"Just roll the friggin' track," I told the engineer.

There are a few things you should know about recording in Sierra Leone in case you happen to find yourself in this very situation. First, when you tell the engineer to "roll the friggin' track," a great number of people within shouting distance of where you are playing will appear out of nowhere and suddenly fill the room; second, all of the room's fans will be turned off and its windows shut to protect the recording from stray noise, even though anyone capable of making this noise will have already gathered inside the studio; and third, those stilled fans and shuttered windows will mean that you have no choice but to work fast to record your new guitar part for a song you've only just heard lest you end up as a hot pool of melted flesh.

As it turned out, I only had to nail down a small measure of riffing. Because the construction of hip hop is, generally, a few bars of instrumentation looped from the beginning to end of the song, all I needed were two bars of gold. Lus was at my shoulder the whole time, counting me through the bars, making sure that I was tight to the end of each measure, and coaching me through the "ya-da-da-da-da's," which, each time, came on the heels of the chorus – "Stand up!" – which was also the song's title.

I'd had so much fun with my young African friends the weight of the session didn't hit me until playback. I thought about where I was and what we were doing and whether people had died in the compound's fire and what the streets beyond the studio door had looked like during the war and the fact that we were making Afro-Canadian hoser hip hop where, five years earlier, the only sounds in Freetown were gunfire and wailing voices rending the dreadful, birdless silence. Stirred by the drama of these thoughts, I told the engineer: "Gimme one more track." Lus and Barmmy shouted that what I'd done was fine, but I repeated my demand: "Gimme one more track."

He spun around in his chair to face the screen and counted me in. This time, I played my fat nasty chords with the whole of my forearm, kerranging them as the weight of my body rose then fell heavily against the bridge. I planted my legs and leaned my shoulder into the riff, striking my strumming hand against the strings like a scythe and trying to show the kids the soul and heat and power of *London Calling* and *Road to Ruin* and every other record they'd ignored in the music room. I played fiercely, blindly. I tried to show them that, even though I'd never lived through war or had had to fight for my next meal, I was playing this way because *they'd* had to. I wanted to show them that my music was terrifying and real and honest, and that, as a forty-two-year-old rock 'n' roll veteran, I didn't give a shit what any of them thought. Barmmy Boy and Lus deserved the best that I could give them. For a few minutes, they got it.

I finished the track bathed in sweat. "Yeah, Super D!" said Barmmy, rising out of his chair. I gave him a look that explained what I'd done, put my guitar on the ground, punched open the door, and walked into the deep African sunlight.

The following night was Party Night at an oceanside club called Paddy's, where Lus and Vickie were scheduled to perform some-time between midnight and four in the morning.

Before heading off to the show, I found myself, as every trav-eller does at least once during their trip, waiting for a man named Yusef. When he finally arrived in his taxi, he turned out to be a small, wiry man in beach shorts and a tank top who drove me, first, to a restaurant for dinner before heading off to the club. I was shown to a table on a terrace just above Man O' War Bay with a view of the water and the surrounding hillside, which lay against the sky like hip and shoulders of a reclining nude. At one point, there was a great groaning sound, then the city sighed and went completely dark. The only thing visible were the shadows of fishing boats bobbing on the water. Within minutes, the generators started grumbling, and one by one, the lights of the surrounding hotels appeared like a succession of matchsticks being lit.

A long beachside drive delivered me to Paddy's, a flat cinder-block building at the top of a rising driveway. Inside, a classic beach bar, open to the sea, had a stage at one end and an enor-mous grass deejay hut planted beside it. Wednesday night was Ladies Night, so there were lots of bodacious Sierra Leonean women dressed to the nines in hot pants and tank tops in the bar, and working girls straddling the bar stools. Vickie – who, like most of the AUCAYD crew, was a friendly, unassuming African teenager – and Lus had submitted their names to the deejay for consideration for the evening's program, but they both stressed that it was never a sure thing whether they'd be chosen. Often, young artists were bumped from the bill if other better-known artists showed up during the proceedings. Lus said that because the AUCAYD singers were young and not yet established, they were usually the first to be excised.

Barmmy had decided not to participate because he wasn't totally confident that he knew his latest composition well enough. Besides, he told me, he'd already set a high standard at the club, having killed in his first live appearance there.

"The first time I ever rapped on stage was at this club," he said. "Some people like to dress boldly for the stage, but I showed up looking modest, without any flash. After they called my name, I didn't even know how to get to the stage. I went the long way around and it took me a moment to get there. When I reached the stage, you could see the crowd thinking to themselves, What is this guy going to do? But that made it sweeter, you know, because once I started rapping, people couldn't believe that this sound was coming from me. I was deep into the music, just zooming. Even after the show, people came up to me and asked me to sing a little, still unconvinced that it was me. They weren't sure it was possible that this sound could come from such a normal-looking person."

Before the show started, Ed Sawyer joined us at our table. Ed was a little preoccupied thinking about how Paps's CD release would play out on the weekend, and whether he'd sell enough VIP tickets to make his money back. At the larger Sierra Leonean shows, VIPs paid a higher price for the good seats, and for food and drink, which Ed had to supply. He was also concerned about a truck and driver that he'd hired for the day of the show, which would drive Paps around Freetown while he rapped from the flatbed. The weight of Ed's mood wasn't brightened either by the prospect of sitting through another performance by his least favourite Sierra Leonean act: a popular comedy duo who, he said, dressed in skin-tight body suits, covered their mouths with foam, and shouted nonsense for five minutes straight. These performers were at almost every gig and sometimes showed up at the heliport to separate departing tourists from their last leones.

On my way back to Accra from Freetown, I encountered two equally bizarre vaudevillians: a purple-goggled, broad-tied goofball dressed like a Funkadelic dropout whose job it was to shout safety instructions at travellers, and a clumsy acrobat named Africa Man with war paint striped across his bare chest who performed somersaults on the concrete while eating two Fanta bottles worth of broken glass.

I hoped that the comedians would make an appearance at Paddy's, but as the evening's emcee – a fellow named Budu, who was no Abbie Kamara – strutted on stage under purple fluorescent lights and told us how lucky we were to have found ourselves at "the finest entertainment complex that has ever happened in West Africa" and "the total university of West African entertainment," the foam-mouthed funnymen weren't part of the program.

The first artist, Budu told us, had come "twenty miles from Waterloo to be here at this fabulous complex." He was called Cos, and his song had a chorus that went "Suga Suga Tee-Tee." Halfway through Cos's song – which he lip-synched using a fancy gilt microphone – the deejay stopped the track dead, and that was the end of Cos. The singer walked to the deejay's window and protested, but Budu stepped in and promptly thanked him for coming out. Slump-shouldered and defeated, Cos shuffled off stage as the next performer was announced.

This is how I learned that club deejays in Freetown wield an unreasonable amount of power and influence. Because most performers mime to studio tracks, they have to hand their CDs over to the deejay, who, like this one, work the stop, pause, and start functions like trigger-happy riflemen. Fortressed in his hut, the deejay at Paddy's dictated the performers' fate without any recrimination, and his ill-tempered behind-the-curtain act was as integral to the show as the performers who showed up each week to be humbled by the impatient wizard. When I asked why

Freetown musicians hadn't given up their pre-recorded tapes, Barmmy said that a lot of people were insecure about their abilities, and that music videos had made lip-synching the norm.

The next performer, a fellow with a Krio name that I couldn't decipher, didn't even attempt to lip-synch to his song. He just whipped his arms around his head and bounced up and down while his track played, making it just beyond the three-quarter mark of his song before the deejay pulled the plug. I was reminded of ZZ Top on the American Music Awards, when the band's drummer threw down his sticks in the middle of the song and danced at the front of the stage while his pre-recorded beats thundered on.

The deejay's routine continued with the evening's next performer, a rapper with the Kraftwerkian name of Nature X, who, were he partnered with Africa Man, would have made an interesting Justice League duo. I half-expected him to walk on stage dressed in cyborg futureman gear, but he looked like all the other men, dressed in a flowery beach shirt and jeans. During his number, the deejay started one song, stopped it, punched the next track, stopped it as well, and moved on to a third track while Nature X waved two fingers in the air, requesting the previous track. The deejay temporarily acquiesced, but stopped it after the first chorus, then moved on to the third track, as if having his sport with the singer. At this point, I wanted to crawl through the window of the deejay hut and pummel him over the head. When I expressed my outrage at the table, Ed said that, in fact, Nature X had tried the oldest trick in the Sierra Leone pop handbook: he'd got the deejay to play snippets of as many tracks as possible to give the crowd a fuller impression of his music. It was a bonkers way of winning approval, but I don't think Nature X would have fared any better had he riffled through his collected works while conducting a live orchestra with his feet.

For him, as for every performer to that point, the audience offered a show-me attitude, no matter how hard they tried.

This didn't bode well for Lus or Vickie, but the next performer, a round, hirsute man with a pendulous belly and overgrown Afro who reminded me of a black George Costanza, greased the crowd with an exaggerated dance routine. Judging from the reaction, the audience found it hilarious. It didn't hurt that he was joined on stage by two loose-hipped women who shook and swang to a generic Afro-beat. Nor did anyone object when he leapt into the crowd and started to grind lasciviously against a few women sitting at a table near the stage. His song wasn't much more than a chorus – "Tumbo! Tumbo!" repeated over and over – but it didn't matter. The crowd had loosened and was ready to party.

A parade of generic Freetown hip-hoppers followed Mr. Costanza. A man named Alfonso – who dedicated his song to "all the Manchester United fans out there!" – gave way to a rap duo called Manchu who gave way to Kamel, who wore a Lite-Brite belt buckle and lasted only a quarter of a song. After he was chased from the stage, Budu called Vickie's name – "Welcome Vickish!" he said, forgetting to mention Lus – and the two teenagers bolted from their chairs.

The thing that struck me while watching the AUCAYD kids on stage was how much younger they were than anybody else, by a good five years. Not only that, but their song, about sustaining peace in Sierra Leone, was easily the most profound tune of the evening, though I suppose "One, Two, Three Red Light" would have sounded trenchant next to songs such as "Suga Suga Tee-Tee." Vickie stood at one side of the stage and lip-synched the verses, while Lus danced opposite her, pumping his arms and rolling his hips to a track that he and Barmmy had created. The crowd treated them respectfully and, when they were done, gave them a round of applause. It was a small triumph that the deejay had laid off the stop button, which was good for him, otherwise I would have brought down his booth in a hail of patio furniture.

The kids skip-hopped back to our table as Barmmy and I cheered. I was the only one whoo-hooing in the crowd – this holler has yet to find its way to West Africa – and I was proud and happy that they'd done well. Lus dropped into his chair and showed the stage his back, challenging any of the evening's other performers to make him turn around. Budu returned to the stage and said, "Right here at the finest entertainment complex in the world, you can see, my friends, that we also have some of the greatest and raw talent in West Africa at what you and I know is the best place for live music in the country."

At least he was half-right.

MASSEY HALL

THE WINGS OF ADVENTURE DELIVERED ME HOME IN TIME
to end what I'd helped start twenty-seven years earlier. In March
2007, the Rheostatics bowed out of being a band in a concert at
one of Canada's oldest and most storied music venues: Massey
Hall, located in the heart of my city. The date had been offered
to us while we were still together, and after Tim quit, it hung
there like a plump, ripe fruit. I knew that playing a farewell show
in the grand old hall was the right thing to do, but I was just as
happy to say fuckit and let the band die a cruel and ugly death,
partly as a vindictive gesture and partly because I didn't see the
point of throwing a party for a band who'd thrown in the towel.
But one evening, when Martin and I were sitting around trying
to figure out whether a new Rheos' lineup could work, Michael,
our ex-drummer, told me, "Dave, you're not good at endings.
You've never had to deal with them. Me, I'm all about endings."
This made me want to be good at endings, and to prove my
former bandmate wrong. Besides, passing up the opportunity to
play the hallowed theatre would be wrong-headed under any circumstances, and the more I thought about the weight of the
event, the more I realized that the Rheos' death could be as profound as its beginning.

Because my year of travelling and playing around the world had been heavy, great, and exhausting, I wasn't particularly emotional, at first, about what was easily the most profound and bittersweet concert of my life. But slowly, the event engulfed me. At first, I resisted helping to plan it – figuring out what songs to play, who to invite to perform with us, or whether to spend seven hundred dollars on a snow machine. I was tired, having done these kinds of things for so long. Even though I was thrilled with the idea of striding across one of the fabled rock 'n' roll stages of Canada – which we'd never played from before, save a two-song dropin at a poorly attended benefit show a few years back – having to discuss set times, press schedules, and T-shirt designs felt pedestrian after playing shows in places where none of that mattered.

The significance of the show became impossible to avoid. We sold tickets fast and in great quantities, and for the first time in our lives, the sense of excitement was palpable: a hot box office, commercial radio hosts discussing the importance of the show, trade ads, posters, and our name spelled out on the marquee that hung on the old building's stone facade. Secretly, I think we were all giddy at being considered an "attraction," rather than a club date on a listing grid in a city music guide. The band's name scrolled alongside Sting and Rod Stewart's on the city's twenty-four-hour news and weather television stations, and Sam the Record Man – the great record store of my youth, where, after countless Boxing Day sales, Tim and I rode the subway home studying the album jackets, sleeve notes, and pro-duction credits of great and formative albums such as *Highway to Hell*, *Drums and Wires*, and *More Specials*, which we'd bought on sale for $5.99 – assembled a tribute section near the front of the store, our albums elbowed between racks of crap, which is how I'd started to view all other forms of music, such is the prerogative of a person in a dying band.

At one point, someone suggested that we were the first and only Toronto band to play the Edge, Maple Leaf Gardens, and Massey Hall. I don't know if this is true, but even if it isn't, that we were even considered for such a distinction quickened my heart. This made all of those years being denied whatever it was we wanted but could never have – these regrets, too, tasted less sour in the shadow of our demise – feel like so much rock 'n' roll armour, replacing the weakened spirits and creative cynicism that had affected me during the band's later days. Coming home from distant lands to be crowned by the press and Canada's musical establishment helped too, and the excitement surrounding our gig – although to call it a "gig" besmirches the glitter of its appeal – filled me with pride and happiness. After a while, I affected a prosperous showman's bluster, decrying, "Get me the snow machine at whatever cost!" and "Whatever quantity of T-shirts we're making, triple it!" I scribbled out a defining set list, and it was met with roaring approval. Even Tim – always the most careful and fretful Rheostatic – strode abreast our triumphant marching banner, agreeing to every dint of the evening's program. The Rheostatics' death throes couldn't have been more lively, making me wish we'd broken up more often.

An emotional weight gathered around the event. Strangers stopped me in the street to ask if I was doing all right *because it can't be easy* and *how's Martin doing?* and *what do you think you'll do now?* while looking at me as if I couldn't possibly do anything else. Others told me, less gravely, but with just as much personal concern, that a cousin had bought fourteen tickets in the first balcony and that everyone was going to be there cheering and going crazy, *even my mom and dad, who got me into you guys, playing the* Whale Music *soundtrack every night before I went to bed.* Someone else told me that their best friend in high school had phoned them out of the blue and invited them to the show *even though I haven't seen them in a hundred years because we lost touch when I moved out west, but that didn't work out too well,* and that they'd be sitting together in Row G *stoned and bawling our friggin' eyes out.* Another person told me that she'd mended ways with her ex-husband, *can you believe it?,* and could we please play "Record Body Count" or "Self-Serve Gas Station" or "Fan Letter to Michael Jackson" *because those were the useless bastard's favourite songs.* Some fans were more plaintive, describing what the band had meant to them over the aural history of their lives; others were humble and soft-voiced while revealing that they'd named their son or daughter after one of our songs, usually "Claire," although I always held out hope for "Onilley" or "Alomar" or "Uncle Henry."

Word reached us that fans were driving across the province and flying in from other parts of the world to see the show. We received a torrent of e-mails and a pile of letters, which I added to one of the enormous green garbage bags that I had stored in a dark corner of my basement. It wasn't hard to remember the stories buried in those bags: the fellow who'd left his car at the roadside in flames and for whom the cops climbed back inside the wreck to rescue his autographed Rheos CD collection; the wilderness traveller who was lost for two days in the deep bush and preserved his sanity by repeating the words to one of our songs like a mantra before he was found; the fan who wrote to tell us that his brother had tried to kill himself, but who was nursed back to health after he gave him a box with a CD player and a copy of one of our records; and Jake, who, after a terrible accident, emerged from a deep coma without any memory of birds or chocolate or television, but singing "Me and Stupid."

The notion that they would all be sitting in the darkness of Massey Hall watching their band die when they'd come so close to dying themselves overwhelmed and terrified me.

My heart edged into my throat as the concert neared. One evening, we were asked to appear on Dave Bookman's radio show in Toronto. We hadn't been together as a band since Tim and Michael had quit. Between my trips, Martin Tielli and I had written and performed music for a play based on my erotic hockey stories, so we'd kept our musical shorthand sharp. But Mike hadn't played drums in nine months, and Tim, our bassist, had mostly played rhythm guitar as the front man for his new solo group. Yet as I approached the station from across the street and saw the fellows gathered in the entranceway, they looked no less of a band to me, standing shoulder to shoulder and joking as Martin reached into his pocket for a cigarette. This raised the obvious question about whether we'd ever *not be* a band, why we were breaking up in the first place, and how a bunch of people who seemed so normal together could be so fucked up.

Dave's radio station, CFNY FM, was the same one that Tim and I had driven to at its old location in Brampton to hand the station manager our demo cassette recorded with our parents' money and pleading with him to play it, which he did. CFNY – which had since largely descended into a new rock formula, redeemed only by Bookman's irresistibly bold, passionate, and funny drive-time broadcast – was the first station to play our music, and it would be the last. Once, a deejay at 97 Power Rock in Buffalo played our first single – "Satellite Dancing" – on the last Sunday before the start of Grade 13, right after he played "Take This Town" by XTC. Back then, I was thrilled every time I heard our songs on the radio. One of the tragic yet beautiful realities of an artist's life is having to pass on the ownership of one's work. Even in those dark moments on stage when

I wondered what might happen if a Bengal tiger were loosed from one of my bandmate's speaker grilles, I knew that if the music wasn't working for me, it was working for others who were hearing it for the first time. If my world travels had taught me anything, it was that even though the Rheos would never play "Horses" or "Fan Letter to Michael Jackson" again, maybe some kid in the Hunan or an African carpenter was whistling the melody, keeping it alive.

Dave gathered us around the interview bench and asked, "Why are you doing this? You're just going to get back together, right? You're just like the Who and all the rest of them." He sounded bitter, which dumbfounded us. Dave slashed his hand across the air and told his engineer, "I can't do this. Let's just play the band's shortest song and get out of here. This is very hard. Play it and let me think of what to do."

I tried to console my friend. When Bookman had joined us on our English tour in 1994, our band was experiencing similar depths of emotion. We were booked to play two weeks at a university hall in Edinburgh, but the gigs had gone very badly. After one set, I sat in the dressing room and told our soundman, Roger Psutka, that I was quitting the band. This lasted only about as long as it took him to convince me not to – about four minutes – so I returned to the stage for an encore. Nobody talked much for the rest of the tour, and a few months later, Dave Clark quit the band. In that moment, something about the band's essence died. And now here I was, reliving those horrible feelings all over again live on the radio in front of everyone.

Just as "Record Body Count" was finishing and we sat staring at one another on the interview bench, two friends – Dave Ulrich, the former Inbreds' drummer, and Steve Stanley, my Morningstars hockey teammate – came through the door. I was relieved that there'd be someone else to diffuse the tension.

I noticed that Dave harboured something under his arm, and as he approached us, he placed a box on the table, then lifted the latch to reveal a stack of CDs. I looked up to see Bookman smiling and raising his arms.

It was a tribute CD – the Rheostatics' "Secret Sessions" – recorded covertly over the year of our demise without any of us knowing it. Four bands – King Cobb Steelie, the Local Rabbits, Weeping Tile, and the Inbreds – had reformed after breaking up to contribute to the record. On the CD booklet were testimonials from musicians we'd helped along the way. The Barenaked Ladies had recorded one of our songs in a hockey arena in Regina; others had done their versions in the quiet of their home studios. It was an overwhelming moment in which the weight of all that we'd been as a band choked my heart. The interview ended with most of us too overcome for words, and I left the station to find the city consumed in a flash blizzard. I drove through the teeming Lake Ontario snow *feeling stoned and bawling my friggin' eyes out.*

Erected in 1894, Massey Hall ("The Old Lady of Shuter Street") is one of the few remaining buildings in Toronto that connects the past to the present. It's an old Victorian music hall with two balconies, stained-glass windows on the sides, and twenty-seven hundred faded burgundy seats that rattle and sigh when you sit in them. It's the kind of place that's as friendly as it is big – Maple Leaf Gardens, which sits abandoned and catatonic two blocks north, was like that too – whether you're watching AC/DC, who opened for UFO in 1979, or Winston Churchill or Wilfrid Laurier or King George or Jack Dempsey, who fought an exhibition match there. In 1931, Hitler's cousin gave a speech warning Canadians of the evils of Nazism, and during the Second World

War, soldiers gathered in the great hall before being shipped by train to base camps around the country, then shuffled into the war's global conflict. In 1953, Charlie Parker, Dizzy Gillespie, Bud Powell, Max Roach, and Charles Mingus gathered for drinks at the nearby Silver Rail tavern – now gone – before crossing the street to play what is regarded by enthusiasts as the greatest jazz concert ever.

George Gershwin performed at Massey Hall, so did Arturo Toscanini, Glenn Gould, and Maria Callas. Enrico Caruso and Beniamino Gigli sang there. After Gigli's performance, he asked where he could find good Tuscan cuisine in Toronto. My grandparents' parish priest happened to be within earshot, and told him: "The best Italian food in Toronto is at Delpha Bidini's house." The next day, the great Italian tenor sat down to a feast in my grandparents' dining room on Beatrice Street, surely a great thrill for both of them, but especially for my grandfather, an opera enthusiast. The first concert my father ever attended was *The Barber of Seville* at Massey Hall, accompanied my grandfather. The irony that the Rheos' last performance would also happen there was not lost on my family, nor was the fact that, twenty-seven years earlier, my father had driven us to our first show a handful of blocks away at the Edge.

Having reached my emotional peak after Bookman's radio ruse, the remaining days of the Rheos were easy and good. I wished it had been the same for Martin, who came down with a bad case of laryngitis for the first time in twenty-two years. On the day of the gig, he could barely talk, let alone sing. He'd been to see a voice specialist – whose office was busy with photos of Mick Jagger and Bryan Adams – who'd told him to stop smoking and talking, which the guitarist and singer found impossible to do, especially at a time when reaching out and connecting with fans, bandmates, and family was essential to the band's adieu. During the show, he fought to wrench every note from his larynx. It was a courageous musical performance, and it made me admire him all the more, but also again raised the question of why we were throwing away such passion and determination when commodities like this are rare in any artistic discipline.

Having spent the last year playing to strangers – and the last twenty-seven playing to fans who knew the anatomy of our songs – I felt that I had nothing left to prove. I was reminded of the old sports adage about how the best players are unaffected by the pressure in big games having grown up poor and scrambling to survive in the country, the ghetto, or wherever. For us, the pressure of a last concert at Massey Hall was nothing compared to having weathered the vagaries of Canadian alternative rock long enough to be privileged to play this kind of show. One of the Rheos' forces was that we were forever the band who'd debuted at the Edge, and that every show was about hammering back the threat that it was all just an accident, happenstance, a trick, and a cruel joke conjured by some hoser wizard who, at any moment, could cough and make it all disappear. But as we walked out on stage at 8:10 p.m. on March 21, 2007, at Massey Hall, I knew this wasn't going to happen. We'd survived the accident long enough to hear the end of the joke.

Because the gig was glorious in its finality, we played as if the songs didn't have to be. In the days leading up to the show, I wondered whether I'd be thinking, Wow. This is the last time I'll ever play "Making Progress" or "The Tarleks" or "Northern Wish," but it wasn't the case. There were certainly moments rich with the kind of heavy sonic drama that only a performance in a venerable and historic theatre could produce: parts of "Shaved Head"; "Northern Wish," with our two ex-drummers, Don Kerr and Dave Clark, joining us on cello and drum kit, respectively;

the breakdown in "Feed Yourself," with Tim and Martin lying on their backs at the lip of the stage staring into the ceiling; and the aching strains of the intro to "Self-Serve Gas Station." It was the free-mindedness and spontaneity of the show that I'll remember most; I never thought such whimsy and joy would have been possible on such a profound evening. For "My First Rock Concert," four members of a local comedy troupe, the Imponderables, burst into the hall to re-enact the song's Joe Jackson scene dressed as Toronto cops, and during the instrumental section in "When Winter Comes," seven hundred dollars' worth of fake snow was propelled into the air by dual bubble machines, which blanketed the stage in white as it had been on the evening of Bookman's radio interview.

The old hall looked beautiful from the stage. Its dark wooden ribbing absorbed whatever sounds we pushed from our amps. Because of the warmth of the venue and the love of the crowd, it was easy for us to connect despite our estrangement and the years of shit we'd forced on one another: stealing girlfriends and corrupting marriages, betraying trust, exploiting weaknesses, and saying absolutely the worst possible things. Just a few years earlier, Martin had written Tim an e-mail telling him how much he despised his songs, then realized that that message would be better left unsent. But he used the wrong function on his computer and the e-mail found its way to Tim. Not long after that, we sat in the darkness during a power outage at rehearsal and unfavourably graded the songs that Tim was hoping to put on our new record. It was brutal and horrible, but the honesty was exhilarating. Still, it proved too much, and on the liner notes to Tim's solo album, he thanked everyone but me and Martin.

I often suffered the brunt of Martin and Tim's angst. Before a 2006 show in Belleville, Tim told me, after twenty-six years, "Do you realize how fucking difficult you are to work with?"

Then, a week before Massey Hall, Martin called me a "pussy" on stage during a warmup show at the Starlight Lounge in Kitchener-Waterloo. In both cases, I let the bullets pass through me. During my world travels I'd not had to suffer through these kinds of indignities – Al's Shanghai meltdown notwithstanding. I was relieved at being left unbruised, but also curious whether, in the end, I'd miss the pain of contact. After all, no matter how badly the Rheos had treated one another, we spent enough time in that perfect, exultant place celebrating the beauty of art and the glory of rock 'n' roll that our emotional terrorism was neutralized. At Massey Hall, the skies cleared and our hearts softened for a final time. In a way, the show was like one long glorious apology to one another.

For me, the salient moment of the concert came during the last song, "Dope Fiends and Boozehounds," which I'd written at a subway station in Toronto – incorporating a third verse about Pink Floyd that Janet dreamed up – and perfected by the group at the Royal Albert Hotel while on tour in Winnipeg in 1987. In the middle, the song gives way to a repeated drum figure, which, on this night, was played with four guest musicians: Chris Brown, Don Kerr, Dave Clark, and multi-instrumentalist Ford Pier. At a tune-up show at the Horseshoe Tavern the previous evening, Ford had helped lug my equipment from the trunk of my car to the club, bringing with him a set of goalie pads that I'd stashed there, just in case I'm ever waved down by a forlorn hockey team in desperate need of a netkeep. When I asked why he was doing this, he said, "Well, it can't hurt to have them around." They ended up sitting at the back of the stage for most of the show. Then they found their way to our load-in at Massey Hall, where they lay atop our equipment like a pair of sleeping hounds. I threw them to the back of the stage, but by gig time, they'd worked their way to the edge of Michael's drum riser.

During the drum break Ford grabbed the pads and brought them to the front of the stage. He craned a microphone close to the pads, called me over, and we started thumping them with our hands. We played for a handful of bars – the fat leather of the pads produced a fine *whomp* that rolled off the stage – and then Ford stood up, perhaps looking for a jockstrap or helmet to percuss. As he did, I looked down at the pads, stared back at my friend, lifted one of the goalie pillows off the stage and thrashed him in the back, sending the keyboard player ass over tea kettle across the hallowed ground.

Ford picked himself up, then attacked me. The spotlight found us as we wrestled and mock-assaulted each other at the epicentre of the grand stage. Ford finally climbed to his feet, proclaiming himself the victor, and I lay there vanquished, staring at the theatre's beautiful stained-glass windows and decorative ceiling. Because I was lost in the submission of the moment, I don't remember much else. But Ford told me later that, from the ground, I threw out my arms, widened my eyes, and said:

"Africa."

For our encore, we did two acoustic songs in the crowd before saying goodbye. Everywhere I looked people were crying, and for the last verse and chorus of "Record Body Count," they were both crying and singing. Afterward, there was a reception in the theatre bar downstairs for friends, family, and our musical peers. All of our years together were collected there. At one point, Martin, who could still barely talk, said, "I don't know what I'm going to do. I'm going to die." I told him, encouragingly, but half-convinced, "Don't worry, we'll get something going. It'll be great," but it's not what he'd meant. He was describing the impossible depth of the evening, its crushing sense of perspective, and what it had felt like, after years exploring our country

Good. Dead. Gone. (*Trevor Weeks*)

of rock, to watch all that we'd achieved drift away like a great ship leaving shore. Through an ocean of tears, it felt good, partly because we'd died an elegant and good death, and partly because I could see myself standing on the shore, holding a guitar case that I'd carried with me around the world and would carry again.

After the party, Tim, Martin, Michael, and I, with our girl-friends, wives, and a group of friends, ascended into the lobby, where we found our equipment stacked against the doors of the theatre as it would have been after the earliest gigs we'd ever played. There were no smoking roadies waiting to help load it onto trucks bound for another gig in another town; no impatient road manager giving us our plan for the next day; no curious huddle of fans inviting us out for a drink at a cool secret bar that nobody else knows about but them. I loaded my guitar cabinet into the car and pulled away, and all of those miles I'd driven through places strange and familiar on journeys near and far faded in the rear-view mirror, and were replaced by the cold blinking lights of a quiet city in the middle of the night. Once home, I collapsed on the bed and fell asleep to the sound of what, at that moment, was the sweetest music of all:

Silence.

(in order of appearance)

Led Zeppelin, "Hot Dog" (*In Through the Out Door*, 1979)
Willie Nelson, "Changing Skies" (*Tougher Than Leather*, 1983)
The Members, "Stand Up and Spit" (*At the Chelsea Nightclub*, 1979)
John Cooper Clarke, "Beasley Street" (*Snap, Crackle and Bop*, 1980)
Nick Lowe, "Indian Queens" (*The Convincer*, 2001)
Mayor McCa, "Mental Carcus" (*Welcome to McCa Land*, 1999)
Blur, "Tender" (*13*, 1999)
Stompin' Tom Connors, "Farewell to Nova Scotia" (*Stompin' Tom at the Gumboot Cloggeroo*, 1976)
Matti Nykanen, "Topless" (*Yllatysten yo*, 1992)
Motorhead, "Eat the Rich" (*Rock 'n' Roll*, 1987)
Roxette, "Joyride" (*Joyride*, 1991)
Stevie Wonder, "Saturn" (*Songs in the Key of Life*, 1976)
Rush, "What You're Doing" (*All the World's a Stage*, 1976)
Max Webster, "On the Road" (*High Class in Borrowed Shoes*, 1977)
Goddo, "So Walk On" (*An Act of Goddo*, 1979)
BTO, "Down to the Line" (*Rock n' Roll Nights*, 1979)
Queen, "Love of My Life" (*A Night at the Opera*, 1975)
Stan Rogers, "Song of the Candle" (*Turnaround*, 1978)
The Midi-Ogres, "The First Saturday in May" (single release, 1998)
The Lawn, "Shady Street" (*The Lawn*, 1991)
Townes Van Zandt, "I'll Be There in the Morning" (*For the Sake of the Song*, 1968)
The Beatles, "Back in the USSR" (*White Album*, 1968)

Psychedelic Furs, "Pretty in Pink" (*Talk Talk Talk*, 1981)

The Feelies, "Fa Ce-La" (*Crazy Rhythms*, 1980)

Tom Waits, "Time" (*Rain Dogs*, 1985)

Camper Van Beethoven, "(I Was Born in a) Laundromat" (*Key Lime Pie*, 1989)

Marimba Plus, "Rainbow" (*Zebrano*, 2005)

Alun Piggins, "Out in the Woods" (*Balladesque*, 2000)

Chris and Kate, "Go On" (*Go On*, 2004)

Barenaked Ladies, "Hello City" (*Gordon*, 1992)

Rick Moranis, "Hockey" (*You, Me, the Music and Me*, 1989)

XTC, "Earn Enough for Us" (*Skylarking*, 1986)

By Divine Right, "Sofa Tour" (*All Hail Discordia*, 1997)

Smokie, "Liverpool Docks" (*The Collection*, 1992)

Jesus Jones, "International Bright Young Thing" (*Doubt*, 1991)

Sly and the Family Stone, "(You Caught Me) Smilin'" (*There's a Riot Goin' On*, 1971)

Bram Tchaikovsky, "Girl of My Dreams" (*Strange Man, Changed Man*, 1979)

Earth, Wind and Fire, "Shining Star" (*The Best of*, Vol. 1, 1978)

Beyond, "Save Ourselves" (*No Longer at Ease*, 1999)

Steel Pulse, "Leggo Beast" (*True Democracy*, 1982)

The Diodes, "Tired of Waking Up Tired" (*The Best of the Diodes*, 1998)

Local Rabbits, "Play On" (*Basic Concept*, 1998)

Spike Jones, "The Man on the Flying Trapeze" (*The Best of*, Vol 1., 1975)

Loudon Wainwright III, "Road Ode" (*Career Moves*, 1993)

The Move, "Cherry Blossom Clinic" (*The Best of*, 1974)

The Kinks, "Daylight" (*Preservation, Act 1*, 1973)

Joe Jackson, "On Your Radio" (*I'm the Man*, 1979)

Incredible Bongo Band, "Let There Be Drums" (*Bongo Rock*, 2006)

Neil Young & Crazy Horse, "Cortez the Killer" (*Zuma*, 1975)

Meat Puppets, "Up on the Sun" (*Up on the Sun*, 1985)

Mott the Hoople, "All the Young Dudes" (*All the Young Dudes*, 1972)

The Replacements, "Sixteen Blue" (*Let It Be*, 1984)

Johnny Cash, "Drive On" (*American Recordings*, 1994)

The Who, "A Quick One While He's Away" (*A Quick One (Happy Jack)*, 1966)

Talking Heads, "Cities" (*Fear of Music*, 1979)

Frank Sinatra, "I've Got You Under my Skin" (*The Capitol Years*, 1998)

Jonathan Richman & the Modern Lovers, "Abdul and Cleopatra" (*Back in Your Life*, 1978)

Ladysmith Black Mambazo, "Nomakanjani" (*Journey of Dreams*, 1988)

Gang of Four, "To Hell with Poverty" (single release, 1982)

Bob Dylan, "Just Like Tom Thumb's Blues" (*Highway 61 Revisited*, 1965)

Taj Mahal, "Take a Giant Step" (*Giant Step*, 1968)

The Slits, "I Heard It Through the Grapevine" (*Cut*, 1979)

Blackalicious, "Powers" (*The Craft*, 2005)

Super Furry Animals, "Juxtaposed With U" (*Rings Around the World*, 2001)

Lupe Fiasco, "Daydreamin'" (*Food and Liquor*, 2006)

The Pogues, "The Band Played Waltzing Matilda" (*Rum, Sodomy & the Lash*, 1985)

The Ramones, "I Just Want to Have Something to Do" (*Road to Ruin*, 1978)

The Inbreds, "Any Sense of Time" (*Kombinator*, 1995)

Please write,

Dave Bidini

PO Box 616

Station C

Toronto, ON

M6J 3R9